Children's Agency and Development in African Societies

La capacité d'agir et le développement des enfants dans les sociétés africaines

This book is a product of the CODESRIA Child and Youth Studies Institute.

Ce livre est issu de l'institut d'études sur l'enfance et la jeunesse du CODESRIA.

Contents / Sommaire

About the Authors / Les auteurs

Yaw Ofosu-Kusi is Associate Professor of Social Studies and Dean of the Faculty of Social Sciences of the University of Education, Winneba, Ghana. He obtained his doctorate degree in Applied Social Studies from the University of Warwick, United Kingdom. His research interest is primarily in urban childhood and the informal economy, with specific attention given to child migration, street life and labour, and children's agency. He is also a member of the editorial board of *Childhood*, the journal of global child research, and has varied teaching experience from universities in Ghana, Switzerland and Germany. Among his most recent works are: 'Dreams, expectations and experiential realities of street children in Accra, Ghana', in *Narrating (Hi)Stories in West Africa* (Berlin: Lit Verlag 2015), and 'Neo-liberalism and housing provision in Accra, Ghana: The illogic of an over-liberalised housing market', in *Selected Themes in African Development Studies* (New York: Springer 2014).

Deevia Bhana is the DST/NRF South African Research Chair (SARChl) in Gender and Childhood Sexuality at the University of KwaZulu-Natal. She has published widely in the field of gender, childhood sexuality and schooling. Her most recent work is *Childhood Sexuality and AIDS Education: The Price of Innocence* (Routledge, 2016)

Adediran Daniel Ikuomola holds a doctorate degree in Sociology and is currently a lecturer in the Department of Sociology at Adekunle Ajasin University, Nigeria. His primary research interest cuts across issues on youth and deviance, with emphasis on lifestyle and self-control theories. His work has appeared in Peace and Conflict Review; Arts and Humanities; Culture and Development, and Council for the Development of Social Science Research in Africa (CODESRIA). He is a recipient of the prestigious American Council of Learned Society and African Humanities Programme (ACLS/AHP) postdoctoral award in 2013 and the North-West University, Potchefstroom-South Africa postdoctoral fellowship in 2014. Some of his current works are: *The Nigerian Civil War of 1967 and the Stigmatization of Children Born of Rape Victims in Edo State, Nigeria* (2009); *Womanhood and the Media: Nigeria and the Arab World* (2011).

Pamela M.Y. Ngugi is a senior lecturer in the Department of Kiswahili at Kenyatta University – Kenya. She did her bachelors and masters studies at the University of Nairobi and thereafter joined the University of Vienna Austria for doctoral studies. She has interests in children's literature studies, translation and socio-linguistics and has written books for children. She has contributed articles to both English and Kiswahili journals.

Mokua Ombati is a trained sociologist and anthropologist affiliated to the Department of Anthropology and Human Ecology of Moi University, Kenya. He is also an adjunct lecturer in the School of Arts and Social Sciences of Maasai Mara University, Kenya. His research interests centre in the areas of indigenous knowledge systems, security and peace, gender, children and youth, and social stratification.

Ts'epang Florence Manyeli is both an academic and professional social worker. She holds M.A in Social Work (Social Development and Planning) from the University of Port Elizabeth, now Nelson Mandela Metropolitan University, South Africa. She is currently a lecturer in the Department of Sociology, Anthropology & Social Work at the National University of Lesotho. Her social work and academic pursuits focus on social justice for children and vulnerable people at the micro, mezzo and macro levels through involvement in humanitarian operations and participation in seminars and conferences. Her areas of expertise and interest are project management, counseling, community development, social security and child welfare.

Musediq Olufemi Lawal holds a doctorate degree in Sociology and Anthropology from University of Ibadan, Nigeria. He is currently a Senior Research Officer at the Forestry Research Institute of Nigeria. His teaching and research areas include Cultural Anthropology, Health, Social Problem, Environment, Population and Development.

Catherine Mayesero Makhumula is currently enrolled as a doctoral candidate in the Department of Drama at Stellenbosch University, South Africa. She holds an MA in International Performance Research from the University of Warwick, UK and the University of Amsterdam, Netherlands. She is also a lecturer in theatre arts in the Department of Fine and Performing Arts at Chancellor College, University of Malawi. She has been involved in many community projects that use theatre as a way of interrogating social problems, with specific regard to youth and health. Her research interests are in Theatre for Development and Performance Studies.

Tete Jesinta Lebsonga holds bachelors and masters degrees in Sociology of Development from the University of Yaoundé I, Cameroon. As a serial rape survivor, she is actively engaged in the prevention of gender-based violence, particularly rape and incest. She currently works as an independent consultant and trainer in the field of Adolescent Sexual and Reproductive Health; The Prevention of Sex Based Violence in Primary Schools, under the auspices of the German International Cooperation for Development (GIZ), and the National Network of Aunties Associations (RENATA).

Sandra Elvyre Loumedjinon est titulaire, en 2002, d'un diplôme d'Ingénieur en Gestion de l'Environnement de L'Ecole Polytechnique Universitaire de L'Université d'Abomey Calavi au Bénin et en 2006 d'un Diplôme d'Etudes Approfondies Option Environnement et Développement dans la même Université. Depuis 2015, elle est doctorante en Economie des Ressources Naturelles à l'Ecole Doctorales de l'Université de Parakou. Actuellement, elle le poste d'Experte en Suivi Evaluation du Programme Omi Delta de la Coopération des Pays Bas (SNV) au Bénin.

Hippolyte Héli Abanda a une Maîtrise sur mesure en Sciences de l'éducation, équivalent du Master, obtenue à l'Université Laval au Québec et a travaillé sur *Politiques éducatives et genre au Cameroun : inscription des filles dans les filières industrielles.* Il est actuellement Professeur des lycées et Doctorant avec pour sujet : *Colonialité du savoir et du pouvoir dans les études féministes en Afrique. Une étude déconstructionniste du phallogocentrisme à la lecture de L'Aventure Ambiguë de Cheikh Hamidou Kane.* Ses activités de recherche portent sur la problématique du genre en Afrique et au Cameroun en particulier avec un point d'honneur sur la citoyenneté et l'autonomie des femmes. Il est Directeur de l'ONG le Relais Enfants-Parents du Cameroun qui œuvre pour le maintien des liens parentaux entre les détenus-es et leurs enfants à travers un accompagnement psycho social.

Edmond Mokuinema Bomfie est professeur au Département de Sociologie de l'Université de Kisangani (RDC). Plusieurs fois lauréat et personne ressource aux activités du CODESRIA, il est un ancien Chef de Département de Sociologie, Vice-Doyen honoraire chargé de l'Enseignement à la Faculté des Sciences Sociales, Administratives et Politiques, Doyen honoraire à la Faculté de Droit et actuellement Directeur du CRIDE (Centre de Recherches Interdisciplinaires pour le Développement et l'Education). Ses intérêts de travail portent sur les mouvements sociaux (religieux, identitaires), la gouvernance de l'eau en Afrique Centrale et le travail des enfants dans les zones de conflits armés.

Bra-Amba Dolo est Psychopédagogue de formation initiale. En entamant sa carrière dans les ONG, il est vite allé à la diversification des expériences tout en alliant travail et formations. Ainsi, il découvre le travail social, notamment dans l'administration pénitentiaire, la consultation privée, l'enseignement secondaire et supérieur privé et la recherche. Dans le même temps, il passe un master professionnel en Management de projet, un DEA en Décentralisation de l'Éducation, un Certificate of Advanced Studies (CAS) de l'Université de

Genève en Protection et Droit de l'Enfant puis de nombreux certificats en Droits Humains et Droits de l'Enfant. Actuellement Coordinateur de Programmes pour World Education Inc. au Mali, ses recherches doctorales sont orientées vers l'analyse des interactions entre le système éducatif malien et les comportements infanto-juvéniles violents dans les centres urbains.

Kabran Aristide Djane a un Doctorat en Sciences Sociales, avec une spécialité en Sociologie de l'Environnement obtenu à l'Université Felix Houphouët Boigny de Cocody (Côte d'Ivoire). Il est actuellement Maître-assistant des Universités (CAMES), enseignant d'enquête qualitative et quantitative au département de Sociologie de l'Université Peleforo Gon Coulibaly de Korhogo (Côte d'Ivoire). Ses activités de recherche se focalisent sur la socioconstruction de l'environnement d'une part et sur la modélisation du comportement environnemental d'autre part.

1

Introduction: Children's Agency and Development in African Societies

Yaw Ofosu-Kusi

Introduction

The Council for the Development of Social Science Research in Africa (CODESRIA) organised its 2011 edition of the annual Child and Youth Institute under the theme, 'Children's Agency and Development in African Societies'. This volume is the outcome of that Institute. The theme is apposite principally because many African children are experiencing a life of neglect, marginalisation, and destitution in spite of the potentials of family and society to properly care for them. This neglect and sometimes disdain for children and their welfare is grounded in the belief that children, as developing social and cultural beings, have limited rights, capacity and authority to fully participate in society. In reality, however, millions of African children play constructive roles in their families and social environments. For example, they work to support their families; in some situations they assume responsibility for their siblings when their parents succumb to death through diseases and/or wars. Why then should children not be taken seriously?

The United Nations (UN) and a number of its institutions have thrust childhood into the spotlight. The relevance and inevitability of the various UN conventions, especially the United Nations Convention on the Rights of the Child (UNCRC) and International Labour Organization (ILO) conventions on human rights, child trafficking, child labour and exploitation has led to a reconstruction of childhood and reassessment of children's role in societies around the world. In tandem with this repositioning is the emergence of a new paradigm of childhood that perceives and treats children as capable beings. However, a good deal of current research and the debates grounded in this paradigm and the extant literature have a western-world orientation and so are sometimes criticised as Eurocentric by a section of Africans. In any case, the spotlight, epitomised by the UNCRC, is not a coup that bestows unbridled power and resources on African children in the determination of their life courses. At the moment, there are many challenges that undermine the potential underlined in those international agreements. One way to appreciate this is to ground African research, and to place African childhood within the emerging paradigm by interrogating and relativising it to African traditions and realities. It is against this background that this volume, comprising sixteen chapters, and steeped in research around the continent, variously examines children's agency, the inherent contradictions and vulnerabilities, their search for identity and representation and development.

While not disassociating the African situation from the global context because it is a futile exercise, it is imperative however to anchor the emerging discourse on African specificities. The 2011 Child and Youth Institute, benefiting from the scholarship and experience of Phil Mizen of the University of Warwick, United Kingdom, Deevia Bhana of the University of Kwazulu-Natal, South Africa, and Edmond Mokuinema Bomfie of the University of Kisangani, Democratic Republic of Congo as resource persons, was meant to do exactly that. With seventeen laureates from Western, Central, Eastern and Southern Africa, the Institute provided a platform for seasoned and budding researchers to share research experiences and unpack theories and conceptual viewpoints. The intellectual exercise lasting three weeks was a direct response to exhortations of the Deputy Executive Secretary of CODESRIA, Professor Bernard Mumpasi Lututala, at the opening ceremony, for Africans to engage in rigorous and objective African research that aims at solving problems and improving conditions on the continent by creating new knowledge, challenging existing ones, constantly questioning building tensions, and where necessary, deconstructing them.

Establishing a Context

Africa's population is a youthful one. According to UN-Habitat (2010), by 2015 Africa's estimated population will be 1.2 billion. UNICEF's State of the World's Children 2012 indicated that approximately 477.3 million of Africa's population in 2010 were below 18 years, of which 155.1 million were under 5 years. At the estimated average population growth rate of 2.1 per cent from 2010 to 2030 (UNICEF 2012), the population will continue to be a very youthful one for many years to come. While this could be courageously interpreted as positive for the continent, the paucity of resources and opportunity for the majority raises serious concerns about the future of generations of children and young people unless concomitant efforts are made. For now, millions of children have limited or no access to education, irregularly attend school if enrolled at all, are exposed to hazardous labour conditions, and live under harsh traditions and child-rearing practices (UNICEF 2012), or extreme impoverishment in slum-like conditions that are characterised by insecurity of tenure, lack of basic services, over-crowdedness, and low standard housing (Davis 2006; UN-Habitat 2010).

The orthodoxy on childhood centres on models that are influenced by the dual themes of socialisation and development. In both cases, children are seen as entities under training and preparation towards adulthood. All societies possess shared values and norms adherence which ensure continuity and reproduction. If children are in the state of development, then they must internalise those values and norms through socialisation in families, schools and relevant institutions to become full-fledged, functional members of their society. This is a direct complement to psychology's core premises of childhood which sees it as a series of stages through which children progressively accumulate skills for life. Developmental psychology also equates adulthood with rationality. Therefore, by going through a 'natural growth', children will mature biologically into rational adults (James and Prout 1990:10). This evolutionary process in either case represents a transition from 'simplicity to complexity of thought, from irrational to rational behaviour' (ibid:11). Both paradigms therefore are forward-looking and anticipatory.

Both however have been critically discussed since the 1970s. Socialisation for instance has been criticised as being overly dependent on what the adult has to offer. Children are essentially passive in their own socialisation because little regard is paid to their views, experiences, social worlds and capacity to influence both their lives and those around them (Mayall 1996; James and James 2001). Moreover, to the extent that socialisation ensures continuity of shared rules and preferred behaviour in a society, it ignores change and conflict. The psychological model of development has also come under critical scrutiny. For instance, Mayall (1996:19) cautions that the 'designation of children as developing non-people and socialisation projects' places them in the natural and biological context but neglects the 'social and political status of children and childhood'. Children's development is not a function of only biological and natural stimuli, but as Corsaro (2005) submits, is critically shaped by the social environment as well. Since there are multiple social environments, there must also be considerable variations in children's physical and cognitive development and, for that matter, different childhoods. If social practices governing childhood and affecting the lives of children are also not universally consistent, then it is presumptuous to model children's cognitive development on universally applicable stages of development.

As a result of such criticisms, contemporary paradigms place more emphasis upon children as 'beings' rather than 'becomings'. This shift in understanding, as James and James (2001) point out, means that children have to be considered for who they are now rather than in terms of what they may or may not become in the future. Upon this basis, three important premises are widely acknowledged as the building blocks of the new ways of conceptualising childhood (ibid): first, childhood is a social construct; second, children deserve to be studied for what they are, rather than as appendages to adults; and third, children are capable of forming their opinions and developing perspectives, so we as adults must pay attention to those views. But within this diversification is also the fact that childhood as a social space is common to all children. All children, regardless of the culture in which they are raised and are developing, go through the similar biological process of change and maturation towards adulthood. This is a natural and biological commonality, though the content of that could vary according to the social and economic environment. As noted by James and James (2001:27), '... childhood is, at one and the same time, common to all children but also fragmented by the diversity of children's everyday lives'.

Against this background, it is important to strike a balance between children's social maturity which depends on the social and cultural settings in which children are located and their biological maturity which can be universalised. For instance, all 10-year-old children, regardless of where in the world they live, are biologically immature and physically underdeveloped. That is a universal truth. But 10-year-old children have different levels of social maturity in different societies. For example, whereas they may be considered socially mature in some African societies and therefore assumed to be capable of performing certain familial responsibilities, cultural and institutional practices may designate such children as incapable of those responsibilities in other societies.

An inevitable consequence of the new conception is children's agency. That children have agency and are socially competent is acknowledged and exemplified by their actions in society. The sanitised, unproblematic notion of children's agency is their capacity to act independently, make decisions, and engage in actions out of their own volition. In a bid to answer their own question: 'What is agency?' Emirbayer and Mische (1998:962) conceptualised it as 'a temporally embedded process of social engagement, informed by the past ... but also oriented towards the future ... and toward the present'. Agency variously evokes personal will, ability, capacity, drive, motivation, choice, innovation, creativity, resourcefulness and action in the social agent to act in ways that create change or reinforce the status quo (ibid). The temporal nature of the social agent's actions is important here because as Eminbayer and Mische (1998) point out, agency is dynamic and over time assumes variations and different configurations.

Corsaro's theory of 'interpretative reproduction', rooted in sociology's agency and structure, provides an important conceptual basis for us to discuss the agency of African children. Corsaro (2005) argues that children actually make efforts to actively interpret their world through the development of their own peer cultures while concurrently participating in the prevailing social institutions and relevant adult cultures. The collective or aggregate activities of children on their social environment must therefore be taken into consideration since children negotiate, share and create in their engagement with both adults and their peers. The actions of individual children may be insignificant at the present but incrementally signify new ways of seeing and knowing childhood. As Sewell (1992:20) points out, agency engenders 'some degree of control over the social relations in which one is enmeshed, which in turn implies the ability to transform those social relations to some degree'. All individuals, no matter the level of their cognitive development at some point in time conceptualise things, construct intentions and act in certain ways that generate some impact, however minimal it may be.

In this respect, African children, in spite of some traditional and cultural barriers, are not passive recipients of adult culture; they collectively produce their own social world by utilising the information they appropriate from the adult world. The probable reason is to take responsibility for, and to address their concerns thereby acting as agents of change and social reproduction. Such actions, like those of adults, are pregnant with positive or negative consequences. Indeed, contemporary events in Africa provide illustrations of children and young people's active participation in every aspect of life. For example, in South Africa, they were actively involved in the struggle for liberation from the yoke of apartheid and dictatorship (Kurtz 2010); in many Sub-Saharan African countries, they migrate to cities in search of work and improvements to their lives (Kwankye, Anafi, Tagoe and Castaldo 2007; Hashim 2007), engage in productive activities in rural and urban areas (Ofosu-Kusi 2002; Hashim and Thorsen 2011), and make contributions to the family economy and community development (Kohler 2012; Mahati 2012; Spittler 2012).

Agency, Work and Development

Children engage in the foregoing actions for a number of reasons. Variously, they do so to gain their independence, escape from dysfunctional families, or destitution. A central issue in this is rural-urban migration arising from pervasive under-employment and unemployment in the rural areas, children's pursuit of status, dignity and material things (Kwankye *et al* 2007; Agbu 2009; Ofosu-Kusi and Mizen 2012). The fact that children work is an inevitable consequence of African culture because over the ages children have accompanied their elders and learnt the traditions and culture of their society through work. This is why the debate on child labour in Africa is not so much about the productive form of child engagement that enhances socialisation and aids cognitive, physical and social development. Rather, it is about the exploitative dimensions and inherently unproductive elements that have been incorporated into child socialisation. It is estimated that over 100 million African children between the ages of 5 and 14 years will be engaged in child labour across the continent by 2015 (Agbu

2009). In this respect, both the UNCRC, ACRWC and various African national constitutions are emphatic about the worst forms of child labour. For example, children's involvement in fishing expeditions, mining and quarrying, prostitution, and 'porterage' of heavy loads is clearly detrimental to their development. It is equally negative for the long term development of society since the generation of children who should be educated and helped to acquire proper skills are marginalised through exploitation and disentitlement.

Against this background, Ofosu-Kusi addresses children's bid to gain a foothold in the informal sectors of Ghana's urban environments in Chapter 2. He argues that the rampant spatial and economic 'informalisation' of urban environments serves as a magnet for children to migrate or for urban poor children to desert their homes for the streets and markets. The rising social disorganisation, due in part to a blossoming informal economy, the failure of state institutions to regulate socio-economic activities and to enforce laws on child labour and school attendance reinforces the children's perception that they can assume independent lives in the streets. Under the broad theme of 'street life as labour', a number of street boys and girls were interviewed about their daily lives in Accra in relation to 'expectations, friendships, adaptations and personal survival'. While the majority of adults in the country consider such children as recalcitrant and in search of illusive city attractions, the children in their view were making rational decisions and choices that match their agency with the challenges they encounter in families, schools and society. But with those decisions come inherent or tangential challenges that sometimes disrupt their hopes and aspirations of fashioning a life of their own on the streets. He concludes that although children's potential to solve their problems cannot be idealised as an alternative to the normative obligation of adults, it is the inaction of responsible adults and governmental institutions that compound their vulnerabilities and so motivate them to deploy their personal capacities to solve problems that ostensibly should be the responsibility of adults.

In furtherance of this theme, Ikomola's contribution in Chapter 3 focuses on the dynamics of child fosterage in some markets in Lagos State, Nigeria. Even though fostering is an age-old age tradition in Nigerian societies, he argues that the practice has been abused to the extent that children in urban areas are made to engage in economic activities rather than being nurtured and cared for as demanded by tradition. In his view, the neo-liberal economic policies that have created armies of unemployed and redundant labour in Nigeria have a pride of place in the brutal exploitation of children as supplementary labour in the family economy. The extent of their engagement, he notes, negatively affects their mental, physical, psychological and social development. Using in-depth interviews and observation that spanned four markets in Lagos and 115 boys and girls, he concludes that foster children do not do well at school because they have little time for academic work. Since fostering appeared to impact negatively on children's socialisation, he advocates enforceable legislation to regulate the practice.

In chapter 4 also, Olufemi writes about issues and challenges confronting working children in cocoa-producing areas of Ondo State, Nigeria. His study examined schooling activities, challenges and the coping mechanisms of a number of boys and girls aged between 12 and 17 years. Other significant adults, mostly parents and teachers, were also interviewed. Contrary to most people's expectations, he concludes that children who work on cocoa plantations are not adversely affected by their work, as the children themselves do not consider what they do as child labour. Rather, they consider it as part of their socialisation as others before them have done. Nevertheless, the pressures of work had resulted in academic distraction, loss of interest in studies and eventual dropping out of school by some children in those communities. The children however are not passive recipients of the demands and instructions of their family because they have devised ingenious coping mechanisms such as cooperation and pooling of resources to shorten their work-time so that they could do their personal studies regardless of the circumstances.

The issue of child migration is taken up further by Dolo in Chapter 13, where he argues that child migration as a problematic issue in social development is driven by the logic of child protection. This may be so because of the persistence of the traditional conception of childhood that tends to ignore children's agency. Based on a study of the migration experiences and agency of under-age house-maids in Sikasso, Mali, he argues that increasing levels of child migration raises the need to reappraise children's capacity. He focuses on the processes and circumstances surrounding children's migration, living and working conditions, and their reactive strategies against the challenges they encounter. He cautions that despite the difficulties that the girls face, we must not fail to take into consideration their own abilities to recognise, react and deploy strategies to overcome their challenges and adversities. He therefore concludes that the historic images of household girls, presented as excessively abused people, needs some degree of revision since their own visions of migration and work are more positive.

Agency and Vulnerability

Within the context of the new paradigm, we note that children are active makers of social life rather than passive recipients of psychosocial development. They develop coping mechanisms and show resilience even in times of wars and conflict and under disintegrating family situations (Boyden and Gillian 2005). As Mizen and Ofosu-Kusi (2010) point out, children refuse to be negated by developing a capacity to live through relations of reciprocity, mutuality and friendship. However, children's power to act is not without limits because power in all its forms is mediated by structural difficulties and contextual realities. The daunting reality in many African societies thus constrains children in what they can do. If they choose to work in the informal sector for example, they do so as low wage earners, face job insecurity and exploitative and dangerous conditions and end up being what Davis (2006), labels as 'surplus humanity'. Generally, child vulnerability is manifested in child-child, teacher-pupil, boy-girl and parent-child relations, among others.

It is along this line that Bhana reconfigures the conventional view of African youth in relation to sexuality in Chapter 5. She argues against a construction that is framed in marginalisation and passivity, and a childhood sexuality that projects children, especially girls, as docile victims. Instead, she advocates a more complex construction in which the intricacies between children's agency and their vulnerabilities are brought to the fore. She argues that the most effective way to minimise transmission of HIV and children's vulnerability, while at the same time recognising agency, is to develop a thorough understanding of the structural inequalities. A failure to do so, she warns, might result in the bracketing of young people's sexuality 'within the gender binary of passivity and domination', while little consideration is accorded their sexuality in relation to desires, intricacies of love and joy, expectations, fears, and so on.

In relation to females, she raises the need to deconstruct the discourse that associates young African femininities with pain and disease. Instead, young African girls must be accorded a capacity to influence the situations and occurrences around them, rather than being viewed as passive recipients of infections and sufferers of the consequences. Even though this reorientation is hampered by their emotional and financial dependence on men and the warped distribution of power, she points out that young women are challenging the status quo in relationships by being more assertive, bearing in mind the multiplicity, fluidity and contextual nature of power. Bhana concludes that for policy formulation and implementation to be more successful, children's and young people's vulnerability must not be over-emphasised to the exclusion of sexual agency.

In Chapter 6, Makhumula innovatively applies 'theatre for development', a dramatic technique, to study children's agency within the confines of cultural and structural rigidities. The study investigated how young people define, negotiate, and perform roles and identities in high risk situations of HIV transmission, in relation to youth self-efficacy and the socio-cultural and psychological influences on behaviour. Situating her study in young people's capacity to negotiate and take charge of life-transforming situations, she proposes a holistic approach in a bid to transform their health behaviours. Makhumula's study is fully situated in the new paradigm in which the child actively engages with the social world in spite of the constraints and vulnerabilities, as opposed to the orthodoxy of marginalisation and passivity. In the dramatic depictions of situations of vulnerability to HIV infection, four major narrative forces emerged as the major propellants of the actors' actions. These were 'communion', 'serendipity', 'agency', and 'fatalism', all of which showed that the children were actively engaged in generating, re-presenting and interpreting their experiences in a reflexive manner.

The theme of children's agency, vulnerability and resilience is also addressed by Manyeli in Chapter 7, where she explores the contribution of the community home-based care model in building children's resilience in child-headed households in Malawi. Basing her study on a purposively selected sample of four households with twenty orphaned, abandoned or deserted children aged between 7 and 18 years over a period of time, she explored their experiences, relationships with extended family members and resilience in the face of adversities such as grief, depression, withdrawal, inability to cope, and aggression. She provides a gripping account of the impact of HIV/AIDS-related deaths on the country and children in particular. For children, the greatest effect is their vulnerability to the various socio-economic problems of society as they are thrust into the adult world of caring for themselves and their siblings. Witnessing the death of their parents, the ensuing hardships and the resulting stigma creates lasting mental scars on many of them. All these problems, she notes, combine to make some of the children vulnerable to crime, drugs and alcohol use, forced labour, begging, prostitution or early marriage.

Even though the external family system was found to be a significant alternative for orphaned children, what is instructive about Manyeli's contribution is the effort that children put into managing the affairs of their lives and family after the demise of their parents in order to 'persevere and restore balance'. While stressing the primacy of the children's agency in constructing normality in the midst of their physical/material and emotional vulnerability, it is their resilience, ability to rise from the depths of grief and abandonment that inspires most.

In the ideal world, children are expected to stay in school when they are enrolled; however, for one reason or the other many of them drop out of school. As a result of the increasing difficulty of retaining enrolled children in schools, Elvire's contribution, written in French in Chapter 14, focuses on the causes of school dropout and subsequent reorientation in Abomey-calavi, Benin. Situating her study in the social construction paradigm and social adaptation theory, she found that factors such as lack of finance and school materials, fear of teachers, and health conditions weighed heavily on children's decisions to quit school. Although, she concludes, the drop-outs usually evolved strategies to fit into the society, their success depended on their ability to overcome the social trauma of being labelled as school failure or dropout.

One instance in which the vulnerability of children becomes not only glaring but also disturbing is when they are caricatured in the images of their parents. Writing in French in Chapter 15, Abanda discusses the impact of parents' incarceration on their children's development. Even though imprisonment is a punishment for the law breaker, he argues, it also represents the loss of a bread winner and caretaker for a child. This development endangers the wellbeing and future of the child who might become marginalised, lose respect and be subjected to mockery. His conclusions are based on a study of how fifty children utilised their agency and strategised to overcome their problems and challenges at a time their parents were imprisoned in Yaounde, Cameroon. Although the children put in their best effort, their vulnerability was evident in the fact that many of them did not get the necessary attention from their relatives; some had to abandon school, those who remained in schools obtained poor grades, while others were stigmatised. He concludes that children's wellbeing is greatly hampered by the incarceration of their parents, hence appropriate measures must be taken to shield them from social rejection and abandonment.

Imagination, Participation and Development

Article 12, a general principle of the UNCRC, entreats African countries to grant children the right to freely express their views on matters concerning them according to their age, maturity and ability. Similarly, Article 7 of the ACRWC advocates freedom of expression for a 'child capable of communicating his or her own views...' Nevertheless, both articles draw the ire of sceptics of children's right on the continent, even as many African countries, Kenya and Ghana for instance, have incorporated the right into their national legislations. A careful thought shows the critical nature of the right since participation allows children to develop and strengthen their capabilities to understand, question, and facilitate change in their socio-economic and political environments. Thus, whether children are perceived as biological or social constructs, the right of participation provides a scope for them to mature as responsible social actors.

No doubt, children have a capacity to confound; they have vivid imaginations as well as perceptive views about situations and events, when given the chance to be expressive. In order to understand the world in which children are expected to live in, and to avoid framing our understanding of them on the basis of what others say or presume to be the case, we 'must take seriously the commitment to listening to what children have to say...' (Mizen and Ofosu-Kusi 2010:254). Generally however, adults tend to be presumptuous of children, because we are confident of our understanding of their world. But those views are not sacrosanct since the more we listen to children and see the world through their perspectives, the more fallible our knowledge appears to be.

In reality, children are not completely ignorant of the adult world; they have views and develop opinions based on information gleaned from their surroundings. This is evidenced in Chapter 8 where Mokua Ombati writes on children's perceptions of Kenya's two foremost political leaders. The projective or associative technique was adopted to study how engaged Kenyan children are by seeking their attitudes towards and perceptions of Kenya's two principal politicians, President Mwai Kibaki and Prime Minister Raila Odinga. In this respect, thirty-six Kenyan school children, aged between 7 and 10 years, in the

Eldoret Municipality of North Rift Valley, were interviewed and observed to probe their levels of political socialisation, imagination and identification.

He argues that children, just like adults, build images of political leaders and construct views about them through an active search for political information, and knowledge of the political leaders. All these shape their attitudes towards political authority and represent important elements in their civic development. This is critical because the political exposures that children are subjected to at the early stages of their lives can have significant impacts on their political behaviour much later in life. On these bases, the findings showed that children idealised and demonstrated more pronounced favour towards President Kibaki but were less charitable towards Prime Minister Odinga. An ominous outcome of the study however, was the children's interpretation of political power as wealth, an unfortunate association that projects politics as an opportunity to amass wealth rather than to serve one's country.

Based on the premise that children are relegated to the status of passive and irrational beings by the socio-anthopological orthodoxy, Lebsonga argues in Chapter 9 that children should be considered as active participants and producers of social action. In a bid to prove this point, she studied children's participation in school governance as part of the child-friendly school (CFS) initiative in Cameroon. Applying qualitative techniques of in-depth interviews, focus group discussions and observations to gauge the behaviour of the pupils and teachers, she hoped to determine how participation in the children's government in schools engenders and reinforces children's capacity, and how the dynamics of the process promotes the school as a child-friendly environment. It was apparent that both pupils and schools have benefited from their involvement in school governance because it instilled a sense of consciousness and discipline in the participants and made them work harder on both their academic and non-academic activities.

In Chapter 10, Pamela Muhadia Ngugi discusses the deployment of children's assembly to encourage children to actively participate in the Kenyan society. The thrust of her argument is that when children are properly handled and facilitated at their own pace, they become more receptive to new ideas and so are able to contribute more effectively to the fulfilment of their rights and responsibilities as embedded in the UNCRC, ACRWC, and national legislations. Her study focused on the National Children's Assembly that consists of forty-seven representatives from counties around the country. Among issues raised by the children were accessibility of education in terms of opportunity and distance, child labour, the plight of disabled children, corporal punishment in schools and homes, and the failure of some adults to exercise care-taking responsibilities for their children. The study gives credence to the argument that if given the opportunity, children can confound adults with their insightfulness, sense of identity, responsibility and competence. She concludes that the children's assembly clearly enhances children's agency and is a timely reaction to the new perspectives on childhood in Kenya since the assembly provides a platform for social participation and engagement. Thus, while it is important for children to participate in decision-making, it is essential that they are engaged in national debates since it is an opportunity to extend 'democratic rights to a disenfranchised group'.

Children's social and cultural environments are significant in how they structure their lives, personal identities and participate in that society. In Chapter 11, Bomfie, writing in French, shows how Banali and Mbuti children of the Democratic Republic of Congo (DRC) represent themselves in relation to their environment. The central argument is that children's socio-cognitive development depends on the information acquired from their environment. The environment therefore is instrumental in the construction of the child's self-identity and representation. In a qualitative study, the participants were required to draw objects to represent their desires and role models. Children in Banali, a diamond-mining community, were found to be reconfiguring their self-representation on the most successful mining entrepreneurs, Pikolo and Sheriff. Their objects of desire were diamonds, motor bikes, dollar notes and luxurious houses, all symbols of wealth in that environment.

Mbuti children, on the other hand, represented themselves with simple and basic objects associated with the forest in which they lived rather than with modern symbols even though efforts were being made by authorities and NGOs to 'modernise' them. The children were therefore more likely to follow the footsteps of their parents, and engage in hunting or trapping which were the traditional practices dictated by their environment. In both cases, there was a dominance of local culture in the development of children's character as they evidently applied their agency, positively or negatively, in the pursuit of local vocations. On this basis, he concludes, there is a multiplicity of childhoods shaped by children's milieu rather than an individualised and homogenised one that can be branded as a quintessential African childhood.

Children have imaginative concerns about their environment and are inherently motivated to initiate actions based on their evolving capacities as well as participate in social efforts to restructure and protect it. In Chapter 12, also in French, Djane writes on children's environmental behaviour and argues that, though modelling of human behaviour in the social sciences has greatly contributed to strengthening the link between the humanities and the physical sciences, it is difficult to reconcile them epistemologically. Nevertheless, he attempts to bridge this gap by modelling the environmental behaviour of a randomly selected sample of elementary school children on the basis of seven indicators. It emerged that children were environmentally aware, troubled by the filth engulfing their environment and willing to participate in initiatives to redeem the environment. On the basis of this, he develops a predictive model of children's environmental behaviour and how they apply their agency to act in socially acceptable ways.

Conclusion

Children are critical to every society because they are every society's hope for the future. When properly nurtured, they will blossom and become agents of constructive change, but if neglected, they could become agents of destructive change. Ideas and perceptions that we hold about children, just like other aspects of life, change over time and raise the need for a review of age-old traditions and culture. It is for this reason that the 2011 Institute chose to anchor the imperatives of the new and old discourse on children in African specificities. It is not an attempt to disassociate the African situation from the global context or to blindly copy the global view, but simply to 'relativise' knowledge to Africa. In this development, we see a clash of views between modernisers who recognise the capacity of children and therefore advocate for more space for children to operate, and traditionalists who are sceptical about children being anything but children.

It is obvious however, that we can shape our children into the future force of the continent if we devote time and resources, and recognise their capacity to develop physical and socio-cognitive abilities. In this respect, the various chapters have traversed the continent by dwelling on opportunities and hopes, as well as teasing out the challenges and despair that constrain our efforts to promote the welfare and well-being of African children. Regrettably, majority of our children do not have the privileged childhood that others experience in the developed world. But their greatest asset is their enthusiasm, resilience and capacity to surprise in spite of the meagre opportunities and resources. Our greatest failure as adults will be to turn away and pretend that all is well with African children. The reality is quite obvious.

References

Agbu, O., 2009, 'Introduction: Children and Youth in the Labour Process', in Agbu, O. ed., *Children and Youth in the Labour Process in Africa*, Dakar: CODESRIA.

Boyden, J. and Gillian, M., 2005, 'Children's Risk, Resilience, and Coping in Extreme Situations', in M. Ungar, ed., *Handbook for Working with Children and Youth: Pathways to Resilience across Cultures and Contexts*, London: Sage Publications.

Corsaro, W.A., 2005, *The Sociology of Childhood*, London: Pine Forge Press

Davis, M., 2005, *Planet of Slums*, London: Verso.

Emirbayer, M. and Mische, A., 1998, 'What is Agency?' *American Journal of Sociology*, Vol. 103, No. 4, pp. 962-1023.

Hashim, I.M., 2007, 'Independent Child Migration and Education in Ghana', *Development and Change,* Vol. 38, No. 5, pp. 911-931.

Hashim, I. and Thorsen, D., 2011, *Child Migration in Africa*, London: Zed Books

James, A. and James, A.L., 2001, 'Childhood: Towards a Theory of Continuity and Change', *Annals of the American Academy of Political and Social Science,* Vol. 575, pp. 25 – 37.

Kohler, I., 2012, 'Learning and Children's Work in a Pottery-Making Environment in Northern Cote d'Ivoire', in G. Spittler and M. Bourdillon, eds., *African Children at Work: Working and Learning in Growing Up for Life*, Berlin: Lit Verlag, pp. 113-141.

Korboe, D., 1997, *A Profile of Street Children in Kumasi*, Legon: Centre for Social Policy Studies, University of Ghana.

Kurtz, L.R., 2010, 'Anti-Apartheid Struggle in South Africa, 1912 – 1992, www.nonviolent-conflict.org/images/stories/pdfs/kurtz_south_africa.pdf Accessed 14th April 2014.

Kwankye, S.O., Anarfi, J.K., Tagoe, C.A. and Castaldo, A., 2007, *Coping Strategies of Independent Child Migrants from Northern Ghana to Southern Cities*, Regional Institute of Population Studies (RIPS), University of Ghana, Legon.

Mahati, S.T., 2012, 'Children Learning Life Skills Through Work: Evidence from the Lives of Unaccompanied Migrant Children in a South African Border Town', in G. Spittler and M. Bourdillon, eds., *African Children at Work: Working and Learning in Growing Up for Life*, Berlin: Lit Verlag, pp. 249-277.

Mizen, P. and Ofosu-Kusi, Y., 2010, 'Asking, Giving, Receiving: Friendship as a Survival Strategy among Accra's Street Children', *Childhood*, Vol. 17, No. 4, pp. 441-454.

Mizen, P. Ofosu-Kusi, Y., 2010, 'Unofficial Truths and Everyday Insights: Understanding Voice in Visual Research with the Children of Accra's Urban Poor', *Visual Studies*, Vol. 25, No. 3, pp. 254-267.

Ofosu-Kusi, Y., 2002, 'Migrant Child Labourers in Ghana: A Case Study of the Making and Adjustment Generation', Ph. D Thesis, University of Warwick, UK.

Ofosu-Kusi, Y. and Mizen, P., 2012, 'No Longer Willing to be Dependent: Young People Moving Beyond Learning', in G. Spittler and M. Bourdillon, eds., *'African Children at Work: Working and Learning in Growing Up for Life*', Berlin: Lit Verlag, pp. 279 – 302.

Spittler, G., 2012, 'Children's Work in the Family Economy: A Case Study and Theoretical Discussion', in G. Spittler and M. Bourdillon, eds., *'African Children at Work: Working and Learning in Growing Up for Life*', Berlin: Lit Verlag, pp. 57 – 85.

UN-Habitat, 2010, *The State of African Cities: Governance, Inequalities and Urban Land Markets*, Nairobi: UNEP.

UNICEF, 2012, *State of the World's Children, 2012*, New York: UNICEF.

2

Establishing a Foothold in the Informal Economy: Children's Dreams, Agency and Street Life in Ghana

Yaw Ofosu-Kusi

Introduction

Children and young people's relations with their families and the larger society are influenced by factors such as tradition and culture, modernisation, law, education, and socialisation. These factors variously shape their competencies and how they engage with their worlds, often in positive but sometimes negative ways. Many African children for example, engage in strenuous work as an integral part of their socialisation or migrate independently to live and work elsewhere (Ofosu-Kusi 2002; Kwankye, Anarfi, Tagoe and Castaldo 2007; Hashim and Thorsen 2011; Dougnon 2012). While such actions may have diverse implications on the individual or others, they are also a reflection of children's capacity to address recurring challenges in their lives. One way for some Ghanaian children[1] to negotiate challenges relating to family life, school, and the broader social relations is to travel to the cities, or in the case of children from poor urban households, seek independent lives on the streets. A life on the streets is possible because of the highly informal nature of a good part of the city economy and spaces often symbolised by make-shift structures, open markets and the accompanying opportunity to earn money for one's daily needs.

The rampant informalisation of Ghanaian cities and children's belief in their capacity to do things for themselves underlines the discussion in this chapter. The central argument is that rising social disorganisation, as a result of the state's failure (or inability) to regulate social and economic activities in the streets and markets, reinforces the perception of Ghana's city streets as zones of employment for children. This development encourages child migration as well as an upsurge of urban poor children onto the streets, often in the belief that they are acting in ways that promote their self-interest and personal development. But exercising one's agency to do things in the cities is just one side of the coin; the other side entails tensions and challenges of urban living that in the majority of cases expose children to considerable degrees of vulnerability.

Children in the Terrains of Informality

In the 1960s, Keith Hart studied how the *Frafras*, a migrant group in Nima (a slum in Accra) managed to survive the rampant inflation, insufficient incomes and difficulty of gaining employment in the formal sector. He described what he saw as a 'world of economic activities outside the organised labour force...' where legitimate or illegitimate work was undertaken without regard to permanency or regularity of employment, and fixity of wages (Hart 1973:68). Writing about the informal sector in India, Harriss-White (2009) provided further contextual clarification by categorising activities under 'small-scale' and 'intestitial' informality. In the former case, much of the production and distribution is small and/or embedded in households' daily activities. Virtually unorganised and severely underemployed, the majority of workers here operate on the blind side of laws on registration of businesses, location, health and sanitation, and taxes among others. In the latter case however, the operation levels might be relatively larger and could lie somewhere between formal and informal sectors with the actors here also deliberately circumventing laws and regulations (ibid). Two overlapping trends are similarly discernible in Ghana. The first is structural or spatial informality which gives rise to shanty towns, informal settlements and, in its most dramatic forms, slums such as Nima and Old Fadama. The second is economic informality which involves the side-stepping of state bureaucracy in the production and distribution of goods and services. The two systematically reproduce each other.

Since the 1970s, the size of the informal sector around Africa has rapidly expanded in terms of production and occupation of space, especially public land. Currently, the African Development Bank estimates that in Sub-Sahara Africa, the informal sector accounts for 55 per cent of the gross domestic product and employs 80 per cent of the labour force, with most of them being women and youth (African Development Bank [AfDB] 2013). The untrammelled expansion of the sector in Ghana can be partially traced to its dedicated pursuit of neo-liberal economic policies from the mid-1980s at the behest of the International Monetary Fund (IMF) and the World Bank. Ghana's acquiescence to the demands of the two institutions resulted in liberalisation of its foreign trade, unprecedented devaluations of its currency, mass redundancies and contraction of the public sector, while state institutions were privatised. The basis for this governmental retreat, as Kiely (1998) points out, was the neo-liberal contention that governments cannot efficiently intervene in an economy. The economy improved somehow and so motivated the IMF and World Bank to tout Ghana as a successful case of structural adjustment programmes (SAP) in Africa.

However, the lay-offs and state's disengagement from its traditional responsibilities diminished the size of the formal sector. In the face of dismantled social welfare programmes, the only option for redundant labour was to seek redemption in myriads of marginal activities. Furthermore, because of the major contraction in government expenditure and deflationary nature of policies, the private segment of the formal sector reduced its production capacities, thus cutting down on their rates of labour absorption (Sowah 1993; Konadu-Agyemang 2010). It is widely known that almost all labour made redundant in the restructuring process ended up in the informal sector, thus leading to its phenomenal expansion (Verlet 2000; Davis 2006; Sparks and Barnett 2010). The figures are instructive: in 1990 the informal sector accounted for 49 per cent of total employment in Ghana, but by 1997 it had increased to 89 per cent (Overa 2007), while in 2000, it was estimated to have contributed $1.9 billion to the economy (Schneider 2002).

For an apathetic state, there are many advantages of a blossoming informal sector. For example, it saves considerable resources by either fully or partially disengaging itself from the infrastructural requirements of the sector (Harris-White 2009) thus setting in motion a process of structural and social disorganisation. It can also afford to neglect welfare needs and abandon its reproduction roles because the actors are generally undocumented and unorganised *(ibid)*. Besides, it supports the formal sector through cheap sources of labour, including those of children, without the pressure and associated cost of organised labour, a development that has prompted Ninsen (1991:3) to argue that it is the informal sector that props up 'reproduction of the labour force' in peripheral economies like that of Ghana.

The phenomenal expansion of African cities and the concomitant structural or spatial informality from the 1980s is also closely linked to neo-liberalism. Davis (2006:17) succinctly notes that, 'rapid urban growth in the context of structural adjustment, currency devaluation, and state retrenchment has been an inevitable recipe for the mass production of slums'. Denied a fixed income, thrown out of jobs and unable to afford accommodation, it is inevitable that victims of SAP will gravitate towards informal dwellings in African cities for residence and income-earning activities. Davis (2006:152) goes on to speculate that slums will hold the key to the future of cities 'not just for the poor rural migrants, but also for millions of traditional urbanites displaced or immiserated by the violence of adjustment'. A clear evidence of this is that the physical growth of many African cities from the 1980s far exceeded their economic growth rates, thus resulting in a deficit of infrastructure (*ibid*). For example, while the city of Accra grew by 4.4 per cent in that period, its infrastructure grew at a much smaller rate (Ghana Statistical Service 2010).

A good proportion of the people swelling the populations of Ghana's cities are independent child migrants, poor urban children and young people. The rising number of these people is closely related to the increasing rate of urbanisation in the country, fuelled especially by rural-urban migration. For example, from 1948 to 2000, there was a 'four-fold' increase in urban settlements, thus causing the urban population to surge to 8.3 million, a 'six-fold' increase (MOWAC and UNICEF 2011:14). Children who are part of this surge either live at the informal settlements or undertake their daily activities there. The International Labour Organization (ILO) estimated in 1998 that 12 per cent of working children in Ghana did so in commercial or economic situations (ILO 1999). UNICEF's 2012 State of the World's Children indicated that 34 per cent of children aged between 5 and 14 years were engaged in child labour between 2000 and 2010. While the majority worked in the rural areas in agricultural settings, the most visible were children at markets, bus stations and traffic junctions and slums carrying loads, hawking foods and wares, loading and unloading trucks. The official numbers, often not reflective of the entire picture, are revealing. For instance Catholic Action for Street Children (CAS), counted 10,420 and 19,165 in 1997 and 2002 respectively, in Accra alone (CAS 1997, 2003). That was an astonishing 83 per cent increase in just a period of five years. A joint census undertaken by the Department of Social Welfare, Ricerca E Cooperazione and CAS in 2010 found the number of street children in Accra to have tripled in just a decade to 61,492 (Department of Social Welfare *et al* 2011).

What is responsible for the rising number of street children in Ghana's urban environments? From the perspective of rural children, the conflation of arduous agricultural work with socialisation, school-related factors such as distance, deplorable infrastructure and inadequate teaching and learning materials, motivate some to look for alternatives to their lives (Ofosu-Kusi 2002; World Bank 2000; Ofosu-Kusi and Mizen 2012). Logically, children who are unable to attend schools for reasons of poverty or discrimination in favour of boys (Tuwor and Sossou 2008) are likely to engage in all-day child labour, a development Grootaert and Kanbur (1995) found to increase a child's susceptibility to labour. Research over the years have also shown that family poverty, strict parenting practices, sometimes culminating in domestic abuse, push children to leave homes and where possible migrate to the cities (Beuchemin 1999, Department of Social Welfare et al 2011; UNICEF and MOWAC 2012).

The ubiquity of children on the streets has engaged the public's attention and imagination for a long time. In a study in the 1990s, it emerged that the public perceived them as recalcitrant children who equate the streets to a place of glamour and good life (Korboe 1997:3). A large part of the blame has been heaped on irresponsible parents, especially fathers who for one reason or the other do not assume responsibility for their children. As part of the public debate, the Minister responsible for Basic and Girl Child Education in 2001 blamed 'irresponsible fathers who bring children into the world and ignore their responsibilities, leaving helpless mothers to carry the burden of raising children alone' (Lartey 2001:2). The evidence soon manifested as the 2008 Ghana Demographic and Health Survey (GDHS) found that a little over half (53.8 per cent) of Ghanaian children lived in two-parent households (MOWAC and UNICEF 2011). However, 22.8 per cent lived with their mothers who generally are less educated, have less social capital and are more likely to be only marginally employed. Only 5.6 per cent lived with their fathers. Even more surprising is the fact that 14.3 per cent of people below the age of 18 years lived with neither parent even though the parents are alive somewhere. Regrettably, more of that is occurring on the streets because the study by the Department of Social Welfare and others, found that 5.1 per cent of the children surveyed were born on the streets, often with the fathers either unknown or making virtually no contribution to their upbringing.

Although the actions of migrant street children are usually condemned in the popular press, they represent a bold step that even some adults are unable or unwilling to take. The decisions to leave home, migrate, live and work in an uncertain environment are reflective of their agency, the individual capacity to do things on their own volition. Those actions portray children as having a reasonably good knowledge of their social world. As social agents, their actions culminate in the creation of work, making of friendships and what they believe to be improvements in their personal wellbeing, when they migrate for example. That children can operate as active agents is in opposition to the traditional notion of childhood as a period of biological and social dependence during which they are held captive to the actions or inactions of adults. The danger in refusing to be necessarily passive recipients of adult's behaviour is that their actions may undermine the authority of adults, especially their parents, and so create tensions even if they had sought to make a contribution to the family's wellbeing (Mizen and Ofosu-Kusi 2013). It is such children who utilise their personal resources to reshape their lives that we encounter in the streets and occupy our attention in the following sections.

Researching with Street Children

Since 2004, we have adopted a programme of qualitative research to research 'with' street children and urban poor children. The various segments of the research were conducted in the streets and markets of Accra with different groups of children invariably working and or living in the streets, markets, transport stations, and informal settlements in western and south-western Accra, particularly Old

Fadama, as well as Kaneshi Market, Obtsebi Lamptey Circle, Kwame Nkrumah Circle, the Central Business District of Accra, especially Rawlings Park, and CMB. Basing the study on their 'street life as labour', interactions between us and the participants centred on their journeys to Accra, expectations, friendships, adaptations and personal survival strategies, and in particular, their everyday experiences of work.

By 2012, we had run through a combination of participatory research methods such as photo-elicitation, which provides the participants 'a visual means of expression and communication' (Ofosu-Kusi 2014:44), in-depth interviews through individual or group conversations, and observations researched 'with' 130 boys and girls, aged between 9 and 17 years. The multi-method approach created an opportunity for us to collaborate with the participants by drawing them more actively into the research process. Through photography for example, the participants created visual topics and scenes that enabled construction of themes and engendered discussions between the researcher and the researched beyond the formal process of interviews. Besides, regular visits to the study sites created deeper familiarity with the social context and trust amongst the participants. As a result, an interactively-generated set of narratives that takes 'seriously the commitment to listening to what children have to say...' (Mizen and Ofosu-Kusi 2010:254) as against what we as the 'other' construed the case to be, was developed. The data in this paper is based on a segment of the research in 2012 that involved 31 (15 male and 16 female) participants aged between 10 and 17 years at Old Fadama.

Old Fadama, the principal research environment, is a densely-populated archetype of economic and structural informality. Even though it occupies a physical space of only 31 hectares on the banks of the Odaw River and Korle Lagoon in the south-western part of Accra, it is inhabited by approximately 80,000 people from all parts of the country and beyond (Housing the Masses 2010). The labyrinth of structures found here double as residential and production units, hence the community is practically open to anyone with or without capital to engage in small-scale or interstitial informal activities, legitimate or otherwise. The irrelevance of the state is felt in the absence of legal provision of electricity and water, public health and social care, as well as public schools, within that community. With 65 per cent of children at Old Fadama not attending school (Housing the Masses 2010), the market and adjoining streets offer attractive places for work and socialisation.

Conversion of Aspirations into Actions

Children's desire to travel or seek some form of independence in the cities can only be effectuated through the possession of the necessary capacity or resources to do so. Such resources are not only external – natural or social – but also the powers they posses as human beings After all, agency as Sewell (1992:10) notes, "… arises from the actor's control of resources", and the "capacity to reinterpret or mobilise…." them to exercise that power. As human beings, children possess their own resources, albeit limited, which could be mobilised to engage or manipulate the worlds around them. They possess individual mental and physical abilities to work, engage others through acceptable means of persuasion or even coercion in the bid to promote their interest.

The exercise of agency in this particular case is demonstrated in the voluntary pursuit of dreams through migration to the cities of the country. In spite of the dominant perception that persistent exposure to the vagaries of streets and markets is inimical to children's development (UNICEF 2012), they drift in their numbers to Accra under the conviction that it is a place of redemption from rural drudgery, dysfunctional families, inconstancy of parental behaviour, poverty-imposed vulnerability, and loss of entitlements (Mizen and Ofosu-Kusi 2013). But once there, they can only join 'the ensemble of small, non-wage, income-generating activities' (Ninsin 1991:3) that dominate the urban landscape and represent the subsistence opportunity of last resort for many people.

Unsurprisingly, the expectations of children who migrate to Accra are founded on riches, better lives, urban lifestyles, greener pastures and the grand idea of being able to assume some temporary responsibility for themselves. This desire could be so over-riding that sometimes resources are wrongly appropriated to achieve that objective. Thus, while 13-year-old[2] girl, Shetu, without hesitation, noted that she had come to Accra "to look for money; to seek for greener pasture" regardless of the consequences of the dirty work of scrap-metal collection she was doing, 17-year-old Efe, "was so determined to be in Accra" that she stole her aunt's money to pay for her fare to Accra. Even though her parents had arranged for her to live with her aunt in another city, her inexorable pursuit of an independent life in Accra negated every other suggestion about her future, as expressed in the following words:

> … They were taking me to go and live at Sunyani but they said my relatives were in Accra so I picked my auntie, who was a Police Officer….I picked her money and came to Accra. When I came I took the lorry fare out of the money and gave the rest to my grandmother to be given to her anytime she came around… [Girl, 17 years; Sells sweets]

Another participant, Kweg, was born to a Ghanaian mother and an Ivorian father in a suburb of Abidjan, Ivory Coast. In his community the weighing card, an evidence of early childhood care, is a requirement for school enrolment. He claimed his was lost in a fire outbreak and so was denied enrolment into the local school. Unable to attend school, he started roaming the streets. One day, in an act of considerable bravery, he decided to come to Ghana, at the age of 12 years. He recounted:

My mother did not want to bring me to Ghana. She took all my younger siblings except me. Many times, I overheard my siblings mentioning Ayensu [in Ghana] as where we come from. One day, I took some money my mother had saved…

Int: How much was the money?
Kweg: In Ghana cedis it would be more than 2003. I boarded a vehicle to Takoradi, when I got there I asked and was directed to Ayensu. When I got to the house, my younger aunt was there…. [Male, 16 years, Porter].

It is astonishing that a 12-year-boy would travel hundreds of kilometres from one country to another in search of his roots. But the tenacity of his action gives credence to the significance of some children's capacity to marshal minimal resources to achieve their objectives. His next stop after some time in Ayensudow was the streets of Accra.

What provides concreteness to such decisions is the firm belief that they can have a place as well as means of sustenance on the streets. Hardly has any of the children we have encountered in our research acted purely on impulse in quitting school or leaving their families to embark on those life-changing experiences. In most cases, there was some degree of deliberation to find transport fares or link up with somebody already familiar with the prospective environment. Tilly, a 17-year-old iced-water seller for example recounted that, "….my friend brought me to Kokomba … she said that if I come here I will get something to sell, that's what brought me here". Her decision and resultant action was motivated by her sister-in-law's failure to enrol her in school, even though she had assured her mother that she would do so. Her suggestion that they "should go and look for some work to do" was the confirmation she needed to activate her thoughts after assurances from her friend that she would take her along because, "…. if I sell things there [Old Fadama] I will get money and no one will take the money away from me…" When TJ (another participant) was asked why he stopped schooling to come to Accra, his unhesitating response was:

Because of my friend … He is the one I followed to come to Kaneshie and then I continued to Kokomba (Old Fadama).

Int: And what happened?

TJ: learnt how to work; I carried things and I became happy here… [Boy, 15 years, Porter]

The participants obviously put a great store by the information they received from their peers, especially returning migrants and, typical of most human behaviour, there was a tendency to act on the positive news of earning one's own income, having the freedom to decide for oneself, or learning a trade while disregarding information about the harshness and uncertainties of street life. It is probable that they were fed with distorted information by the returnees in a bid to justify their actions. In this respect, the participants' quest for independence was to a large degree influenced by the perceived success of others, the so-called 'demonstration effect' and the unintended call to action it engenders in some children.

For Val, a chain of misfortunes first forced her to quit schooling and then to contemplate a life in the streets. According to her:

> .... one day when I was going to school, my father said he was going to town. When I came back they said my father had passed away; my mother had just given birth at that time so she could not work. I also could not work at that time to look after myself that is why I stopped schooling... [Girl, 15 years, Iced-water seller]

The extended family is the social insurance for the majority of Ghanaian families (Kutsoati and Morck 2012), especially children, hence a member of the family should have assumed immediate and future responsibility for Val. But that familial institution is creaking and becoming unreliable because of the growing focus on the immediate family, sparse economic resources, migration and urbanisation. Many of the participants therefore cited the lack of support in times of adversity as the primary driver for their migration. Ama summed up children's frustrations in the following words:

> Well, some of ... the children are out there because of poverty, some are obstinate, some want to go to school but they have no one to help them, that is why they have come to live at Kokomba (Old Fadama). [Girl, 17 years, Iced-water seller]

Most adults associate street children with recalcitrance; they see them as people who are unwilling to yield to the authority of adults. Thus, when Efe was asked to reflect on how people see children who work in such places, she argued that it is not just obstinacy, but dereliction of parental duty to children:

> They see them as people who do not respect their mothers or their mothers are not responsible for their needs; that is why they are here. Some children ... their families have the means, but it is because of their own stubbornness that they have come here. Some too, the family does not have anything so they have allowed them to come here to struggle.

It is therefore not surprising that while some of the participants left home because they wanted they control their own lives by themselves ("stubbornness", according to Efe), others saw their exposure to work in Accra as critical to their personal future development, or even an opportunity to make a contribution to the family economy. According to Adel, a girl of 16 years selling iced-water, "I use some (of my income) to buy dresses, shoes, I feed on some, and I save some and remit to my grandparents". Kweg also said, "Yes I make *susu*[4]. When I collect the savings at the end of the month, I send the money to my mother".

Apparently, the absence of control and regulation in the informal urban environment offered an attractive alternative to the restrictive rural life or urban households. That knowledge tended to accentuate children's dissatisfaction with the status quo of homes and families. For example, 15-year-old Gabby preferred loading and off-loading vehicles to the daily routine of having to go to farm and the familiar instruction of "get up and let's go" every morning. For TJ, such routine chores conflicted with his desire to do things he preferred, usually to play with his friends back home, yet he was punished each time he did what he preferred in opposition to what the familial obligations of making a contribution to the household entailed. He recollected:

> Sometimes they told me... they commanded me to do it but sometimes I didn't do it and would go out to play.

Int: So when you didn't do it, what happened?

TJ: They would beat me....they forced me to do it...

Int: I see. But don't you think you were doing it to help them?

TJ: I knew that if I did it I'd be helping them.

Int: But why didn't you want to help them?

TJ: Because I liked to play with my friends.

Not all the participants saw their contribution to the family in the one-dimensional way TJ and Gabby did. For example, Val believed that undertaking domestic chores, even at an early age of 5 years, was a constructive activity that would have telling impact on her identity as a person. She believed it would make her appreciate the value of work, else "....when I grow up I will become lazy and will not like work".

In virtually all cases, the participants gathered information, processed it and made what could be considered as informed decisions that are reflective of their (agents') desire for self-promotion. Although their actions might symbolise to adults (and others) misbehaviours such as disrespect or disobedience, the outcomes of those actions were ostensibly more important than the consequences. The dream and aspiration of staying in Accra and their enactment into concrete actions of travelling and living independently are significant efforts in children's negotiation of their agency. Their journeys to and efforts in Accra are reminders of human power to pursue courses of actions as ends (to find something 'better' to do with their lives) in opposition to normative expectations of staying at home (to help parents) (Archer 2000, cited in Mizen and Ofosu-Kusi 2013). TJ exemplified this when he stated, "I work for myself and put it [money] in my pocket... what I like is that when I do the work I get a lot of money (about 20 Cedis per day)". Adults, in the belief of their rationality, are likely to brand such actions as reckless, a betrayal of family and unwillingness to succumb to the authority of adults and society as was observed by Korboe (1997) in his study of street children in Kumasi. In fact, many of the participants' families agonise over their actions and are unable to fathom out their abandonment of families and the safety of their homes for the streets. Adel, who came from a not-so-poor urban household in another part of Accra, revealed the worries her family expressed each time she went home:

> They ask what is wrong with me to abandon my home and sleep on the streets and visit occasionally. I tell them there is nothing wrong with me..."

But a careful scrutiny unearths rational choices and actions that match their agency with the structural difficulties in their lives. For Adel, the real reasons for leaving home were the "noise, insults, beatings; these caused me to leave the house". However, the opportunity of a life of independence and ability to earn an income and spend it the way one pleases is also pockmarked with challenges that test one's capacity to manage the uncertainties of an informal environment.

Challenges of Being on One's Own

The fact that children possess agency does not mean they are in complete control of the challenges inherent in or tangential to their actions. A major challenge in this regard is the very difficult terrain in which the participants were trying to shape a life of their own. For example, every aspect of their lives at Old Fadama and the other places is 'monitised'. It is therefore impossible to survive without money. They have to pay to bath, wash their faces and clothes, use the toilet, even to cross a wooden bridge linking Old Fadama to the Timber Market, in addition to normal expenditures on food, clothing, health, entertainment, and so on; all these in a physically challenging environment. As recounted by TJ, "When it rains you see that the whole place becomes soaked up, there is stagnant water everywhere and actually some of the areas become flooded". Efe was more concerned about the excessive noise: "... there is noise ... morning afternoon, evening and dawn. Everyday there is noise there". For Val, "... the living conditions here are terrible, I can't continue to live here for many years"; while Evans, a 16-year-old scrap-collector concluded that besides his friends, "...there is nothing good about this place". Ama confirmed:

> Yes, it's very difficult; sometimes when the landlord comes for his rent and we don't have, he comes again for the second time and if we are unable to pay, he packs our things outside until we are able to pay.

Int: And if someone comes to pay for your place?

Ama: Then we lose it and will have to look for another place or sleep outside.

Attractions and associated freedom of the city could be overwhelming for impressionable boys and girls, but they must earn money to have any stake in that. Indeed, finding something to do in Accra's informal sector is not a herculean task for child migrants, but there are challenges that continuously test their capacity to manage the vicissitudes of the streets. A major issue is the competition for work.

For example, one of the common activities girls undertake is selling iced-water. But it entails walking long distances in the scorching sun, as noted by Val who had been selling iced-water for two years and earned around GHc5 a day, "When the sun is out and you are going up and down, you will feel that it scorches your body". The easier way will be staying at one place for the customers to go to her to purchase the sachets of water, but that would be a worthless strategy because there are many other children trying to sell the same product or undertaking similar activity. Besides, she is paid on a piece rate basis, so she needs to work as hard as possible. When TJ who worked as an off-loader was asked about the major challenge in his work, he replied that:

> TJ: You chase cars and there will be nothing in it and you have to chase another until you can get some. That makes the work difficult, and those that you have to carry and send ... may be heavy. There are some that are so heavy that if you carry them your neck will pain you but still you will be forcing yourself to do it.

'Forcing yourself to do it", as TJ has pointed out shows some degree of perseverance, but it is also an evidence of the severe pressure under which they have to perform for subsistence. In fact, they are regularly exposed to dangers of falling in the gutter or being knocked down by vehicles or bumping into others, sometimes with unpleasant consequences. When 14-year-old Bibi was asked about some of the routine occurrences in her everyday work, she said:

> Sometimes accidents happen, for example when someone calls and you are running.... Some children get knocked down as a result of the rush to sell their water.... [Girl, 14 years, iced-water seller]

Old Fadama and the adjoining places with their haphazard distribution of shacks, half-built concrete stores, food stalls and so on, offer minimal security and protection to children. Despite the presence of a police station in the vicinity, existential security is insubstantial as various governments have sought to eradicate the community in its present form rather than offer protection. Not surprisingly, the public and official perception of such a place is that of a den of criminals, notwithstanding the fact that majority of people are hardworking and law-abiding. Thus for people like Efe, the issue is not about watching out for pick-pockets but also dreading what the Police might do if they suspected you of having some money:

> ... the Police have some people who check if you have money then they will go and inform them. They know that this place is full of thieves; so no matter what, you 'stole' it, so they will tell you and they will come for your money or they will come and collect all the things in your room.

A palpable absence of security is therefore evident in their working and social environment. The relatively older and more seasoned street children obviously have all the advantages over the younger and late arrivals as they adjust to the situation. Thus, although the participants willingly talked about their personal tragedies, they had reservations about reporting the perpetrators of violence to any authority. A survival strategy in this respect is a partial assimilation of violence as an occupational hazard. In confirming the degree of violence, Tilly noted that:

> It is bad…The adults here disturb the children. It has made their lives difficult; sometimes when you sell they can beat you up and take the money from you.

The challenge of insecurity sometimes emanate from the children and young people themselves in the form of squabbles and violent confrontations. According to Cila, a street-smart 17-year-old girl, "… a lot of things happen all the time, some fight, others claim their boyfriends have been snatched and in some situations they stab one another. Women fight women and men fight men…"

Though their desire for independence from controlling adults pushed some of the participants to the streets and markets, their existence in that environment is closely linked to adults as employers, landlords, *susu* collectors, and social workers. After all, it is adults' demand for their services as porters, hawkers, domestic workers, *chop bar* (informal restaurants) workers and even prostitutes, sometimes under fictitious family connections to give a sense of normalcy to the relationships, that gives concreteness to their decisions to work in the informal economy. Kweg, for example, regularly worked for a store-keeper under arrangements that clearly fit what Verlett (2000:77) calls 'domestification of working relations'. It suited him that he had something to do every day but he disapproved the way he was being treated: "I don't want her to lord over me or for her to use the little mistakes I make against me… and the boasting of her wealth at my displeasure". Ama also, like many others, regularly incurred the displeasure of her employers, "… she gets angry and insults me". The relatively older street children, especially boys, also pose challenges to weaker ones like TJ because they drive them away from some working places in order to minimise the competition, while others rob them in the night as described by him:

> TJ: There are some people… they have not made up their minds to work, they will be there and someone will suffer, and when he is asleep then they go to take their money from their pockets.

The participants' idea of unbridled freedom is merely wishful, as even in the absence of parents and other family members, the 'social control' of their lives is driven by similar 'paternalism' inherent in familial relations (Morice 2000:195). But while this reality evidently limits the extent of their expectations and abilities, they appear to internalise the challenges, learn lessons and evolve ways of dealing with them.

Thus, in spite of the gloom that sometimes permeate the participants' account of their lives, they also display remarkable optimism about how they would exploit the tangible and intangible resources they have gathered to advance their lives. They variously talked of going back to school, learning a trade, and finding means to help their families. According to Efe:

> I am preparing to go and look for a better work to do. We hear they are coming to demolish this place, that is what I am afraid of. So I am going to look for money to hire a proper house so that when I am there, there will not be any problem.

In comparing the present difficulty of earning an income to the past, Naa, a 16-year-old girl from Togo, warned that, "Of late there is no money, if you don't look for a trade you will not eat"; Ike, a 15-year-old boy working as a driver's mate planned to learn a trade and then "I will move to a new house", because he could not endure the environment for too long; while May, 17-year-old girl who sells iced water wished to move her parents out of Old Fadama, "because this place is not good, so if I grow up and start working, I will take all of them out of this place".

Conclusion

There is no doubt about the profound implications of neo-liberal economic policies that have been implemented in Ghana since the early 1980s on families and their children. The resulting unemployment, withdrawal of subsidies, rising costs of living and the large-scale privatisation of critical social services, such as health care and education, have considerably impoverished families (Brown and Kerr 1997; Ofosu-Kusi 2006; Konadu-Agyemeng 2010). An unintended outcome of this has been a phenomenal expansion of the informal sector as Ghana continues to drift towards a neo-liberal state. The consequent colonisation of public spaces, associated small scale or interstitial informality and the state's inability to enforce child labour and school attendance laws have attracted hoards of children to cities such as Accra, Kumasi and Takoradi. And with the same forces that touted the potential of neo-liberalism in the 1980s now projecting the informal sector as the future of Africa, it is likely that more children would be tempted by the opportunities of urban informality as African governments embrace and rebrand it.

Children and young people's dependence on parents, family and the government in many cases has yielded less tangible results than expected. But while the proper places for children to develop are homes and schools in the company of trustworthy people, their voluntary immersion into the informal sector must also be seen as a physical expression of their dissatisfaction with the status quo and a desire to mitigate personal challenges. No doubt, some of their actions (like independent migration) compound issues for them and their families, but there are sometimes positive implications for their development as well. Regardless of the outcome, they seek to address their problems in ways that conflate their developmental needs with their agency.

The potential of children and what they do for themselves under adverse conditions cannot be idealised as an alternative to the normative obligations of society to them. But it is the inaction of society that exacerbates their vulnerability and so propels a deployment of their innate capacities as human beings. In fact, the words and actions of children in our many years of research show that they are not entirely helpless and are able to effect changes in their existence. Such changes do not always yield the best outcomes, but they indicate reactions to adults' inactions or misguided actions.

Notes

1. The term 'children' is used in accordance with Ghana's constitutional definition of anybody below the age of 18 years, and Article 1 of the United Nations Convention on the Rights of the Child.
2. The participants' ages were those given at the time of the interviews. Since many of them had been in Accra for periods ranging from a few months to 4 or 5 years before we met them, they were apparently much younger when they came to Accra for the first time.
3. At the present (June 2014) exchange rate of 4 Cedis to 1 Euro, this would be approximately 50 Euros.
4. *Susu* is a form of saving in which a person makes a daily contribution to an informal mobile banker. This is done for a fixed period of time after which the saver is given his/her money minus a commission to the mobile banker.

References

African Development Bank (AfDB), 2013, 'Recognising Africa's Informal Sector', www. afdb.org/en/blogs, Accessed 10/03/2014.

Archer, M.S., 2000, *Homo economicus, homo sociologicus, and homo sentiens, rational choice theory: Resisting Colonization,* Archer, M.S. and Tritter, J.Q., London: Routledge.

Beuchemin, E., 1999, *The Exodus: The Growing Migration of Children from Ghana's Rural Areas to the Urban Centres,* Accra: Catholic Action for Street Children and UNICEF.

Brown, L.R. and Kerr, J., 1997, 'Ghana: Structural Adjustment's Star Pupil', in Brown, L.R. and Kerr, J., eds., *The Gender Dimensions of Economic Reforms in Ghana, Mali and Zambia,* Ottawa: Renouf Publishing Company.

Catholic Action for Street Children, 1997, *Field Report,* Accra: CAS.

Catholic Action for Street Children, 2003, *Statistics,* Accra: CAS.

Davis, M., 2006, *Planet of Slums,* London: Verso.

Department of Social Welfare, Ricerca E Cooperazione and CAS, 2011, 'Census on Street Children in the Greater Accra Region', Accra: Department of Social Welfare.

Dougnon, I., 2012, 'Migration of Children and Youth in Mali: Global Versus Local Discourses', in G. Spittler and M. Bourdillon, eds., *African Children at Work: Working and Learning in Growing up in Life,* Berlin: Lit Verlag.

Ghana Statistical Service, 2010, *Population and Housing Census: Provisional Results,* Accra: Government of Ghana/GSS.

Harriss-White, B., 2009, 'Work and Wellbeing in Informal Economies: The Regulative Roles of Institutions of Identity and the State', *World Development*, Vol. 38, No. 2, pp. 170-183.

Hart, K., 1973, 'Informal Income Opportunities and Urban Employment in Ghana', *Journal of Modern African Studies*, Vol. 11, No. 1 (1973) pp. 61-89.

Hashim, I. and Thorsen, D., 2011, *Child Migration in Africa*, London: Zed Books.

ILO, 1999, 'A New Tool to Combat the Worst Form of Child Labour, ILO Convention 182', Geneva: ILO Campaign Office.

Kiely, R., 1998, 'The Crisis of Global Development', in Kiely, R. and Marfleet, P., eds., *Globalisation and the Third World*, London: Routledge.

Konadu-Agyemang, K., 2010, 'The Best of Times and the Worst of Times: Structural Adjustment Programs and Uneven Development in Africa: The Case of Ghana', *The Professional Geographer*, Vol. 52, Vol. 3, pp. 469-483.

Korboe, D., 1997, *A Profile of Street Children in Kumasi*, Legon: Centre for Social Policy Studies, University of Ghana.

Kutsiati, E. and Morck, R., 2012, 'Family Ties, Inheritance Rights, and Successful Poverty Alleviation: Evidence from Ghana', *Working Paper 18080, National Bureau of Economic Research*, http://www.nber.org/papers/w.18080, Accessed 25/06/2014.

Kwankye, S.O., Anarfi, J.K., Tagoe, C.A. and Castaldo, A., 2007, 'Coping Strategies of Independent Child Migrants from Northern Ghana to Southern Cities', Legon: Regional Institute of Population Studies (RIPS), University of Ghana.

Lartey, C., 2001, 'Street Child Phenomena: Irresponsible Fathers to Blame', The *Ghanaian Chronicle*, Vol. 9, No. 136-August 8, 2001.

Ministry of Women and Children's Affairs and UNICEF, 2009, *Children in Ghana*, Accra: UNICEF.

Ministry of Women and Children's Affairs and UNICEF, 2011, 'A Situation Analysis of Ghanaian Children and Women: A Call for Reducing Disparities and Improving Equity', Accra: UNICEF.

Mizen, P. and Ofosu-Kusi, Y., 2010, 'Unofficial Truths and Everyday Insights: Understanding Voice in Visual Research with the Children of Accra's Urban Poor', *Visual Studies*, Vol. 25, No. 3, December 2010, pp. 254-267.

Mizen, P. and Ofosu-Kusi, Y., 2013, 'Agency as Vulnerability: Accounting for Children's Movements to the Streets of Accra', *The Sociological Review*, Vol. 61, No. 2, pp, 363-382.

Morice, A., 2000, 'Paternal Domination: The Typical Relationship Conditioning the Exploitation of Children', in Schelemmer, B., ed., *The Exploited Child*, London: Zed Books.

Ninsen, K.A., 1991, *The Informal Sector in Ghana's Political Economy*, Accra: Freedom Press.

Ofosu-Kusi, Y., 2002, 'Migrant Child Labourers in Accra: A Case Study of the Making of an Adjustment Generation', Ph.D Thesis, University of Warwick, UK, *http://wrap.warwick.ac.uk/3646*

Ofosu-Kusi, Y., 2006, *Development in Ghana: Resources, Utilization and Challenges*, Accra: City Publications.

Ofosu-Kusi, Y., 2014, 'Children's Motivation for Migration and Engagement in Work in the City of Accra', in Bourdillon, M., ed., *The Place of Work in African Childhoods*, Dakar: Council for the Development of Social Science Research (CODESRIA).

Ofosu-Kusi, Y. and Mizen, P., 2012, 'No Longer Willing to be Dependent: Young People Moving Beyond Learning', in Spittler, G. and Bourdillon, M., eds., *African Children at Work,* Berlin: Lit Verlag.

Overa, R., 2007, 'When Men Do Women's Work: Structural Adjustment, Unemployment and Changing Gender Relations in the Informal Economy of Accra, Ghana, *The Journal of Modern African Studies,* Vol. 45, No. 4 (2007), pp. 539-563.

Schneider, F., 2002, 'Size and Measurement of the Informal Economy in 110 Countries Around the World', Presented at the Workshop of Australian National Tax Centre, ANU, Canberra, Australia, July 17, 2002.

Sewell, J.H., 1992, 'A Theory of Structure: Duality, Agency, and Transformation', *American Journal of Sociology*, Vol. 98, No. 1, pp.1-29.

Sowah, N.K., 1993, 'Ghana', in Adepoju, A., ed., *The Impact of Structural Adjustment on the Population of Africa*, London: James Currey.

Sparks, D.L. and Barnett, S.T., 2010, 'The Informal Sector in Sub-Saharan Africa: Out of the Shadows to Foster Sustainable Employment and Equity?' *International Business & Economics Research Journal,* Vol. 9, No. 5, 1-12.

Straker, J., 2007, 'Youth, Globalization, and Millennial Reflection in a Guinean Forest Town', *Journal of Modern African Studies,* Vol. 45, No. 2 (2007), pp. 299-319.

Tutu, R.A., 2010, 'Determinants of the Estimation of Return Migration Propensities among Young People in the Face of Risk: Accra, Ghana', *Journal of Applied Sciences,* Vol.10, No. 8, pp. 620-627.

Tuwor, T. and Sossou, M-A., 2008, 'Gender Discrimination and Education in West Africa: Strategies for Maintaining Girls in School', *International Journal of Inclusive Education*, 12:4, pp.363-379.

UNICEF, 2012, *State of the World's Children 2012,* New York: UNICEF.

Verlet, M., 2000, 'Growing up in Ghana: Deregulation and Employment of Children', in Schlemmer, B., ed., *The Exploited Child*, London: Zed Books.

World Bank, 2000, *Entering the 21st Century: World Development Report 1999/2000,* Oxford: Oxford University Press.

3

Child Fosterage Dynamics in Selected Markets in Lagos State, Nigeria

Adediran Daniel Ikuomola

Introduction

The fostering of children is an ancient phenomenon in Africa. Many researchers and non-governmental agencies have noted that child fostering, the practice of sending one's biological children to live with another family, is widespread in Sub-saharan Africa (Eloundou-Enyegue and Stokes 2002; Verhoef and Morelli 2007). This is because in Africa, especially Nigeria, children belong not only to their biological parents but also to the entire community; hence, both are supposed to play a significant role in their upbringing. Children are also seen as useful helpers by their parents; the belief is that engaging children in work enhances their usefulness to themselves and the entire society (Aderinto 1997; Ayobade 2008). Generally, the basic aspects of fostering in Nigeria are 'traditional' and connected to customary child training, and also to the apprenticeship system for certain professions such that a child not only learns from the master, but also lives with and works for him (Goody 1982). Describing the uniqueness of West African fostering in terms of its tradition, prevalence and the early age at which children are sent out, Isiugo-Abanihe (1985), noted that:

> Fostering here is rooted in kinship structures and traditions, children are sent out not only in the event of family crisis or when one or both natural parents cannot, for some reason, manage to bring them up. Rather, the sending out of children is practised by both stable and unstable families, married and single mothers, healthy and handicapped parents, rural and urban homes, and wealthy and poor parents (p.56).

Goody (1973) also echoed the disciplinary aspect of fostering to involve the sending out of male children to their uncles' homes to be raised, while female children might be claimed by their aunts in infancy or early childhood. Also, in matrilineal societies, children on occasion are raised by maternal kin with claims and responsibilities over those children.

In recent times however, the quest for children to be brought up or educated in the cities, temporary and long-term migration and economic crisis often prompt some parents to foster out their children (UNICEF, UNAIDS, and PEPFAR 2006; Grant and Yeatman 2012). Fostering has also become one of the ways through which some young couples, particularly women, are able to combine labour force participation with motherhood (Vandermeersch 2002; Alber 2004; Grant and Yeatman 2012). The change in parental roles in households as well as the demands of urban economy has resulted in the introduction of even more younger children into the practice (Fiawoo 1978; Bledsoe 1994; Evans and Miguel 2007). According to Isamah and Okunola (1997), the complexities of structural, economic, social and demographic changes in many African societies have affected and altered traditional fostering practices. For example, the Nigerian Demographic, Health and Educational Survey (2004, 2008) notes that most out-of-school children in Nigerian cities are living outside their biological homes, most likely in foster homes and undertaking economic activities their parents may not be aware of. Even where they are allowed to attend school regularly, evidence suggests that education expenses made on them tend to be lower than those made on the household's biological children (Nigerian Demographic, Health and Educational Survey 2008). In spite of the exploitative dimension some people have introduced into the practice of fostering, the unadulterated form serves a useful cultural function where children of less privileged members of the extended family can benefit from the generosity of the more capable ones.

The incidence of child labour in fostering practices seems to have risen during and after the oil boom in the 1970s in major cities in Nigeria (Ebigbo 2003). The post-boom era witnessed major economic deterioration, manifested in dwindling returns on investments, retrenchment and unemployment as well as migration from rural to urban areas. The cumulative effects of these challenges disempowered many families to the extent that some of them had to send their children to live with others in order to minimise the economic hardships they were experiencing. However, such children are increasingly pushed into the performance of menial jobs such as hawking, loading and off-loading of wares in the streets and in homes (Ayobade 2008). Such activities may be inimical to their long-term physical, mental, social and moral development, especially if they affect the children's schooling. Yet, the importance of children in society cannot be over-emphasised because they are the future and for that reason their right to education, self-expression and freedom from exploitation ought to be upheld (UNESCO 2003).

Developmental theory provides a useful framework through which some of the more proximal causes of fostering and its implications on the welfare of the child can be understood. To survive and thrive, children and adolescents need to grow up in a family that provides for their changing needs. Recent theories like Thomas and Chess's (1986) goodness of fit, and Scarr and McCartney's (1983) gene/environment interaction have shown why children should remain with 'extended' families in indigenous care system. The latter concluded that children's need to survive and to thrive simply explains fostering, while children respond differently at different environments, depending on their level of physical, cognitive, emotional, and psychological development. A young person's developmental stage will also be a factor in determining the kinds of support and protection the child needs to survive and possibly thrive. This is a crucial period for establishing survival, growth trajectory, and development of brain function – language acquisition, curiosity, and the emerging understanding of cause and effect (Fabes and Martin 2002). To some extent fosterage arrangements, if not well probed, might jeopardise these important milestones. For example, while children become easily attached if they have a good caregiver, there are also specific risks to their agency, survival and development if they are not afforded the necessary care and attention (Foster 2000). This evolved balance of vulnerability with potential for attachment makes being fostered early in life both a liability and an asset. For obvious reasons, putting children into fosterage is easier than when they are much older, or adults (Townsend and Dawes 2004). Older children in such situations face dilemmas relating to physical growth, self-regulation, appreciation of rules and responsibilities, peer relationship and family identity (Schaeffer 2000). According to Aptekar (2002), these challenges impact on children's physical development and schooling and so any failure to properly resolve them may elevate paid and/or exploitative labour in the streets of major cities as viable option for some boys and girls. It must however be noted that fostering as a socio-cultural practice is not intrinsically bad; in fact, it leads to redistribution of wealth and responsibility in Nigerian families. It is the reduction of the practice into economic exploitation of children that raises concern.

In spite of this, research on child labour as an integral part of fostering has been limited, thus bringing to the fore the need to examine the relationships between child labour and fostering practices. It is in this regard that the study sought to investigate the effect of foster children's activities on their social well-being by taking into consideration gender, types of commercial activities undertaken in foster homes, the role of biological parents on foster children's social and economic wellbeing as well as the factors that lead to child labour under such circumstances.

Methodology

In order to appreciate the problem under study, a descriptive survey comprising both quantitative (questionnaire) and qualitative (in-depth interviews and observations) techniques was adopted. The combination of the two approaches enabled the extraction of descriptive, observational, and narrative data about foster children in the four markets where the study was conducted. The study population consisted of an estimated 20,000 foster children in the major markets of the twenty local government councils in Lagos State (Iginla 2007).

A convenient sample size of 115 boys and girls between the ages of 9 and 17 years was selected through key informants and market-heads in various lines of business. The market heads were identified through a pilot study embarked upon earlier to ascertain the presence of foster children in the selected markets. They were also instrumental in directing us to key informants that aided in the identification of key subjects of the research. Thirty respondents were selected in Oshodi market, twenty-eight from Lagos Island market, twenty-nine from Mushin market, and twenty-eight from Kosofe market, all in the three senatorial districts of Lagos state.

Discussion of Results

Socio-demographic Characteristics of Respondents

Of the 115 respondents in the study, sixty-eight (59.1 per cent) were female while forty-seven (40.9 per cent) were male; all were below the age of 18 years. In terms of their religious affiliation, 71.7 per cent were Christians, 20 per cent Muslims, and 8.3 per cent animists. The majority of them (27 per cent) were 14 years old while 23 per cent were 17 years old. Other age categories were 9 years (3.5 per cent), 10 years (4.3 per cent), 11 years (21.2 per cent), 12 years (13 per cent), and 13 years (8 per cent). The age distribution reflect the usual ages at which children are usually given out in fosterage (Isiugo-Abanihe 1985; Verhoef and Morelli 2007).

Table 1: General Background of Participants

Age	Male	Female	Children in school	Children out of school	Average working hours per day
9	2	2	3	1	3
10	2	5	6	1	3
11	10	13	17	6	3.5
12	3	12	14	1	3.7
13	2	7	5	4	3.9
14	11	20	23	8	5.7
17	17	9	16	10	6.2
	47	68	84 (73.0%)	31(27.0%)	
Total	115 (100%)		115 (100%)		

Approximately 50 per cent of children in the study were from the South-West region of the country which is populated mostly by the Yorubas; 32.1 per cent were from the South-East, predominantly populated by the Igbos; 17.7 per cent were from the South-South populated mostly by the Ijaws, Ogojas, Ibibios and Efiks, while 2.5 per cent were from the North-Central, populated mostly by the Tivs and Hausas. Since the study was conducted in Lagos, it is not really surprising that the majority of the participants were from the area. The Igbos, the second largest group in the study are known for their entrepreneurial skills and propensity to employ children and close relatives, usually from the hinterlands, as shop assistants (Ebigbo 2006).

Seventy-three per cent of the respondents were still attending school as against 27 per cent who were out of school. Of the out-of- school respondents, 16.5 per cent had stopped schooling at the secondary level, 4.3 per cent at the primary level, while 6.1 per cent had never been to school. Even though the majority of respondents were schooling, earlier empirical evidence shows that the majority of child labourers are out of school (Isamah and Okunola 1997). Nonetheless, the high number of out-of-school children in the study, while not representative of the general situation, implies that a good number of children in cities like Lagos are unable to fully enjoy their right to personal development and education as expected under the United Nations Convention on the Rights of the Child as well as the Nigerian Constitution and related Acts of Parliament.

Table 2: Current Status of Children's Biological Parents

Gender	Status of Parents			No Response	Total
	Both Alive	One Alive	Both Dead		
Male	9 (7.8%)	6 (5.2%)	17 (14.8%)	15 (13.0%)	47 (40.9%)
Female	15 (13.1%)	41 (35.7%)	12 (10.4%)	-	68 (59.1%)
Total	24 (20.9%)	47 (40.9%)	29 (25.2%)	15 (13.0%)	115 (100%)

Regarding parentage, forty-seven respondents (40.9 per cent) had lost either of their biological parents, twenty-nine (25.2 per cent) had lost both parents, while twenty-four (20.9 per cent) had surviving parents. However, fifteen (13.0 per cent) were not interested in revealing any information about the current status of their parents. Information about the status of their biological parents is critical because it provides clues and motives for foster care (Isiugo-Abanihe 1985). Possibly, fear and mistrust of strangers prevented them from opening up to the researcher in spite of the assurances given to them. The main activities the foster children engaged in were selling of sachet and table water, hawking of vegetables, and grinding of ingredients like pepper and tomatoes. The daily incomes arising out of these activities ranged between N1,500 and N2,000[1].

Persistence of Fosterage

The traditional reasons for fostering vary widely but the most common are long-term illness of parents, death, divorce, and parents' separation. On the positive side, the reasons could be mutual help among family members, socialisation and education and the strengthening of family ties. It is for these reasons that child fostering has become a characteristic feature of African family systems. According to Isiugo-Abanihe (1985), it not only serves as a reinforcement mechanism for social bonds, but also helps to maintain the high fertility rates through the redistribution of the economic burden of child rearing. It is therefore an integral part of the extended family structure that underlies African societies.

Table 3: Reasons for Living in Foster Homes

Reasons	Frequency	Percentage
To attend school and learn a trade	25	21.7
To serve as house help	10	8.7
Poverty	7	6.1
Death of Parent(s)	16	13.9
Marital problems (Separation/divorce)	13	11.3
To escape rural life	11	9.6
Migration of parents /transfer	14	12.2
I don't know	19	16.5
Total	**115**	**100**

Table 3 outlines the reasons why children live in foster homes rather than with their biological parents. The paramount reason was the quest for education and artisanal skills. Other key reasons were marital problems between parents (11.3 per cent), poverty (6.1 per cent), and migration of parents to other cities (12.2 per cent). The reasons that emerged from the study are not radically different from the traditional reasons adduced to explain child fostering in Africa, and Nigeria in particular. Some of the reasons clearly show the positive role fostering plays in propping up the extended family system. For instance, the second most important reason was the death of parents which raises the issue of collective responsibility of the extended family in looking after their deceased relatives' children. The foster parents may not necessarily be economically better off but they are obliged to show solidarity by making some sacrifices. However, the strains and difficulties experienced in the foster homes and places of work undermine its role in cementing family relations. It is evident that excessive household demands on foster children leave psychological scars on them and also weaken family ties in the long run (Filmer and Pritchett 1999; Sewpaul 2001).

Impact of Activities on the Children's Well-being

The in-school foster children who were all attending public schools generally had little or no time in engaging themselves with academic work, especially after school hours. Yet, the general perception of public education at both primary and secondary levels is that it is staffed with incompetent or ill-motivated teachers, have limited teaching and learning materials and so generally incapable of providing quality education to children (Okunola and Ikuomola 2009). Seven of the foster children said they were attending evening lessons instead of regular schools because they arrived in Lagos in the middle of the school year. However, they expected to be enrolled in regular schools at the beginning of the new academic year. For the in-school children, 14 years was the minimum age at which they gained admission into junior secondary school. It is evident from Table 1 that the number of hours spent working increases with age, as the older the children became, the more hours they had to work both on weekdays and weekends. Simi, a 17-year old girl from Ijesha explained the difficulties encountered as a senior secondary school student this way:

> Lagos was very sweet when I first arrived because my aunty would pick me when primary schools closed, buy me food and take me home. But all these stopped when she started having children when I was in JSS1[2], because I started work seriously. I thought it was fun assisting in carrying the baby at first, but later it prolonged, both at home and in the market; gradually it became my duty to go to the market and start selling until she joined me. It is not easy because there is usually no time to read since I am always already tired after school but have to go straight to the market (Simi, female, 17 years, Ijesha).

Similar concerns were raised by most of the respondents at the secondary school level. However, children in the primary schools within the age brackets of 9 and 12 years were less concerned with the number of hours they were working; instead, their concerns centred on what to eat and the suitability of the market environment as a play ground as well as a place of work. Fortunately, their work load tended to be less than that of those in the secondary schools.

Table 4: Participants' Attitude Towards Work

Research question	Gender		Total
Do you enjoy both economic and domestic activities assigned to you?	Male	Female	
Yes	34(29.6%)	27(23.5%)	61(53.1%)
No	13 (11.3%)	39(33.9%)	52(45.2%)
No response	-	2(1.7%)	2(1.7%)
Total	47(40.9%)	68(59.1%)	115(100.0%)

Not surprisingly, majority of the female respondents (33.9 per cent) did not enjoy the work, especially domestic chores, that they had to do because they found it too demanding. This was a common complaint from children who lived in homes where the foster parents were in the process of raising a family. As for the male counterparts, 11.3 per cent found hawking and other work in the markets interesting because they could meet and play with their friends. Altogether, 53.1 per cent (29.6 per cent male and 23.5 per cent female) claimed to enjoy the work they did as against 45.2 per cent who did not.

Apparently, respondents aged between 9 and 10 years tended to enjoy their work more than the other groups, probably because they worked largely in the domestic domain or had just arrived in Lagos and were being introduced to life in the neighbourhoods.   However, as they progressed in age, they found work to be less and less pleasant. For instance, for those aged between 12 and 17 years, the working hours rose from 3.7 to 6.2 hours per day since they would have passed the stage of pampering, thus more and more of their time had to be devoted to work. Pampering here represents a period of time when the children are introduced to their neighbourhood and surroundings and are shown the nearby markets and selling points in the streets where they are likely to work later. At this stage, they do little or no work, thus a false sense of security and freedom is created. However after this period, they are assigned more work-related responsibilities which, understandably, they find tedious and uninteresting. As they grew older and approached their teens, they appeared to gradually resign themselves to the realities of their work. This was summarised by a participant from Kwara State, in Ojuwoye Market at Mushin:

> I remember when I came two or three years ago, my in-law used to pamper me; the first time, he took me to the market where he was selling building materials then to see things, not knowing that his intention was to gradually introduce me to the work. Initially I was unhappy, but after two months, I had to stop complaining and to see my future in it… (Deji, male,14 years, Mushin).

This knowledge may ultimately be converted into economic capital within various fields upon entering adulthood, thus enabling the youth to develop survival skills and competencies in the street economy. While this is the basis of the traditional concept of fostering, that the knowledge could become 'embodied cultural capital' (Bourdieu 1986), it is often exploitative; hence, some of the children's negative perception of the practice. The relationship between age and social wellbeing was also found to be more favourable for younger foster children between the ages of 9 and 12 years as opposed to those from 13 years onward. The younger ones were apparently better cared for, so they appeared   more relaxed even while they were being interviewed; their school uniforms were cleaner and sometimes well ironed, unlike their relatively older counterparts whose school uniforms and house wears were unkempt and in some cases tattered. Children with foster parents working in the clothing business were better dressed because they had to look nice to attract customers to the shops, as noted by Tola, a 14-year-old participant:

> Once it is time to go to the market, I am always told to put on my best clothes, because it attracts customers. I have been severely beaten a number of times for not dressing well to the shop. Ever since, I have learnt my lesson (Tola, female, 14 years, Mushin).

On dietary habits, the culture of buying foods piecemeal from vendors was observed among a sizeable number of respondents in the mornings. However, there were a few others (7 per cent) who sometimes ate at home before going to school, especially on Mondays as the leftovers from Sunday meals were served as breakfast. Otherwise, they were given between N10[1] and N20[2] for breakfast, depending on their age. Those whose schools were not far from their homes or the markets were asked to return home or go to the markets during school break for their breakfast; others had to forfeit their meals because they had too much work to do. Others preferred to be given money, because it gave them the freedom to make their own choices about food and drinks, as noted by Tola:

> The money is what I am used to, whenever we eat at home, aunty will not give us the money (Tola, 14 years, Mushin).

More than half of the respondents, 62 out of the 115, noted that most often they ate late because by the time they finished their work in the market and managed to get home through the heavy traffic, it would already be late in the night. For those who lived around the market place, 53 of the 115 participants had the privilege of eating around normal times in the evenings. However, most of them (71) could not get regular morning meals before going to school. Responses from in-school children showed that lunch was often late and irregular. The earliest time was estimated by the children to be between 3pm and 5pm, depending on the distance of the participants' school from the market. Regarding their health, the majority (77.4 per cent) noted that their health concerns were attended to whenever they fell ill. However, there were those who were afraid to report any ailment to their foster parents because of the harsh reaction they might receive. This is made clearer from the account of James below:

> It is always difficult for me to tell my foster parents that I am ill because of the scolding that usually comes with it. The last time I had malaria, I could not eat and I did not tell my aunty and uncle not until I fainted and my neighbours rushed me to a nearby chemist shop, before I was eventually taken to the hospital (James, male, 13years, Kosofe).

Probing into the reason why he was scared of reporting the ailment to the foster parents, James responded:

My aunty and her husband do complain a lot that I am fond of wasting their money and resources, so I find it difficult to tell them I need malaria drugs. The malaria is the result of exposure to mosquitoes in the market, because we usually close late at night, and our shop stand is directly on top of the drainage.

The experiences of James reflect some of the findings of (Bledsoe 1990; Bicego, Rutstein and Johnson 2003) to the effect that a number of foster children experience more work, less well-being and education, compared to other children in the same household. As a result of such developments, researchers like Foster (2000) have concluded that the fostering system in urban areas has been stressed and damaged beyond repair.

Gender Preference and Activities of Foster Children

According to Mrs. Edem, a mother of two with a male foster child, the nature of the work or business activities of foster parents and the age and gender of the foster child are basic determinants in child fosterage. These will also determine the type of work the foster child will be asked to do at home or in the market place. She explained:

> This boy (pointing to him) is a relative of my husband; when I needed someone to assist me at home after my second child's birth, my husband went to the village (Eastern Nigeria) and arrived with Emeka. Although I would have preferred a girl, he felt that a boy would be more helpful to both of us at home and in the shop (Mrs. Idem, Kosofe),

Three of the five foster parents interviewed corroborated Mrs. Idem's view that, to a large extent, the genders of foster children determines the duties that are assigned to them. They pointed out that, even among their own biological children, responsibilities are distributed according to gender. Another interviewee claimed that:

> In fostering a child, I went for a boy because training a male child is an investment one can reap from, it is even cheaper than paid house help. This particular boy with me has been very helpful to me, especially when my wife was at school in Lagos State University two years ago. He does virtually everything from domestic to commercial activities at home and in my shop, a female would have run away, as was the case with a neighbour last year (Mr. Ojogbane, male, Kosofe).

His wife added:

> Girls are even more difficult to train; they are exposed to a lot of problems ranging from rape, molestation, harassment.... From my own experience as a child, my niece was a victim, at an early age of 16, although this was partly due to my auntie's fault and neglect, she became pregnant and was eventually sent packing (back to the village). The problem it created between her biological parents and mine is best imagined (Mrs. Ojogbane, Kosofe).

The exploitative element that sometimes characterises fostering is evident in Mr. Ojogbane's classification of the relationship as an investment, something to profit from at an appropriate time. While foster children are engaged in all sorts of domestic activities regardless of their gender, the interviews however show that functions such as babysitting are reserved for female foster children. In addition, the foster mothers claimed that even though they preferred fostering girls at the early stages of their marriage, they would be indifferent to gender at the latter stages when they would no longer be bearing children. With regard to commercial activities however, there appeared to be a gender preference. For example, according to the two male foster parents in the study, male children were preferred as assistants in trading activities such as wood, iron, cement, and ornaments, that are dominated by men. In contrast, female foster children are preferred in trading activities that deal with 'feminine' things like vegetables, cooking utensils, and beauty products.

Table 5: Gender Distribution of Work

Type of Work	Gender		
	Male	Female	Total
Domestic activities/Assistance in the market	11(9.6%)	21(18.3%)	32(27.7%)
Sale of wares at the market	7(6.1%)	15(13.0%)	22(19.1%)
Sale of wares both at home and market	12(10.4%)	19(16.5%)	31(27.0%)
Learning trade/working	17(14.8%)	13(11.3%)	30(26.1%)
Total	47 (40.9%)	68 (59.1%)	115 (100.0%)

Table 5 shows that 9.6 per cent of male respondents were variously involved in domestic activities and providing assistance in the market as against 18.3 per cent of female respondents. For those who engaged solely in commercial activities (selling of goods) for their foster parents, 13 per cent were female compared to 6.1 per cent male counterparts. Similarly, there were more females engaged in the sale of wares both at home and in the markets than males. However, more males than females served as both apprentices and workers earning incomes for their foster parents. Evidently, most of the children are in one way or the other involved in commercial activities as confirmed by a 14-year-old female participant, Adama, in Mushin Market:

> I have to work with my uncle's wife everyday in her nylon-cutting and soap-making shop here in Mushin, I am on her pay roll now; she saves the money for me and sends it home to my mother in the village every month; she is sick and this is the only way my uncle said he can help her, so I have to leave the village in Oyo to learn a trade and work so as to struggle for myself and my mother since the death of my father (Adama, Female, 14 years, Mushin).

Though most of the children do not see their income-generating activities as negative, it was observed that many of them were usually overworked by the end of the day. This was even more noticeable among children who combined schooling with after-school work in the markets.

The Influence of Biological Parents on Foster Parents' Duties

Efforts were made to determine the influence of biological parents on their children's schooling while they were with the foster parents. To begin with, of the thirty-one (30 per cent) respondents who were not attending school at that time, nineteen (16.5 per cent) had stopped schooling altogether, while five (4.3 per cent) had stopped schooling at the primary level. Apparently, children whose biological parents were from the Western part of Nigeria (Yoruba-speaking area) were frequently in contact with them, compared to those from the other parts of Nigeria. Two reasons could account for this; the first is proximity. Lagos State is situated in the western part of Nigeria, thus it was much easier for the parents to travel to visit their children or keep in touch through mobile phones. The second is the state's free education policy at both primary and secondary levels. It has also been argued that the average Yoruba family takes children's education more seriously than any other ethnic group in Nigeria (NDHES 2008). In the case of other participants from across the River Niger (Igbos, Calabar, Effik and Ibibio-speaking), much emphasis was placed on the acquisition of trading skills as the path to future success. There was also a widely-held belief amongst the participants that 'coming to Lagos will make them successful'. This view is common to most people in the rural areas because they see the city as a place of unending opportunities that could transform their situation in life. Those who fared worst in terms of parental influence on their education were respondents from Calabar and Akwa Ibom. The obvious explanation for this is the hundreds of kilometres that separate the children in Lagos from the parents back home. For example, five of them had never seen their parents in the two years preceding the study, neither were they able to contact them through telephones. Of the total number of respondents who had at least a surviving parent (twenty-four with both parents alive and forty-seven with one single parent alive), twenty-one had not seen their parents in the past two years, as against thirteen participants from the western state. Five of the respondents could not recall when they last saw their biological parents; one of them said in Pidgin English "e don tai oh wen I see my family since I come" (meaning he has not seen his family since his arrival). However, they were in touch through phones. Simon, a 13-year-old native of Calabar, who was living in Ijesha pointed out:

> My parents live in far away Calabar, and the family I am staying with just does not want me to school, they do not believe in education because they themselves are not educated.

According to Kolomoh, a 14-year-old Yoruba boy living in Aguda, a relatively highbrow area, compared to Ijesha:

> In my own case, I was just lucky to have been placed in a school, not just a school but also a private one for that matter! I was also schooling before coming to Lagos, my parents do not play with education. Every holiday my dad visits and monitors my performance in school.

For Uduaken, a 17-year-old boy from Akwa-Ibom, "They found out that I was brilliant, that was why I am in school today, not necessarily because of my parents! They have not visited me since l left home".

Apart from schooling, the majority of biological parents had little or no influence on the way and manner in which their children were being raised in the foster homes, even though some of them were well-informed about the wellbeing of their children. Apparently, those who were not doing well at school or were engaged in deviant and sometimes criminal behaviours were either sent back home or cautioned by emissaries. Sometimes, people travelling to Lagos were asked to visit the children on their behalf, thus maintaining some contact, and through that exerting some form of influence on the lives of their children.

Conclusion

The differential engagement of foster children in the public sphere in laborious economic activities, in comparison to biological children, defeats the major reason and philosophy behind child fostering. With the varying degrees and circumstances found surrounding fostering practices in selected markets in Lagos State, Nigeria, foster children can be said to be disadvantaged, relative to other children within the same household. The study observed the engagement of children as young as 9 years hawking wares for their foster parents. Unfortunately, as with many social practices in Africa, fostering tends to impact more on girls than boys, since the former usually have to sacrifice their education for the wellbeing of the foster family because of the domestic responsibilities they are assigned to do. According to Verhoeff and Morelli (2007), the cooperation between the donor and recipient family colours the experience and outcomes of children in their foster home. This means that the true extent of the child's experiences is difficult to ascertain since it is shrouded in family relations. For example, even though some biological parents of foster children worked and lived close to the foster parents, they did not pay regular visits to their children. This is consistent with the fact that fostering is often initiated by the biological parents of the child as a way of minimising their dependency burden or sometimes aspiring for better chances in life for their children. But this shirking of biological responsibility means that some of them may not be aware of the laborious and time-consuming activities their children are expected to undertake in opposition to the quest for their overall development.

Even though child fostering has always been an integral part of the African culture, it was never intended to be an avenue for foster parents to exploit the child for their own economic gains. The study therefore recommends that biological parents and relatives should carefully examine the socio-economic intentions of would-be foster parents before giving out their children. It is also imperative that the laws regulating child fostering in Nigeria are implemented to the letter.

Notes

1.   Between US$10 and US $15 daily.
2.   Junior Secondary School.

References

Aderinto, A.A., 1997, *Home Dissertation among Juveniles in Lagos and Ibadan Metropolis: Causes Patterns and Consequences,* unpublished PhD Thesis, Department of Sociology, University of Ibadan.

Alber, E. 2004, 'Grandparents as Foster-parents: Transformations in Foster Relations between Grandparents and Grandchildren in Northern Benin, *Africa* Vol. 74, No.1, pp. 28-46.

Aptekar, L., 1996, 'Street Children in Nairobi', *Africa Insight,* Vol. 26, No. 3, pp. 250-259.

Ayobade, A., 2008, *A Critical Appraisal of Parents' Poverty and Children's Street Entrepreneurship in Lagos Metropolis,* A paper presented at the 6th Annual Lecture and Workshop of the Department of Sociology, University of Lagos.

Bicego, G., Rutstein, S., and Johnson, K., 2003, 'Dimensions of the Emerging Orphan Crisis in Sub-Saharan Africa', *Social Science and Medicine,* Vol. 56, pp. 1235-1247.

Bledsoe, C., 1990, 'The Politics of Children: Fosterage and Social Management of Fertility among the Mende of Sierra Leone', in W.P. Handwerker, ed., *Births and Power: Social Change and the Politics of Reproduction*, London: Zed Books. pp. 88-100.

Bledsoe, C. 1994, 'Children are Like Young Bamboo Trees: Potentiality and Reproduction in Sub-Saharan Africa', in K. Lindahl-Kiessling and H. Landberg, eds., *Population, Economic Development and the Environment.* Oxford, England: Oxford University Press. pp. 105-138.

Bourdieu, P., 1986, 'The Forms of Capital', in J. Richardson, ed., *Handbook of Theory and Research for the Sociology of Education,* New York: Greenwood.

Ebigbo, P.O., 2003, 'Street Children: The Core of Child Abuse and Neglect in Nigeria', *Children, Youth and Environments,* Vol. 13, No. 1, pp. 1-12.

Ebigbo, P.O., 2006, *A Profile of Child Trafficking in Nigeria,* Enugu: Fourth Dimension.

Eloundou-Enyegue, P.M. and Stokes, C.S., 2002, 'Will Economic Crisis in Africa Weaken Rural-Urban Ties: Insights from Child Fosterage Trends in Cameroon', *Rural Sociology,* Vol. 67, No. 2, pp. 278-298.

Evans, D.K. and Miguel, E. 2007, 'Orphans and Schooling in Africa: A Longitudinal Analysis', *Demography,* Vol. 44, No. 1, pp.3-17.

Fabes, R.A. and Martin, C.L., 2002, *Exploring Child Development: Transactions and Transformations (2nd edition)*, Boston: Allyn & Bacon.

Fiawoo, D.K., 1978, 'Some Patterns of Foster Care in Ghana', in *C. Oppong*, G. Adaba, M. Bekombo-Priso and J. Mogey, eds., *Marriage, Fertility and Parenthood in West Africa*, Canberra: Australian National University Press, pp. 278-288.

Filmer, D. and Pritchett, L., 1999, 'The Effects of Household Wealth on Educational Attainment', *Population and Development Review*, Vol. 25, No. 1, pp. 85-120.

Foster, G., 2000, 'The Capacity of the Extended Family Safety Net for Orphans in Africa', *Psychology, Health and Medicine*, Vol. 5, No. 1, pp. 55-62.

Goody, E. 1973, *Contexts of Kinship: An Essay in the Family Sociology of the Gonja of Northern Ghana*, Cambridge: Cambridge University Press.

Goody, E., 1982, *Parenthood and Social Reproduction: Fostering and Occupational Roles in West Africa*, Cambridge: Cambridge University Press.

Grant, M.J. and Yeatman, S. 2012, 'The Relationship Between Orphanhood and Child Fostering in Sub-Saharan Africa, 1990s-2000s', *Population Studies*, Vol. 66, No.3, pp. 279-295.

Iginla, S.L., 2007, *Area Boys' Activities: An Underground Economy*, Lagos State Judiciary Report, Wednesday, 11 April 2007, Lagos: State Secretariat Publication.

Isamah, A.N. and Okunola, R.A., 1997, 'Family Life Under Economic Adjustment: The Rise of Child Breadwinners', in I.J. Guyer, H. Denzer and A. Agbage, eds., *Money Struggles and City-Life: Devaluation in Ibadan and Other Urban Centres in Southern Nigeria 1986-1996*, Portsmouth NH: Heinnemann, pp. 63-72.

Isiugo-Abanihe, U.C., 1985, 'Child Fosterage in West Africa', *Population and Development Review*, Vol. 11, No. 1, pp. 53-73.

Nigeria Demographic and Health Survey, 2008, 'EdData, 2004/2008', Lagos: National Population Commission and ICF Macro.

Okunola, R.A and Ikuomola, A.D., 2009, 'Corporate Establishments' Preferences and the Quest for Overseas' Qualifications by Nigerian University Students', *Educational Research and Review*, Vol. 4, No. 12, pp. 626-633.

Scarr, S. and McCartney, K., 1983, 'How People Make Their Own Environments: A Theory of Genotype-environment Effects', *Child Development*, Vol. 54, pp. 424-435.

Schaeffer, D., 2000, *Social and Personality Development (5ᵗʰ edition)*, Belmont, CA: Thompson Wadsworth.

Sewpaul, V., 2001, 'Models of Intervention for Children in Difficult Circumstances in South Africa', *Child Welfare*, Vol. 5, pp. 571-586.

Thomas, A. and Chess, S., 1986, 'The New York Longitudinal Study: From Infancy to Early Adult Life', in R. Plomin and L. Dunn, eds., *The Study of Temperament: Changes, Continuities, Challenges*, Hillsdale, New Jersey: Erlbaum. pp. 41-45.

Townsend, L. and Dawes, A., 2004, 'Willingness to Care for Children Orphaned by HIV/AIDS: A Study of Foster and Adoptive Parents', *African Journal of AIDS Research*, Vol. 3, No. 1, pp. 69-80.

UNESCO, 2003, 'EFA Monitoring Report on Foster Care and Schooling in West Africa: The State of Knowledge', New York: United Nations Educational, Scientific and Cultural Organization.

UNICEF, UNAIDS and PEPFAR, 2006, *Children Affected by AIDS: Africa's Orphaned and Vulnerable Generations*. New York: UNICEF.

Vandermeersch, C., 2002, 'Child Fostering Under Six in Senegal in 1992-1993', *Population*, Vol. 57, No. 4/5: pp. 661_688.

Verhoef, H. and Morelli, G., 2007, 'A Child is a Child: Fostering Experiences in North Western Cameroon', *Ethos*, Vol. 35, Issue 1, pp. 33-64.

4

Educational Challenges Facing Children in Cocoa Plantations in Ondo State, Nigeria

Musediq Olufemi Lawal

Introduction

Across the world, the future of every culture is reposed in its children; hence there is the need for effective guidance and protection as they are brought up. In Africa, children occupy a central place in society and are raised in close family groups with the responsibility for their social development shared amongst members of the community. Even where the parents are dead, a child will usually have traditional surrogate parents as a cushion against the odds (Ajiferuke 2007). In recent times however, high mortality rates in some African communities and the challenges of urbanisation and modernity have resulted in the abandonment of some children to their own devices after the demise of their parents. Throughout childhood, it is in the home and family that children experience the first impulses and input towards socialisation. In this process, the parents transmit values, rules and standards about ways of thinking and acting, and provide an interpretive lens through which children view social relationships and structures (Ennew 1994; Super and Harkness 2002). Not limited to this, the input from the world equally comes to the child in many cultural and social forms, such as in literature, art and the mass media. The experiences gained from there form the psychological foundation for the child's interaction with the world and enables the child to become a self-reliant individual who enters into social relationships by personal choice.

An appreciation of the roles of children as future leaders has led to both national and international policy initiatives, laws and conventions to guide their growth and development. The expectation is that children will be properly groomed and adequately equipped with what they need for a fruitful adult life if standard rules and laws are applied to certain aspects of their lives. The progress made so far in Nigeria comes in the form of policies initiated to facilitate children's access to education across the nation and protect them against all forms of child abuse. For example, the federal government has developed educational policies such as the Universal Primary Education (UPE), Education for All (EFA) and Universal Basic Education (UBE) in order to address the problem of school drop outs, dwindling enrolment in primary and secondary schools and the general deterioration of education in the country (Ikwuyatum 2010). The UPE scheme was instituted in 1976 to develop the educational capacity of Nigerians generally while the UBE was initiated in 1999 to ensure the provision of free and compulsory basic education for all Nigerian children. The initiative aimed to put an end to child labour (ILO 2004) and improve the relevance, efficiency and quality of schools, as well as address the basic education needs of nomadic, out-of-school and vulnerable children generally.

In spite of this, thousands of children are involved in many work situations and activities rather than being in schools (World Bank 2007) or combine schooling and work. However, it is impossible for working children to find the time and/or energy to attend school regularly, hence most of them drop out of school. About 6 million of such children are working in Nigeria (Ikwuyatum 2010). According to UNICEF (2006), over 8 million children in Nigeria combine schooling and work so that they can cover their education expenses. Gross primary school enrolment declined in Nigeria from approximately 86 per cent in 1993 to 70 per cent in 1996 (Ikwuyatum 2010). There was also a sharp decline in the primary school gross enrolment ratio (GER), from 82 per cent in 1985 to 68 per cent in 1990. An insight into the attendance ratio at both primary and secondary schools level is presented in Table 1.

Table 1: School Attendance Ratio: 2007/2008

Background Characteristics	Net Attendance Ratio				Gross Attendance Ratio			
	Male	Female	Total	Gender Parity Index	Male	Female	Total	Total Parity Index
Primary School								
Residence								
Urban	75.9	72.2	74.1	0.95	99.5	95.5	97.5	0.96
Rural	60.3	53.5	57.0	0.89	84.4	72.7	78.7	0.86
Zone								
North Central	71.7	69.2	70.5	0.97	104.4	97.8	101.2	0.94
North East	46.8	40.4	43.7	0.86	66.4	55.8	61.3	0.84
North West	49.8	37.1	43.4	0.75	68.4	49.2	58.7	0.72
South East	82.4	83.2	82.8	1.01	109.5	110.7	110.1	1.01
South South	80.1	80.1	80.1	1.00	109.1	105.6	107.4	0.97
South West	77.8	75.2	76.6	0.97	101.0	98.9	99.9	0.98

Secondary School							
Residence							
Urban	66.2	62.5	64.3	0.94	99.2	88.0	93.5	0.89
Rural	44.7	38.0	41.4	0.85	70.4	54.6	62.6	0.77
Zone							
North Central	50.1	41.6	46.0	0.83	84.9	62.2	73.9	0.73
North East	29.4	22.1	25.7	0.75	47.2	30.3	38.6	0.64
North West	33.8	19.3	26.7	0.57	54.6	28.7	42.0	0.52
South East	68.7	68.7	68.7	1.00	98.0	91.5	94.6	0.93
South South	66.7	65.5	66.1	0.98	100.6	93.6	97.2	0.93
South West	68.5	68.9	68.7	1.01	101.7	98.6	100.1	0.97

Source: National Population Commission, 2009.

Table 1 shows primary school and secondary school net attendance ratio (NAR) and gross attendance ratios (GAR)[1] for the 2007/2008 school year by residence and zones. The overall NAR for primary schools is 62, while the GAR is 84. Comparatively, the NAR is much higher in urban areas (74 per cent) than in rural areas (57 per cent). The GAR is also higher in urban areas than in rural areas (98 and 79 per cent respectively). There is a slight difference in the NAR between males and females at the primary school level (65 and 59 per cent, respectively). Males also show a higher GAR at the primary school level (89 per cent) than females (80 per cent). There are significant variations at the zonal level; the primary NAR and GAR are highest in the South East (83 and 110 per cent, respectively). North West has the lowest NAR and GAR, with 43 and 59 per cent respectively. The NAR at the secondary school level is 49 per cent, while the GAR is 73 per cent. This is an indication that fewer people attend secondary school than primary school. Both ratios are much higher in urban areas than in rural areas. The NAR and GAR at the secondary school level for males and females follow a similar pattern as the primary school level, with males recording a higher proportion in both cases (52 versus 46 for the NAR and 80 versus 66 for the GAR). South East and South West have the highest NAR (69 per cent each) for the secondary school level while North East has the lowest (26 per cent). South West also has the highest GAR (100 per cent) while North East has the lowest GAR (39 per cent). The forgoing indicates that a large number of children, especially those in the rural areas, are excluded from the school system and are therefore pushed into alternative activities, such as work.

Children's perspective on why they abandon school is still muted despite the vast array of research and scholarship on working children. A good part of the effort has focused on blaming society for the exodus of children from classrooms.

While this is true, it is also critical to appreciate children's perspectives on their active involvement in work if we are intent on finding lasting solutions to this recurring problem. It is against this background that this study sought to examine children's perception of education and their engagement on the plantations, the effects of work on their education, challenges confronting them as well as their coping mechanisms. This was premised on the researcher's familiarity with cocoa plantations and Ondo State as the largest producer of cocoa in Nigeria.

Methodology

The study was an exploratory one that applied qualitative methods for an in-depth understanding of the problem. The study began in May 2011 with a familiarisation visit followed by data collection from the study sites in June 2011. The specific study sites were Oke-Igbo/Ile Oluji (Igbo Olodumare, Ajeloro), Odigbo (Asewele-Korede, Omifon) and Akure South (Ipogun and Ibule) Local Government Areas (LGAs) of Ondo State. These are LGAs known to be the largest producers of cocoa in the state.

Children and youth between the ages of 12 and 17 years, who were actively involved in cocoa farming in the sampled cocoa plantations, were regarded as the population for the study. In addition, teachers in the schools within the communities were involved in the study as key informants due to their daily interactions with the children and their parents. In all, the participants in the study were thirty-six children and twelve teachers, all of whom were selected through a multi-stage sampling technique. The first stage was a purposive selection of eight notable cocoa-producing LGAs out of a total of fifteen cocoa-producing LGAs in the state. In the second stage, two cocoa settlements from a zone in each of the selected LGAs were randomly selected, while the third stage involved selection of children from each of the sampled cocoa settlements. In each of the communities (Igbo Olodumare, Ajeloro, Asewele-Korede, Omifon, Ipogun and Ibule), six respondents, male and female working on cocoa farms, were selected through convenience sampling method to participate in focus group discussion (FGD). The teachers were sampled through purposive, accidental and snowballing techniques. The main criteria for inclusion of respondents (children) was residency of three to four years in the sampled communities, while the teachers must have taught in the local schools for some time so that they would have a wealth of information and knowledge of the study areas.

The primary data were collected through focus group discussion (FGD) involving the children and key informant interviews (KIIs) involving the teachers. The participants' interests were taken into serious consideration at each stage of the research process. They were informed of their right to withdraw from the study anytime they desired and advised not to answer particular questions if they did not want to. In addition, they were assured of the necessary confidentiality while each of them was given a pseudonym to ensure that no information provided could be traced back to them. The qualitative data were analysed through the strategy of content analysis and ethnographic summaries. Some important quotations from respondents during FGDs and KIIs were reported verbatim for further illustration of issues under focus.

Social Background of the Participants

Out of the thirty-six children who took part in the study, eighteen were boys while the rest were girls. All of them were natives of the communities, except two who were born elsewhere. Only three of the participants had been fostered into families producing cocoa. Four of the participants had parents who were blacksmiths and traders by profession, thus not directly involved in cocoa production. None of the children was a migrant since children are forbidden from migrating to work on cocoa plantations in the area. Of the twelve teachers who acted as the key informants, only two were females. A good number of them had working experience and knowledge of the communities since they have been residing there for at least three years.

Table 2: Age and Class Distribution of the Children

		Frequency		
		Female	Male	Total
Age	12 – 14	09	08	17
	15 – 17	09	10	19
Total		18	18	36
	JSS^2 1	08	07	15
Class	JSS 2	06	05	11
	JSS 3	04	06	10
Total		18	18	36

Source: Field Survey, 2011

As indicated in Table 2, all the participants were below 18 years, with a slight majority of them between 15 and 17 years. Regarding school enrolment, there were more girls in first and second years of junior secondary school than boys, while the third year had more boys than girls.

Table 3: Background of Teachers

		Frequency		
		Female	Male	Total
Age	31 – 40 years	03	02	5
	41 – 50 years	02	02	4
	Above 50 years	01	02	3
Qualification	National Certificate of Education	02	02	4
	Bachelor of Education	04	04	8
Years of residency in the study Area	Less than 3 yrs	01	-	1
	3 – 5 years	02	01	3
	5 – 10 years	02	02	4
	Above 10 years	01	03	4

Source: Field Survey, 2011

The teachers were relatively well-qualified, as the majority of them had degrees from universities. They had also resided in the communities for a substantial period of time and had therefore accumulated sufficient information to be of help to the researcher.

Engagement on Cocoa Plantations

Children who live in cocoa settlements engage in a variety of activities on cocoa plantations. Notable among them are weeding, spraying of cocoa trees and pods, harvesting and processing. All children who participated in the study were involved in post-harvest activities that entailed splitting of cocoa pods, removal of seeds from the pods, washing of seeds with water, removal of poor or diseased seeds from the lot and preparations for fermentation of the seeds.

The periods spent by the children on farming activities could be divided into two, namely school and vacation periods. Each of these periods was further classified into weekdays and weekends. During the school period, the children worked mostly on weekends for four to five hours a day, but worked for an average of two hours in the evenings of the school days. In contrast, during vacations they worked mostly during the week days, usually spending five to six hours, and about three hours on weekends. Much of the work on school vacations was done in the mornings so that they could get some time to rest in the evenings and also attend to other personal commitments.

During the week days of the school period, the children spent an average of two hours a day, usually between 3pm and 6pm so that they could return home on time. However, during weekends, they worked from about 8am to 1pm.

Normally, the evenings of the weekends were either used to take care of domestic demands such as clearing of surrounding bush or community services, as may be prescribed by the community elders. When weekly community market days fell on the weekends, work on farms might be suspended for the females so that they could go and sell items in the markets to generate income for the family. At times, dried cocoa seeds were carried to the nearest stores for onward transportation to the big city. Sometimes, the children were expected to remain in the house to assist in the sale and loading of bags of cocoa seeds into vehicles. During the vacation periods, the schedule of work on farms changes to 8am – 1pm, from Mondays to Saturdays. The Sundays are used for general cleaning of the house and for attending church services. They may also go to farms in the evenings to assess what work must be done the following day. Besides this, the children use one hour (7pm to 8pm) daily on private lessons where the local teachers or members of the National Youth Service Corps on national service in the village provided support and assistance. The children usually undertook private independent studies from 9pm to 10pm, though the effectiveness of this was compromised by the constant distractions and fatigue from earlier engagements.

Perception of their Work

An initial inquiry was made in order to ascertain the children's perception of the concept of 'child labour' within the context of their work on cocoa farm. This was necessitated by the general assumption amongst Nigerians and empirical evidence from the International Labour Organization that children in cocoa-growing areas in West Africa are involved in strenuous activities on cocoa plantations. However, many of the children did not see their involvement in cocoa plantation as 'child labour'; rather, this was seen as a necessary part of the socialisation process, an important part of their cultural assimilation, in fact a family legacy to be voluntarily sustained regardless of their level of education. A respondent from Ibule in the Akure South LGA thoughtfully submitted:

> We don't see this as child labour. It does not start with us; some of our elder brothers and sisters were once involved in such work. We were told that important personalities that are making waves in politics and business in the state and Nigeria at large were once involved in farming activities on cocoa farms. So there is no harm in our involvement (Male, FGD, 13 years old/JSS 1).

The personalities mentioned here include the late Chief Rufus Giwa who rose to the peak of his career as the Managing Director of Lever Brothers Plc and Chief Olu Falae a former presidential candidate in Nigeria. The belief of the people here is that if those people were able to pursue their education alongside work on cocoa farms, then the present generation should be able to cope as well. The children noted however that work on the cocoa farms was stressful and hazardous. Among the common hazards they faced are snake bite, injuries from cutlasses and other sharp objects as well as infections that lead to diseases like whitlow. In the majority of cases, the children had to depend on traditional medicine and occasionally on the local health provider for care and medicines when they have accidents. In a further probe into their reliance on traditional medicine for handling healthcare emergencies, a teacher revealed that:

> .....most of the cocoa farms are of appreciable distance from health centres. The reason is that the health centres were centrally sited to serve the adjoining communities... it is therefore always convenient to treat them on the farm with available and affordable means such as traditional medicine (Female-teacher, Oke Igbo, Ile Oluji/Oke Igbo LGA, KII).

Another respondent also noted:

> The time they would have spent on taking minor cuts or what have you to health centres in Ajeloro amounts to wastage. What if they got there and the health personnel was not on ground, or the necessary drugs were out of stock? To me, it is better to make use of traditional medicine, which is the always accessible and reliable (Male-teacher, Asewele-Korede, Odigbo LGA, KII).

The above is a manifestation of the social context within which these children work and live and their adjustment to the ecological and social peculiarities of their communities. For instance, a more practical solution, considering the distance to the nearest health post, is a resort to local remedies to treat emergency cases like snake bites and injuries from farm implements. A good example is the 'commanding' of snake venom out of the body of a victim of snake bite by incantation (spiritual healing) and subsequent application of venom neutraliser (known as *aporo* in Yoruba language).

In spite of the stressful and hazardous nature of work on the cocoa plantations, some of the children claimed they liked working with their parents on the farms, especially when engaged in the less stressful aspects. Others saw it as an intergenerational activity, since they had witnessed their older brothers and sisters also engaged in it while they were growing up. For others, it was an avenue for making some money to supplement their personal income or that of their family. It was also apparent that many of them did those activities to assist their parents who were too old to engage in the strenuous farm work. In this respect, a 12-year-old girl from Asewele-Korede asked:

> If I don't assist my parents, who will? The Calabar boys that used to be on the ground to help out on farms are no longer here because of the activities of some people from Abuja who constantly pay unscheduled visits to determine whether children from other states or towns are being lured into working on cocoa farms. So, it is necessary for us to assist our parents or else, they will die of stress and leave us stranded (Female, 12 years, Odigbo LGA/JSS 1, FGD).

Moreover, the children's direct involvement in the plantations helped them to ascertain the boundaries and extent of their parents' farm lands so that they could hold on to them as family legacy upon their death or when the parents were too old to tend the farm. Another participant of the study noted:

> Our involvement has enabled us to know the extent of our parents' farm. In case of any unforeseen problem, nobody can short change the family. There are families within this neighbourhood whose farms were sold at giveaway prices due to the absence of capable and interested children who could take over those farms. There is a general belief that we will develop interest in cocoa farming through our involvement because most of our fathers and elder brothers developed interest in cocoa farming through the same medium. (Male, 12 years, Akure South LGA/ JSS 1, FGD).

It is apparent that the participants have deep-seated views on their involvement in cocoa farming activities since they have been socialised into it. They may not like it because even under the care and supervision of their parents there are potential hazards, however, they seem to appreciate the importance of the skills and knowledge gained from working on the plantations to their families and their own development.

Formal Education and Future Aspiration

The children in the study were quite aware of, and knowledgeable about, what formal education entails and its value within the communities. Views expressed by them show that formal education is held in high esteem by the community since they see it as a legacy and avenue for projecting the family name and image. They saw the attainment of formal education as a channel for incorporating contemporary ideas into their ways of life, especially farming; hence they all had aspiration for formal education. For instance, 6 of them aspired to be medical doctors, 7 wanted to be engineers, 4 wanted to be architects, 6 took interest in law, 8 were interested in nursing, 3 in pharmacy, while one each aspired to be a teacher and agriculturist with interest in cocoa farming. With these lofty aspirations, they had adopted strategies to counter the inherent problems of their schooling. Among these were working on part-time basis, reading during rest times on farms, and pooling their labour to speed up their work on the various farms. For some children, these strategies worked to their advantage and also elicited respect from their parents. A 15-year- old male noted in this respect:

> I did not know that my father was noticing my desperation for improvement in my education … I overheard him discussing with a friend that he always feels guilty that I have not been fully allowed to concentrate on my academic work due to cocoa farming. In his words, he "would have excluded me from farm work if not for his failing health and inability to secure the services of mature and committed professional farm hands". However, he has reduced the rate of my involvement on the farm. I only go to farm during weekends… I am happy for this because it has greatly impacted on my education positively (Male, 15 years, Ile Oluji/Oke Igbo LGA/JSS 3, FGD).

Some parents encouraged their children to work harder at their books in spite of the conditions.

> My father always reminds me that education is a must so that we can break the cycle of illiteracy in the family (Female, 14 years, Ile Oluji/Oke Igbo LGA/JSS 1, FGD).

Obviously, some children did not hide their distaste for farm work, especially if they had to do that to meet their parents' or guardians' expectations. For such children, the harrowing experiences of some parents as farmers served as constant reminders for them to obtain education to be able to pursue a career in future. A 16-year-old boy contrasted his responsibilities and aspirations in the following words:

> Though I know I have to assist my parents on farms, still the stress involved has motivated me to be serious with my education because I don't like the farming vocation one bit. My father's elder brother who is not into farming looks younger than my father. It means if I venture into farming, I will look older than my age. (Male, 16 years, Akure South LGA/JSS 3, FGD).

In spite of the children's enthusiasm for a future dependent on education, the key informants revealed that the unfavourable aspects of farming could truncate such dreams. This included distractions arising from stress and fatigue as well as fantasies of wealth from cocoa farming. In the words of a key informant:

> Most of the farmers you see around once had lofty dreams like some of these children. But involvement in laborious work on the farms always leads to distraction from books. I am talking from experience as ex-cocoa farm hand in the late 1960s. I was involved in cocoa farms during my fosterage to a paternal uncle after the death of my father; the experiences then were not palatable despite the fact that there were many migrant labourers around to offer their labour. Most of my colleagues who aspired towards greater academic careers could not realise such dreams due to back-breaking jobs on the farms. Assimilation of what was being taught in school was a tug-of-war. My current academic achievement is a product of my liberation from farm work and discontinuation of my fosterage, which came after a misunderstanding between my uncle and my mother (Male-teacher, Oke Igbo, Ile Oluji/Oke Igbo LGA, KII).

In another submission, a key informant who was once a labourer on cocoa farms confirmed the temptations of money and the temporary good life it brought, when he noted that:

> It takes the grace of God and determination on the part of an individual to remain steadfast in the quest for education, especially where the allure of the proceeds from cocoa farm during the sales period remains stronger. This is because economic situation of the family always changes for better whenever farmers sold their cocoa seeds and everybody is treated like a prince or princess. Those that were very

active and industrious were convinced of a brighter future in cocoa farming.…
However, most of them have regretted their actions and have been lamenting over
such decisions. Those of us who were not lured by the fantasy of such money were
tagged as 'lazy' (Male, Teacher, Asewele-Korede, Odigbo LGA, KII).

In other words, it is one thing for the children to aspire to greater heights through
education, it is another thing for them not to be lured by the reality of their
environment. The practical difficulties of attending school in rural cocoa-growing
areas, the challenges of combining schooling and working, as well as the illusions
of quick money, are all critical factors that impinge on their determination to
stay in school. In this respect, some officials of Non-Governmental Organisations
occasionally visit the children to motivate them to stay in school, although the
ostensible purpose of such visits is to discourage forced labour on cocoa farms.
According to one child-participant:

> Some people came to this community once; I was told they have been going round
> other communities. They told us that we should reduce our rate of involvement
> in cocoa farming. They had discussions with us in the presence of our parents. I
> remember one of them telling us that strenuous farm work or the little money our
> parents are giving to motivate us can lure us away from schools (Female, 14 years,
> Odigbo LGA/JSS 2, FGD).

The children's interest in schooling is also influenced by the life-histories of
successful indigenes who had climbed the educational ladder and become
successful in their careers, as noted by a 15-year-old girl.

> D.O. Fagunwa was born and bred in this community. I was told he worked on cocoa
> farms like we are presently doing; still he was a novelist of international repute. He
> remains the hero of this community till today. My teacher once told me that I can
> be greater than Fagunwa if I put in more commitment into my educational pursuit
> (Female, 15 years old, Ile Oluji/Oke Igbo LGA/JSS 3, FGD).

While her thoughts are possible, the reality is that children are growing up in a
different era where there is greater awareness of the implications of child labour
on the development of children. Besides, that was just one successful case, there
were others who did not have the luck and talent of Fagunwa and so might not
have been that successful.

Educational Challenges and Coping Strategies

According to the participants, the challenges that affect their education are unfriendly
learning atmosphere, high turnover of teachers, industrial action by the teachers,
parents' financial problems, lack of teaching-learning materials and dilapidated
classroom structures. The key informants equally acknowledged the issue of
financial difficulty as a major reason for children's involvement in cocoa farming,
as opposed to their fully concentrating on schooling. The genesis of this problem is

poor harvests arising from poor yields, unstable and low producer prices for cocoa. Parents and guardians of children are therefore unable to provide the necessary resources for their children's education, therefore shirking their responsibilities in some cases. Stressing further on this, a key informant revealed that:

> Cocoa farmers have been utterly neglected by the government for long. Support like provision of seeds, farm implements, accessible roads, provision of utility services like potable water and other things that will make living comfortable for them are not forthcoming. On the basis of this, they see the assistance of their children on farms as the only succour, especially with their passing ages. So, the campaign that children should be discouraged from farming remains mere noise. Even the children have recognised the hopeless situation their parents are in, hence their resolve to make their own contributions to the family (Male-teacher, Ile Oluji/Oke Igbo LGA, KII).

The challenges children face at home when studying were distractions and tiredness from earlier activities on the farms. The greatest challenges were faced by the female participants as they had to engage in both domestic and farm work. Although the teachers corroborated these challenges and even raised the issue of irregular school attendance as a result of some children's desire to earn money on the farms, some of the children were reluctant to talk about them. A key informant threw more light on why the children sometimes claimed that working on cocoa plantations did not adversely affect their educational pursuits. In his words:

> ....by custom, the Yoruba in the southwest part of Nigeria believe that one must not wash his or her dirty linen in the open. It is a tradition that has been inculcated in their children over generations. Except for the rascals, you hardly see a child who will own up that farm work is affecting his/her education. The children have been brought up to view whatever they are doing to supplement the farm efforts either through menial jobs or otherwise as their humble contributions. A child that does something to the contrary is seen as a 'bastard' who is courting the wrath of family ancestral spirits. On this note, when the children are suffering, they will actually tell you that they are enjoying the situation. We (the teachers) know much about the magnitude of the problems the children face while working on cocoa plantations. This is because we've been here for long (Male-teacher, Odigbo LGA, KII).

The implication of this is that the Yoruba family places premium on respect for traditions to the detriment of the child's developmental progress. They believe that no matter how bad one's people are one must continue to cherish and appreciate them, hence the adage, "when you sell your family cheaply, you cannot buy it back in whatever amount possible". By this dictum every Yoruba (both young and old) has been inducted into the value system of being diplomatic when discussing family issues, particularly in public. This explains why people sometimes are economical with the truth in order to protect their family image. It is against this background that the children portrayed their engagement on cocoa farms as a family duty, something others had done which they too have to do as a matter of responsibility.

The occurrence of farming hazards like snake-bites and injuries prevent some children from attending classes regularly. Others withdraw from school or fail to attend classes without their parents' knowledge so that they could work on the plantations to earn money. The eventual outcome of this is that they are unable to cope with academic work which in turn exacerbates their school problems and makes them more and more disinterested in schooling. In this regard, a key informant noted:

> The overall assessment of these children's academic performance is not worthwhile when you compare it with what obtains in urban areas... However, there are those that can be classified as 'gifted children' who still perform brilliantly in spite of the stress and distractions of cocoa plantations, but the prevalence of those children is just one out of a thousand. You can imagine what the performance of such children would be if they were allowed to focus on their education alone (Male, Teacher, Ile Oluji/Oke Igbo LGA, KII).

The foregoing is a pointer to the perennial poor academic performance of students sitting for School Certificate Examinations in Nigeria. The picture here is an indication that the academic foundation of the students are weak and that, in spite of the bright picture painted by the children working on the cocoa farms, there is a herculean task to be performed before they can pass their examinations well. In this regard, the work constitutes a major distraction for their future academic pursuits, with the female participants considered by the key informants to be the most vulnerable. A female key informant provided further insights:

> Apart from the fact that the females are expected to carry out certain responsibility at the domestic level, they are often involved in packing and processing of cocoa seeds, fetching water from a river that may be several kilometres away, and drying cocoa beans... Sometimes, they have to skip classes in order to keep up with the demands of cocoa processing or are sick from the stress of those activities. With my ten years experience as a teacher within cocoa producing areas of Ondo State, I can say that the female child appears to be disillusioned when it comes to educational pursuits (Female-teacher, Odigbo LGA, KII).

This confirms the considerable pressure on female children to respond to competing demands and interests, consequently the poor performance of some of them is attributed to the excessive workload that makes schooling difficult and uninteresting. Not surprisingly, some of them drop out while others relocate to towns and cities to acquire skills in tailoring and other vocations.

The children adopted a number of strategies to deal with the problems. For example, some of them undertook individual private studies at night as well as continued to study during the vacation period. They also interacted with their friends in the big towns and cities like Akure, Ibadan and Lagos for additional knowledge and information on the subjects they were studying. They also partook in school excursions, while students from the tertiary institutions served as a source of inspiration for them when they were on holidays. The key informants also played vital roles in ensuring that the children were not overwhelmed by these challenges, by regularly engaging with and sensitising parents on the need for uninterrupted schooling. In addition, the teachers enlisted the services of faith-based leaders in the community to impress upon parents the essence of regular school attendance. Other strategies included regular involvement of students in debates on the importance of education, invitation of successful ex-students to talk to the children about their experiences, and reminders to parents of their responsibilities during Parents-Teachers' Association meetings. They also embarked on regular visits to the homes of pupils to counsel both the children and parents. The children often pooled their labour to quickly do farm assignments so that they could have spare time for their books. In one of the discussions carried out in the study area, a respondent illustrated further the process of joint execution of individual assignments on cocoa farms as follows:

> Since we know that there was no way for us to opt out of farm work, my friends and I have devised a way out. We are eight in number, what we do is to jointly assist each other in the execution of assignments allotted to each of us on the farms. We operate mostly on weekends and with our numerical strength, we often work on four different farms per day. This translates into uninterrupted schooling during week days and farm work during weekends (Male, 15 years, Odigbo LGA/ JSS 3, FGD).

Speaking on the children's ingenuity in soliciting their teachers' intervention when they are overwhelmed with problems, a teacher noted that:

> They do come to us as their teachers for moral support when their parents become uncooperative in terms of work assigned to them on farms... we have been successful in ensuring that the future of these children are not toyed with while the interest of the parents are equally safeguarded (Male-teacher, Odigbo LGA, KII).

Obviously, the interest and demands of children and parents are not always congruent, especially when poverty and the necessities of farm work push parents to disregard the impact of their actions on children's education. The fact that some prominent people come from the community is not lost on the parents; so one can safely assume that some parents wished that their children would also be able to take advantage of their education for the future benefit of themselves and the family. However, the demands of their rural lives, often as impoverished farmers, force some of them to shelf the lofty plans they have for their children.

Conclusion

Contrary to expectations, the involvement of children in cocoa farming was not generally regarded as child labour; rather it was seen as part of the socialisation process of a community where cocoa-farming is considered an integral part of life. Children are therefore involved in cocoa farming as additional farm hands because of the dictates of their culture. According to Boas and Huser (2006), children in Ghana are involved in cocoa farming during the peak periods only, but in Nigeria and Cote d' Ivoire they are used throughout the year, and more extensively during the peak periods. It must be noted however that, not all the children in the study areas engaged in farming, while most of them did so voluntarily to support their parents, thereby making a contribution to family's sustenance. But does this augur well for children's development? Obviously, a systematic integration into the farming traditions could expose them to productive practices that they could adopt to eke out a living for themselves as they matured. The various coping strategies adopted to manage injuries sustained on farms, speed up time spent on farm work, catch up on their studies, and so on, are indicative of the capabilities of children in managing difficult situations, especially in utilising their agency to advance their interests and development.

While, for cultural reasons, the children may see their engagement on cocoa farms in a different light, the reality is that unregulated labour on farms can be antithetical to the norms of uninterrupted upbringing. For example, many of the children's desire for full time schooling instead of regular engagement in farm work indicates a different set of priorities in their lives. But this might not be achieved unless there is greater commitment towards implementation of socio-economic policies and specific measures that lead to sustainable development in those communities, as well as effective enforcement of laws and regulations relating to children.

Notes

1. The net attendance ratio (NAR) for primary school is the percentage of the primary-school-age (6-12 years) population that is attending primary school. The NAR for secondary school is the percentage of the secondary-school-age (13-17 years) population that is attending secondary school. The gross attendance ratio (GAR) for primary school is the total number of primary school students, of any age, expressed as a percentage of the official primary-school-age population. The GAR for secondary school is the total number of secondary school students, of any age, expressed as a percentage of the official secondary school-age population. The gender parity index (GPI) assesses sex-related differences in school attendance rates and is calculated by dividing the GAR for females by the GAR for males. A GPI less than one indicates a gender disparity in favour of males, that is, a higher proportion of males than females attends that level of schooling (NPC, 2009).

2. Junior secondary school

References

Ajiferuke, A.O., 2007, 'Culture and the Process of Child Caring Among the Yoruba in Nigeria', *Journal of Health and Social Management*, Vol. 14, No. 1, pp. 13-17.

Boas, M. and Huser, A., 2006, 'Child Labour and Cocoa Production in West Africa: The Case of Cote d'Ivoire and Ghana' (Fafo Report, 522), Research Programme on Trafficking and Child Labour, Oslo, Norway: Fafo Information Office.

Ennew, J., 1994, 'Time for Children or Time for Adults', in J. Qvortrup, M. Bardy, G. Sgritta, and H. Wintersberger, eds., *Childhood Matters: Social Theory, Practice and Politics,* Aldershot: Avebury.

Ikwuyatum, G.O., 2010, 'Child Labour and the Progress towards the Attainment of Education For All (EFA) Goals in Nigeria', *eJournal of Educational Policy,* available at https://www4.nau.edu/cee/jep/journals.aspx?id=342

International Labour Organisation (ILO), 2004, Child Labour: A Textbook for University Students, Geneva: International Programme for the Elimination of Child Labour, ILO Office, Switzerland.

National Population Commission (NPC), 2009, *Nigeria Demographic and Health Survey 2008*, Lagos: NPC.

Super, C. M. and Harkness, S., 2002, 'Culture Structures and the Environment for Development, *Human Development*, Vol. 45, pp. 270–274.

UNICEF, 2006, *Information Sheet: Child Labour in Nigeria, 2006,* New York: UNICEF

World Bank, 2007, *Country Report on Child Labour,* Washington, DC: The World Bank.

5

Childhood Sexualities in Africa: Agency and Vulnerability

Deevia Bhana

Introduction

Young Africans are striving to create productive and fulfilling lives for themselves and their families, but the conditions under which many of them do this are depicted by wars, famine, income insecurity, and fragile family structures. A pertinent problem in this regard is HIV which continues to impact those between the ages of 15 and 24 in sub-Saharan Africa, but with great gender disparity in rates of infection. According to UNAIDS (2011), in 2010 about 68 per cent of all people living with HIV resided in sub-Saharan Africa where more women than men were infected. It notes further that young women aged 15–24 years are as much as eight times more likely than men to be HIV positive (ibid). Southern Africa bears much of the brunt of the epidemic with South Africa alone being home to an estimated 5.6 million people living with HIV, again with considerable gender disparity in rates of infection (Shisana, Rehle, Zuma and Jooste 2009).

In many cases , only one side of sexuality has been foregrounded in research and intervention around African children (see for example, Cornwall, Corrêa and Jolly 2008), thus resulting in the framing of childhood sexualities within the domain of vulnerability and pain. Within the context of widespread sexual exploitation, abuse and coercion, research has highlighted the gender inequities and relationship dynamics which create conditions for extreme forms of sexual vulnerabilities (Dunne 2008; Wood, Maforah and Jewkes 1998). However, less emphasis has been placed on sexual attractions, desires and pleasures, and as Cole and Thomas (2009) note, on matters of love.

The absence of representations of love in writing about Africa is noted and criticised in the reduction of African intimacy to sex (Bhana and Pattman 2011;

Hunter, 2010). Cole and Thomas (2009:4) note that the absence has become striking in the context of HIV and AIDS. They note, 'where countless studies have analysed how sexual behaviour fuels the epidemic, few have explored how that behaviour is embedded in emotional frameworks'. However, reducing affective relations to sex fuels arguments that hypersexualise Africans and justify racist tropes that create vestigial images of a rampant male sexuality and a docile femininity (Hunter 2010). In understanding childhood sexualities therefore, it is important to recognise not only the vulnerabilities that men and women in particular face, but also agency, pleasure and desire (Cornwall, Correa and Jolly 2008). This is important in changing understandings of childhood constructions of sexualities in Africa, acknowledging that sexuality is a significant part of young people's lives in ways that imbricate structure, gender inequalities and agency. This is the central tenet of this chapter.

Sexuality, Structure and Agency

Sexuality as it is constructed by young Africans sits in tension with agency and structural inequalities and HIV. Structural inequalities produce differential risk for infection and have adverse outcomes for the majority who are poor and marginalised, and particularly for young African women. As Farmer (2004) notes, affliction is embedded within large scale social and economic structures and is the consequence of persistent historical economic inequalities. For instance, the AIDS problem has been exacerbated by stressed economies, deepening poverty, social inequality and its inherent gender differentials, all of which in tandem increase young people's vulnerability.

In the context of extreme vulnerability and disease, children's sexualities are often framed within the domain of pain, suffering and disease. However, even though in much of Africa the child is constructed as a victim of war, famine, violence, and an orphan of AIDS, studies in the last decades have been challenging these assertions (Henderson 2003). Indeed, it is AIDS that has brought increasing research interests to the construction of childhood sexualities in Africa and in particular from the angle of vulnerability and danger (Bhana 2007). Children's sexualities therefore are constructed in the context of steep gradients of social inequalities, including gender inequalities and cultural and political circumstances that reproduce oppression. In the context of sexual risk, sexual violence, teenage pregnancy, and HIV and AIDS, the sexualities of young Africans have been placed under scrutiny, particularly through the optic of powerlessness in relation to women and girls and sexual violence. Many scholars have argued that pervasive poverty, gender inequalities and other forms of structural inequalities shape sexual practices and heighten sexual risk, decrease sexual wellbeing, have negative impact on sexual and reproductive rights and create heightened vulnerability for the gendered spread of HIV (Anrnfred 2004; Jewkes and Morrell 2011). The problem of rape in South Africa, for example, has to be understood within the context of the very substantial gender power inequalities which pervade society. Rape is a manifestation of male dominance over women and an assertion of that position. This is not to argue that men are naturally aggressive but to assert that male control over women and notions of male sexual entitlement feature strongly in the dominant social constructions of masculinity. Both sexual and physical violence against women form part of a repertoire of strategies of control (Jewkes, Mbananga and Bradshaw 2002).

What can children do in these contexts? We need to understand how gender inequalities, social and economic depression combined with violence and rape maintain ascendant rates of HIV and AIDS. Understanding these dynamics will help address what it will take to intervene effectively in reducing transmission and vulnerability. UNAIDS (2005) in lamenting the missing face of AIDS amongst children notes that the disease is wreaking havoc on childhood and argues that children must be at the forefront of the fight against AIDS, noting further that if countries are to develop, they must put children first. Yet, in the context of African AIDS, children and childhood are often viewed from the perspective of loss of parents and the politics of childhood pity (Fassin 2007). Whilst the concern with children orphaned by AIDS remains legitimate, the representation of the child as an object of pity imbricate with and help reproduce vestigial colonial and racialised images of the African child as a parasitical other (Bhana 2009). Moreover, a more comprehensive understanding of children's sexualities is missing while what is there is constructed within the gender binary of passivity and domination.

Arguing against representations of childhood sexuality within the domain of pity and docility, this chapter notes that in the construction of African childhood sexualities, greater care must be taken to understand the complexities in relation to agency and vulnerabilities through which gender power inequalities are reproduced and challenged. Whilst male sexual power has received widespread attention, particularly in subjugating young women (Cornwall, Corrêa and Jolly 2008; Dunne 2008; Jewkes, Dunkle, Koss, Levin, Ndunae, Jama and Sikweyiya 2006), male power is not automatic and sexuality is both contested and negotiated even amongst young people, both boys and girls, in Africa (Bhana 2007; Bhana and Pattman 2011). Such a view attempts to break down the notion that girls are docile sexual beings in relation to an African vanguard – a rampant African heterosexual masculinity. The positioning of predatory male sexuality stains African boys with a mark of sexual and criminal danger and a vector in the spread of HIV/AIDS (Barker and Ricardo 2005). Conversely, the positioning of a female sexuality in suffering and pain (Reddy 2004) reproduces images of a docile African femininity, waiting to be infected with HIV. Although important contributions to understanding the structural forces that produce the AIDS epidemic have been made, this is not the full picture.

Why Focus on Childhood Sexualities?

As indicated, the context of HIV and AIDS has provided a ripe environment to explore more fully the ways in which young Africans give meanings to sexualities. Statistical information has helped to understand the particular vulnerabilities of young people between the ages of 15 and 24 years. Though clearly important in describing the context of vulnerability, sexuality and HIV and AIDS, the quantitative indicators provide limited understandings of the gendered and sexual processes that give rise to such prevalence. More nuanced micro-level research can open up a theoretical and social space to engage with the construction of gender and sexual identities (Dunne, Humphreys and Leach 2006). As Bhana and Pattman (2009) note, research that focuses on young people and makes their lives and identities central to any prevention programme can provide the potential to inform us about how sexualities are conspicuously gendered, raced and classed. Contextually specific responses to the pandemic and to young peoples' overall sexual wellbeing are important, as much research has argued. The importance of more contextualised and relational understandings of childhood sexualities is required if interventions designed to meet the specific needs of young Africans are to be effective.

There is still a dearth of information in much of Africa around how childhood sexualities are constructed. We know very little about the sexual worlds of young adults, how they see themselves, what they wish for, their desires and passions, their fears and the ways in which the performance of masculinities and femininities are constructed, how it is advantageous and how it can inhibit other potential experiences, as well as how it is vulnerable to disease (Bhana and Pattman 2011). Under the onslaught of danger, however, scholars have missed the young Africans' expressions of romance, love and desire. Vance (1984) reminds us that sexuality is not just a domain of danger but also one of exploration, agency, sensations and connections.

Despite this dearth of information, the conceptualisation of the agency of African children is not new. Historical perspectives in South Africa for example point to the dynamic and nuanced construction of sexuality and childhood. In pre-colonial South Africa for example, Delius and Glaser (2002) argue that the association between children and sexuality was relatively open. Children often played sexual games without censure, with sexual exploration being encouraged, monitored by peer groups and regulated. Sexualised games played by young children have been a long standing feature of normal childhood (Jewkes, Dunkle, Koss, Levin, Ndunae, Jamaa and Sikweyiya 2006). Scholars point to different historical moments and contexts where sex play was a strong feature of African childhoods (that sometimes includes penetration as very common amongst girls and boys from about 6 or 7 until early teenage years).

Importantly, the learning of sex was not frowned upon even as it was monitored and regulated. Under the onslaught of Christianity, colonialism, urbanisation, migration and ongoing cultural shifts, the views about children and sexuality are mutating into   dominant models that see the entrenching of masculinities which demand flesh to flesh sex, a celebration of multiple partners and the commodification and control over women and girls (see Delius and Glaser 2002).

Critiquing the muting of gender and sexuality, new African research foregrounds the ability of children to exercise their sexual agency within the context of danger. In relation to the construction of childhood sexualities in Africa, much of the attention, as has been argued thus far, has been on the ways in which vulnerabilities are created and forged within the context of HIV and AIDS (Bhana 2007). Importantly as Kalipeni, Craddock, Oppong and Ghosh (2004) illustrate, material, symbolic and discursive forces combine to constrain the opportunities and choices available to individuals and create conditions of vulnerability for large sectors of the African population. Thus, agency, sexuality, structure and vulnerability are intertwined and it is important to pay attention to these complexities in the construction of childhood sexualities and the ways in which masculinities and femininities are imbricated in it.

Young Masculinities

Boys are inducted very early in life into the rituals of manhood through which they enact forms of masculine conduct that are not always peaceable. What kinds of young masculinities are being developed in Africa, what can we learn from alternate less harmful forms of conduct and what scope is there for interventions around changing masculine identities beginning from the early years? The literature shows that there is a clear connection between men, boys and sexualities (Bhana, Morrell and Pattman 2008). Men are the main agents of violence. They are more likely to be involved in crime, murder and rape. The fact of male involvement in all forms of violence remains. What can research tell us about the forms of masculine violence and how to obstruct it? Focusing on the agency of young men, research illustrates that whilst the African continent is often viewed as a hive of violent men and boys, this understanding feeds into racist stereotypes around the constructions of African masculinities (Ouzgane and Morrell 2005). Despite the massive forms of structural violence in everyday practices, they are engaging creatively with their social worlds demonstrating resilience, care and agency (Morrell and Jewkes 2010). This however must not detract from the persistence of male involvement in war, crime, rape and violence, more generally. The underlying social inequalities between men and women remain; and despite all the attempts to change the situation, sexual and gendered violence against women and girls remains a pressing concern. Indeed, men and boys on the margins pose dangers for peaceable gender relations (Ragnarsson, Onya, Thorson, Ekström and Aarø 2008). Access to weapons in the factional fights and wars in Africa has led to increasing instances of sexual abuse, perpetuating gender inequalities. Cultural values, combined with persistent economic and social inequalities, are argued to fuel violent masculinities and create widespread vulnerabilities for both women and men (Barker 2005).

Working with boys to address the construction of masculinities has now been established as key to developing peaceful gender relations and addressing girls' sexual vulnerabilities (Morrell and Jewkes 2010). Addressing boys in relation to gender transformative approaches is now key to development work (Cornwall, Corrêa and Jolly 2008). Moving beyond a male-centred agenda that enhances male power, new work with men is beginning to show the value of gender equality, the development of non-sexism and the value of respect and integrity (Bhana, Morrell and Pattman 2008). However, such efforts are complicated by the persistence of wars in Africa and social and economic dissolution which increased male vulnerability to sexual violence. Cleaver (2002) in asking questions about masculinity in developing and postcolonial contexts frames the question: what does an ideal masculinity look like? Young Africans, in the crucible of war, conflict and violence admittedly have fewer options for peaceable relations.

Newer options for the construction of masculinities in Africa are now being forged. Violent African masculinities even reside amongst very young children (see Bhana 2005). Violence, war and conflict in Africa remain a serious problem with men and boys mainly implicated and complicit in the reproduction of violence. The control of women and girls and the acquisition of multiple sexual partners has often led researchers to question a masculinity that is violent and risky (Kallipeni, Craddock, Oppong and Ghosh 2004). Greg, Peacock, Jewkes and Msimang (2008) note that such a masculinity is implicated in gender violence and risky sexualities and the spread of HIV. In Africa, recent research has begun to focus on the forms of masculinity which are vulnerable to sexual risk and violence, to intervene and to foreground alternate forms of masculinity (Morrell and Jewkes 2011). Young men are inducted into rituals of violence very early in life. Not all men however undergo these rituals and yet also present violent forms of behaviour. Violence is a key demonstration of male power and the early learnings of violence are reinforced by constructions of masculinity. The implications of such violence, as argued thus far, are greater vulnerability to social and health complications, not only for girls but for boys as well. One form of peaceable masculinity that recent research valorises is a caring masculinity. Morrell and Jewkes (ibid) note that despite patriarchal constructions of masculinity, African men aspire to be good fathers and argue that caring practices amongst households hold potential for better forms of masculinity, one which is not averse to risky sexuality. This development holds good promise for children and young people located in families and households where gender norms are disrupted. However, material impoverishment and structural inequalities remain a problem as young people have little control over the material conditions which create the vulnerabilities to do violence.

Agency, Sexuality and African Femininities

Whilst much research has justifiably pointed to the pain, disease and danger discourse through which young African femininities are forged, there is need to revise the tendency to see young African femininities as 'the suffering other'. Bhana (2007; 2006) argues that even very young African girls are sexual agents, not just victims. Young African girls are often assumed to be sexually passive, waiting to be infected with disease. These narratives often lead to a totalising narrative on patriarchy and racist tropes that reproduce notions of pitiful African femininity. There is a real danger that an inadequate understanding of the multiple forms of femininities can lead to well intentioned interventions designed around addressing sexual risk to unwittingly reproduce the racist trope of a pathetic African femininity. As Bhana and Pillay (2011) note, in South Africa, the context of poverty, a history of inequality, violence and the calamitous effects of HIV have been important in configuring working class African girls as suffering and passive, while African boys have been vilified as bad, violent and vectors in the spread of HIV (see also Bhana and Pattman 2009). Other studies in Africa have shown how young people negotiate relationships within bonds of affection (Cole and Thomas 2009). Swidler and Watkins (2007) in Malawi find that young women are not just victims of sexuality but actively engaged in relations of love though these are underpinned by culturally sanctioned relations of sex and money.

Admittedly, in the context of sexual disease, sexual violence and risk for African girls, sexual encounters continue to be conducted in a context where young men lack new models of relationship behaviour and 'traditional' sexual scripts still endorse male assertiveness and control, and female passivity (O' Sullivan, Harrison, Morrell, Monroe-Wise and Kubeka 2006). The relative powerlessness and vulnerability of girls is exacerbated by women fearing the loss of their partners and anxious about their men not enjoying sex with a condom, coupled with the fear that a request for condoms will be interpreted as a lack of trust in the men or as an admission of their own infidelity. Power inequity and emotional and financial dependence of women upon their partners seem to present significant obstacles to sexual decision-making. While acknowledging the lack of girl power in negotiating sex, it is equally important not to re-inscribe the dominant stereotype of African women and girls' passivity. The emerging scholarship on girls illustrates that they are not simply passive recipients of boys' antics (Bhana and Pattman 2011). Power is understood to be multiple, fluid and contextual, with instances where women do resist male power and challenge men. Some research has suggested that young African women now have greater agency than in the past (Bhana 2011). Breaking with the regulatory grip that links African girls and sexualities with passive femininity, newer research (Jewkes and Morrell 2010; Bhana and Pattman 2011) argue that it is important to give fuller attention to the ways in which race, class, sexuality and culture intersect, not only to provide opportunities for the reproduction of a vulnerable female sexuality but also to permit the angle to be turned on agency. More recent South African research conducted amongst 17 to 19-year-old girls has demonstrated their resistance to the stereotypical ways in the constitution of sexual subjectivities, where unconventional expressions of female sexual pleasure and desire emerged. Some girls draw on a discourse of female sexuality that legitimates young women's desire and enables them to resist being positioned as sluts by constituting their sexual desire as 'normal' (Bhana and Pattman 2011). Bhana's (2009) research argues that the African women's agency and broader engagement has challenged politics in South Africa and intensified challenges to gender identities and practices. Revising notions of passive femininity, Bhana argues against the homogenous grouping of African girls who exclusively perform conventional gender roles, and rather puts the different manifestations of girls' agency under the spotlight in conditions of social and economic vulnerability, thus negating the perception of women as passive victims of patriarchy.

Conclusion

African childhood sexualities – both their agency and vulnerabilities – have not received adequate attention in research and policy except when the gender optic features violence, death and disease. This chapter has argued that vulnerabilities and structural inequalities continue to mark the sexual experiences of young people and needs attention. However, focusing only on vulnerabilities at the expense of sexual agency is harmful in policy, practice and interventions designed to create safe sexualities, and sexual wellbeing. Too much emphasis has been placed on girls as victims without much voice whereas boys are constructed as sexual predators and violent. Associating young African masculinities only within the realm of sexual violence is unhelpful, particularly as these categories fail to consider the multiplicity of experiences and the power of men and boys to care (Morrell and Jewkes 2011; Jewkes 2010).

Childhood sexualities are constructed through gender power relations and have effects for the ways in which hegemonic masculinities and femininities are enabled. One of the problems in African countries is that not enough work has focused on power, pleasure and desires and sexual self expressions. As Pattman and Chege (2003) have noted, African girls are not expected to be seen as overly sexual whereas boys are expected to demonstrate sexual prowess. Whilst sexual exploitation and the horrors of HIV, particularly for young women, must feature in any research, intervention and debate around childhood sexualities, the denial of agency and pleasure through which young people actually identify themselves, is unhelpful.

This chapter has sought to reconfigure the passive and marginalised image of the African child, drawing attention to sexual vulnerabilities and agency. As economic and social changes abound in Africa, changing gender norms are also becoming apparent with more girls gaining access to school. Education provides the potential for both boys and girls to re-think toxic forms of sexualities. As Bhana, Morrell and Pattman (2008) note, working with boys and girls to change the normative constructions of gender is critical, and HIV and AIDS education provides a fertile ground for this to happen. However, change is never easy and never dramatic. It is about time, however, that African childhood sexualities receive the attention they deserve in relation to their vulnerabilities, agency and pleasures. It remains a challenge in all of Africa to put children's sexualities in the forefront of human rights and democratic agendas.

References

Arnfred, S., 2004, *Re-thinking Sexualities in Africa*, Uppsala, Sweden: Almquist & Wiksell Tryckeri.

Barker, G., 2005, *Dying to Be a Man: Youth, Masculinity and Social Exclusion,* London: Routledge.

Barker, G. and Ricardo, C., 2005, *Young Men and the Construction of Masculinity in Sub-Saharan Africa: Implications for HIV/AIDS, Conflict, and Violence,* Washington, DC: The World Bank.

Bhana, D., 2005, 'Violence and the Gendered Negotiation of Masculinity Among Young Black Boys in South Africa', in L. Ouzgane and R. Morrell, eds., *African Masculinities: Men in Africa from the Late 19th Century to the Present,* London: Palgrave Macmillan.

Bhana, D., 2006, 'The (Im)Possibility of Child Sexual Rights in Young South African Children's Account of HIV/AIDS', *IDS Bulletin,* Vol. 37, pp. 66-68.

Bhana, D., 2007, 'Childhood Sexuality and Rights in the Context of HIV/AIDS', *Culture, Health and Sexuality,* Vol. 9, pp. 309-324.

Bhana, D. 2009, "AIDS is Rape" Gender and Sexuality in Children's Responses to HIV/AIDS, *Social Science and Medicine,* Vol. 69, pp. 596-603.

Bhana, D., Morrell, R. and Pattman, R., 2008, 'Gender and Education in Developing Contexts: Postcolonial Reflections on Africa', in R. Cowen and A. Kazamias, eds., *Handbook of International and Comparative Education,* Amsterdam: Springer.

Bhana, D. and Pattman, R., 2009, 'Researching South African Youth, Gender and Sexuality within the Context of HIV/AIDS, *Society for International Development,* Vol. 52, pp. 68-74.

Bhana, D. and Pattman, R., 2011, 'Girls Want Money Boys Want Virgins, the Materiality of Love Amongst South African Township Youth in the Context of HIV and AIDS, *Culture, Health and Sexuality,* Vol. 13, pp.

Bhana, D. and Pillay, N., 2011, 'Beyond Passivity: Girls' Violence in a Single Sex School', *Educational Review,* Vol. 63, pp. 65-78.

Cleaver, F., 2002, *Masculinities Matter! Men, Gender and Development,* London: Zed Books.

Cole, J. and Thomas, L.M., 2009, *Love in Africa,* Chicago: University of Chicago Press.

Cornwall, A., Corrêa, S. and Jolly, S., 2008, *Development with a Body Sexuality, Human Rights and Development,* London: Zed Books.

Delius, P. and Glaser, C., 2002, 'Sexual Socialisation in South Africa: A Historical Perspective', *African Studies*, Vol. 61, pp. 27-54.

Dunne, M., 2008, *Gender, Sexuality and Development*, Rotterdam: Sense Books.

Dunne, M., Humphreys, S. and Leach, F., 2006, 'Gender Violence in Schools in the Developing World', *Gender and Education*, Vol. 18, pp. 75-98.

Farmer, P., 2004, 'An Anthropology of Structural Violence, *Current Anthropology*', Vol. 45, pp. 305-325.

Fassin, D., 2007, *When Bodies Remember Experiences and Politics of AIDS in South Africa*, London: University of California Press.

Greig, A., Peacock, D., Jewkes, R. and Msimang, S., 2008, 'Gender and AIDS: Time to Act', *AIDS*, Vol. 22, pp. 35-43.

Henderson, P., 2003, *Annotated Bibliography on Childhood with Emphasis on Africa*, Dakar: CODESRIA.

Hunter, M., 2010, *Love in the Time of AIDS: Inequality, Gender and Rights in South Africa*, Pietermaritzburg: University of Kwazulu-Natal Press.

Jewkes, R., 2010, 'Where to for Sexual Health Education for Adolescents in Sub-Saharan Africa?', *Plos Medicine*, Vol. 7, pp. 1-2.

Jewkes, R., Dunkle, K., Koss, M.P., Levin, J.B., Ndunae, M., Jamaa, N. and Sikweyiya, Y., 2006, 'Rape Perpetration by Young, Rural South African Men: Prevalence, Patterns and Risk Factors', *Social Science & Medicine*, Vol. 63, pp. 2949-2961.

Jewkes, R., Levin, J., Mbananga, N. and Bradshaw, D., 2002, 'Rape of Girls in South Africa', *Lancet*, 359.

Jewkes, R. and Morrell, R., 2010, 'Gender and Sexuality: Emerging Perspectives from the Heterosexual Epidemic in South Africa and Implications for HIV Risk and Prevention', *Journal of the International AIDS Society*, Vol. 13, pp. 1-11.

Jewkes, R. and Morrell, R., 2011, 'Sexuality and the Limits of Agency among South African Teenage Women: Theorising Femininities and their Connections to HIV Risk Practises', *Social Science and Medicine*, pp. 1-9.

Kalipeni, E., Craddock, S., Oppong, J. and Ghosh, J., 2004, *HIV/AIDS in Africa: Beyond Epidemiology*, Oxford: Blackwell Publishers.

O'Sullivan, L.F., Harrison, A., Morrell, R., Monroe-Wise, A. and Kubeka, M., 2006, 'Gender Dynamics in the Primary Sexual Relationships of Young Rural South African Women and Men', *Culture Health and Sexuality*, Vol. 8, No. 2, pp. 99-113.

Ouzgane, L. and Morrell, R., 2005, *African Masculinities: Men in Africa from the Late 19th Century to the Present*, London: Palgrave Macmillan.

Pattman, R. and Chege, F., 2003, *Finding Our Voices: Gendered and Sexual Identities and HIV/AIDS in Education*, Nairobi: UNICEF.

Ragnarsson, A., Onya, H., Thorson, A., Ekström, M. and Aarø, L., 2008, Young Males' Gendered Sexuality in the Era of HIV and AIDS in Limpopo Province, South Africa, *Qualitative Health Research*, Vol. 18, pp. 739-46.

Reddy, V., 2004, 'Sexuality in Africa: Some Trends, Transgressions and Tirades', *Agenda*, Vol. 62, pp. 3-11.

Scheper-Hughes, N. and Sargent, C., 1998, *Small Wars: The Cultural Politics of Childhood*, Berkeley: University of California Press.

Shisana, O., Rehle, T., Zuma, K., Jooste, S., Pillay-Van-Wyk, V., Mbelle, N., Van Zyl, J., Parker, W., Zungu, N.P., Pezi., S. and The SABSSM III Implementation Team, 2009, *South African National HIV Prevalence, Incidence, Behaviour and Communication Survey, 2008: A Turning Tide Among Teenagers?* Cape Town: HSRC Press.

Swidler, A. and Watkins, S., 2007, Ties of Dependence: AIDS and Transactional Sex in Rural Malawi, *Studies in Family Planning,* 38(3), 147-162.

UNAIDS, 2011, *Report on the Global AIDS Epidemic,* Geneva: UNAIDS.

Vance, C., 1984, *Pleasure and Danger, Exploring Female Sexuality,* London: Pandora.

Wood, C., Maforah, F. and Jewkes, R., 1998, "He Forced Me to Love Him": Putting Violence on Adolescent Sexual Health Agendas, *Social Science and Medicine,* Vol. 47, pp. 233-242.

6

Application of 'Theatre for Development' in the Promotion of Youth Agency in HIV Prevention in Zomba City, Malawi

Catherine Mayesero Makhumula

Introduction

This chapter discusses a workshop-based Theatre for Development (TfD) project with a group of teen boys in Zomba City urban, Malawi. The project investigates how young people define, negotiate, and perform roles and identities in what they consider risky sexual situations in the context of HIV transmission. While many HIV and AIDS prevention projects in Malawi are geared towards behaviour change, this chapter proposes an approach that departs from an exclusive focus on changing individual health behaviours, and moves to a broader approach of understanding and building youth self-efficacy, while investigating the socio-cultural and psychosocial complexities that influence behaviour. Workshop-based Theatre for Development was adopted as a tool for gathering, reproducing and spotlighting instances of vulnerability to HIV. The participants were actively engaged in generating, re-presenting and interpreting their experiences in a reflexive manner.

The research is situated in the new paradigm of social studies of childhood which considers children as active producers of their own social world (James and James 2001; Corsaro 2005). This paradigm subverts the universal models of childhood as a passive and protected life phase, free of 'adult' responsibilities (Evans 2011:384), such as work and caring for the sick. Children and youth are often perceived through opposition to adulthood and as 'people in the process of becoming rather than being' (De Boeck and Honwana 2005: 3). In what she terms the dichotomous construction of the categories 'children' and 'adults', Julia

O'Connell Davison argues that because adults are constructed as autonomous, self-determined individuals, entirely responsible for their own lives and decisions, children, in order to justify their protection, are constructed as passive, helpless and dependent (cited in Smette, Stefansen and Mossige 2009:369). This dichotomy leaves no room for 'young people', who can assume the characteristics of children or adults, depending on the context – children when talking about their need for protection, or adults when discussing their obligation and the need to make good choices (Smette 2009:369). This particular research involved orphaned teen boys, aged from 14 to 16 years. While the participants considered themselves dependent on their care-givers and youth organisations for the provision of food, shelter and other basic necessities, encountering sexual situations was considered a personal challenge, independent of 'adult' protection. Issues of reproductive health are at the heart of everyday livelihood of these young people who have been affected and/or infected with HIV.

The chapter begins with a sketch of the situation in Malawi, followed by an introduction to Theatre for Development. The last part which focuses on narrative and drama, discusses specific real life narratives from the participants and their reproductions in drama.

Children, Youth and HIV Prevention

The HIV/AIDS pandemic has heavily affected children in Malawi. By 2009, it was estimated that 650,000 children had been orphaned by AIDS (65 per cent of all orphans in the country) while an estimated 120,000 children were living with HIV (UNAIDS 2010). As is the trend with new HIV infections worldwide, the majority of HIV cases occur amongst children and young people, particularly those between the ages of 13 and 24 years (UNAIDS *Global Report* 2008).

Writing about orphan care in Malawi, Gillian Mann argues that research on orphan care has tended to focus on responses at the family and community level (Mann 2005). Even programmes which are specifically targeted towards young people often do not involve them in decision-making at the strategic or programmatic level. This lack of participation has meant that the experiences and perspectives of HIV/AIDS-affected children in Malawi have largely not been considered in programmes and policies to meet their needs. Mann suggests that a lot could be learnt from children regarding the positive aspects of their existing coping mechanisms in order to strengthen the capacity of peers and adults to provide them with support (Mann 2005).

Several significant studies have highlighted the gap often prevalent between adolescent's attitudes, beliefs, knowledge or intentions pertaining to sexuality and their actual sexual behaviour (Mwale 2008).While a myriad of behavioural interventions have been designed to promote safer sexual behaviours among adolescents in Malawi, relatively few have proven effective. One such intervention is Behavioural Change Communication (BCC)[1]. The paradox emanating from BCC is that, while adolescents' awareness of HIV transmission dynamics is generally high, behavioural change relative to the HIV/AIDS pandemic has been limited (Mwale 2008). The reason for this, according to Mwale, is that behaviour communication programmes do not capture some of the socio-cultural and psycho-social complexities that may be proximate barriers to change.

Theatre for Development

Houston and Hovorka have claimed that years of Theatre for Development (TfD), alongside other communication forms in large scale HIV/AIDS programmes were successful as they yielded 'nearly universal HIV/AIDS awareness in Malawi' (2007:205). The TfD movement in Africa emerged in the 1970s as an alternative communication approach premised on the cultural dimensions of development. TfD is believed to have been influenced by the theoretical innovations and experiments of two innovators: the Brazilian adult educator Paulo Freire and the Brazilian theatre director Augusto Boal (Mwalwanda 2009). Boal's work attempted to take theatre back to its original form where everybody could participate and discover alternative versions of reality, and where people could make theatre for themselves. He was therefore concerned with breaking off the boundaries between the audience and performers and for that reason used dramaturgic techniques to turn the spectator into the spect-actor.[2]

TfD became popular in Africa with the experiments initiated by university travelling theatres in different countries from the early 1970s to the 1980s. Since then, TFD has become a key part of HIV and AIDS prevention campaigns in Malawi and other African countries. TfD itself has undergone an evolution since its advent in the past two decades. In this regard, there are three basic types: theatre 'for' the people, theatre 'with' the people and theatre 'by' the people (Pia 2003). These types in turn, could be placed under the performance-based approach which emphasises a finished product being performed for the community or the workshop-based approach where the emphasis is on the process (Mwansa 2009). This research project made use of workshop-based TfD.

In workshop-based TfD, facilitators make a conscious effort to involve the target group in the identification of problems or issue analysis, play making, post performance discussions and follow up. Workshop-based TfD underscores the importance of the process and not the product: the play is regarded as a mirror that extends the work done in the process of creating it (Mwansa 2009:16). In this particular project, participants were actively engaged in identifying moments of vulnerability to HIV, reproducing these moments and critically looking back at them in discussion. Although the participants performed the plays to a larger audience, the workshop content and what happened behind the scenes are the focal points of discussion in the paper.

Research Methodology

The study can be broadly described as a case study research. The nature of the workshop necessitated an approach that utilises a combination of participatory, performative and child-centred methods. The following section therefore makes theoretical links between TfD and participatory, performative and child-centred approaches of research to validate TfD as an alternative and viable way of engaging young people in research.

Theatre for Development as Participatory Research

As research 'for,' 'with' and 'by' the people rather than 'on' the people, participatory research seeks to break down the distinction between the researcher and the researched (the subject/object relationship of traditional research), instead creating a subject/subject relationship (Conrad 2004:7). The group process in participatory methods ceases to convey isolated opinions as with surveys or interviews, becoming instead a springboard for collective reasoning. The knowledge produced is socially heard, legitimised and added to the people's collective knowledge, empowering them to solve their own problems (Fals-Borda and Rahman 1991). Despite the differences between the facilitator and the participants,[3] in the project, the facilitator introduced activities which created an environment of open participation in the workshop. The general workshop included physical activities: play, song, dance, games, group and pair sharing, debates, role-play and drama, such that participation from the members presupposed their being in the workshop. The participants demonstrated the awareness that 'their' meaningful and sincere participation was essential to the workshop. For example, there were instances when songs, games and enactments were rejected by the group, on the grounds of being 'childlike' or 'unreal' and alternatives were immediately introduced. From the formulation of ground rules set by the participants at the beginning of the workshop, the sharing of experiences and knowledge, to the daily goals which the participants set for themselves, the workshop proved to be an effective participatory undertaking.

Theatre for Development as Performative Research

Performative research has roots in the field of anthropology, communication and performance studies, where performance is regarded as both a legitimate and an ethical way of representing ethnographic understanding (Conrad 2004). Recently, the notion of performance (or performativity) has been taken up by qualitative social researchers as a form of critical pedagogy in doing arts-based inquiry (Finley, in Conrad 2004:9). Susan Finley asserts that performance creates an open, dialogic space for inquiry and expression through 'an imaginative interpretation of events and the contexts of their occurrences' (*ibid*) which includes the involvement of the observer (Conrad 2004).

In the project, the participants were not only engaged in the 'mirror-ing' of their ideas and real life actions as they played characters from their narratives, they also scrutinised and interpreted their thinking and doing patterns under the microscope of the workshop environment. In arguing for performative research, Conrad notes that participants are both involved and detached, alternating from one to the other, observing the self in action, comparing the two worlds to arrive at some understanding or meaning (Conrad 2004).

Theatre for Development as Child-Centred Research

Child-centred research methodology is defined as research that utilises methods that are easy for children to understand and meaningfully participate in, acknowledges that children's insights are important in generating knowledge, recognises the importance of children's rights of expression and represents a shift away from the objectification of children and regards them as active subjects within the research process (Jones 2007). All activities in the workshop were rooted in the understanding that the participants already have local knowledge and coping mechanisms which they utilise in addressing their own social problems. As indicated earlier on, all activities in the workshop were either approved or introduced by the participants themselves. Drama proved to be a successful method of engaging the young participants who were intrigued with the use of a 'make believe' way of providing insights in their very real, lived experiences.

In effect, Theatre for Development, as a qualitative research methodology that is rooted in participatory, performative and child-centred approaches to research presented a resourceful approach for investigating how young people define, negotiate, and perform roles and identities in what they consider high risk situations in the context of HIV transmission.

Scrutinising Risk through Workshop-Based TfD

The research involved ten teen boys that were identified through Youth Net and Counselling (YONECO), a local non-governmental organisation in Zomba, southern Malawi. YONECO was established in 1997 to address the social injustice and reproductive health issues affecting the youth, women and children. All participants of the workshop were members of YONECO's Resource and Drop-in-Centre for orphans and vulnerable children in Zomba urban.

The initial plan was to have equal numbers of girls and boys (five boys and five girls) for equal representation. On the first day of the workshop, it became apparent that none of the girls would be available. Some girls had to be drawn from markets where they were selling firewood; however none of the girls attended the workshop beyond the first day. This highlights an important gap with regard to girls' participation in HIV and AIDS prevention, even in interventions that target them. This is perhaps because of the nature of gendered responsibilities for the girls which leaves them with little free time, compared to the boys. As was the case here, all school-going members of the drop-in centre were on holiday. However, only the boys involved found the scheduled times convenient while all the girls found the scheduled times inconvenient.

More than half of the participants did not know their exact dates of birth as such their ages were estimated by the YONECO social worker. The participants' estimated age ranged from 14 to 16 years. The group comprised both single and double orphans. In terms of living arrangements, four of the participants were living with at least one parent while another four were living with slightly older siblings. One lived with an uncle while another participant lived on his own. As clients of the YONECO drop-in centre, the participants were provided with lunch every week day.

All participants were enrolled in schools. However, most of them had dropped out of school at some point in their young lives, and have had an on-and-off relationship with the streets of Zomba, depending on their financial situation and family circumstances. Their classes ranged from the fourth year of primary school to the second year of secondary school,[4] with the majority of the participants still in primary school. Participants' daily routine included school, play and odd jobs at the city centre after school hours. Some of the participants confided in us their positive sero-status, hence equal emphasis was given to issues around infection and re-infection in HIV prevention in the workshop.

The facilitator spent ten days doing three-hour theatre workshops with the group at the YONECO drop-in centre, totalling approximately 30 hours of contact time over a two-week period. Since the participants were on school holiday, it was practical to have the workshops in the mornings. Though none of the participants was conversant with drama, their willingness to use drama as a medium of expression and their openness to exploring issues through drama made its use effective. Central to the project was the question of vulnerability to HIV infection, and so the participants were encouraged to discuss situations in which they had felt vulnerable to HIV. This in turn generated a wide range of narratives, some of which were reproduced in dramatic exploration.

After the project implementation phase of the research process, the researcher compiled scripted, audio and video materials which depicted significant moments from the work, examples of which are included in this chapter. The researcher subsequently drew on these 'texts' to engage in a reflective, interpretive process to decipher the outcome of the engagement with the participants.

Narratives

The two objects of analysis in the research were the narratives and the dramatic reproduction of the narratives by the participants. This section discusses observations on the narratives while the next session discusses the dramatic enactments.

Participants were encouraged to discuss instances in which they had felt vulnerable to HIV. Some of the narratives were 'performed' orally to the group (in group or pair work) while others were in written form. Narratives that were deemed sensitive by the participants were discussed in confidence with the assurance of anonymity from the researcher. Most narratives gathered involved encounters with peers in school, at traditional dances, at 'work places',[5] discos and at home during play time.

The themes of being 'found' in or being 'saved' from risky sexual encounters were common in the narratives at the beginning of the workshop. Later, participants became comfortable to discuss narratives in which they presented the 'self' as initiating or being actively involved in sexual situations. The discussion that follows explores how the participants narrated the forces that drove their actions. There were four major forces which propelled the narrator's actions. These were communion, serendipity, agency and fatalism.

Communion

Participants narrated the forces that drove their action in terms of communion when they attributed much influence to others and to their relationships within their social network in their narratives. An example is Stephan's[6] narrative about how his friend had 'saved him' from having sex with a girl he liked from school.

> We were going home from school and I was telling my friend Martin how this girl I liked had invited me over to her house. I told him I would go because I wanted to have sex with her, you know, to see what it's like. Martin convinced me to go to his house first before I go to the girl's house. At Martin's house I got carried away with play and forgot about my date. It's only then that I realised what Martin had done by detaining me. I thanked him for saving me from a big mistake (Stephan, 14 years).

In this narrative, the participant's action/inaction is entirely influenced by his best friend's gesture of looking out for him. It is Martin's (not Stephan's), strongly motivated and goal-oriented action that changed the outcome of the situation, according to the narrator. A strong bond of communion is shown in Martin's commitment in executing a well calculated act of 'saving' his friend and in Stephan's gratitude to Martin for the gesture.

Serendipity

Participants narrated the forces that drove their actions in terms of serendipity when they presented the series of events in their stories mainly as an outcome of 'randomality', luck, or chance. Dziko's story is an example of a story driven by serendipity:

> The girl wanted to have sex with me. We started touching, I'm very sure I would have slept with her had it not been for the other guy. There was another guy who liked her and he kept following us at the dances. He saved me from having unprotected sex! (Dziko, 14 years).

Lieblich, Zilber and Tuval-Mashiach (2008) argue that serendipity is different from mere luck because it implies taking advantage of, using wisely for one's benefit, circumstances that are out of the actor's control. They note that:

> It [serendipity] represents the individual use of the unplanned aspects of experience and implies three similar elements in one's subjectivity: the absence of preconceived intent, strategy, or goal to reach a certain end state; the lack of awareness of power or internal motivation; and attribution of one's development to external factors such as fate, luck, circumstances, or accidents (Lieblich et al 2008:617).

In the narrative above, Dziko tells a story about how he was 'saved' from having sex with a girl the last time he had attended Mganda traditional dances[7]. Dziko's action/inaction is presented as an outcome of 'randomality', luck, or chance, an act of serendipity as opposed to an internally motivated action.

Well Thought-out Motivated Actions

Sometimes the participants' narratives were propelled by a strongly motivated and goal- oriented action when they presented themselves as free actors with agency. In these cases they projected themselves as beings whose deeds, choices and preferences have determined one's situation (Lieblich et al 2008). Bilo's narrative clearly demonstrates this:

> We were playing Chibisabisa[8] and the two of us went to hide together. I asked the girl if we could have sex. Then I thought about it for a second and then shied away. I quickly went home and didn't come back. (Bilo, 13 years)

In this narrative, Bilo is as an active agent who exercises his will and choice to carry out an action, in this case, walking away from a sexual encounter. After probing further, Bilo revealed two motivating factors that made him walk away: firstly, because he did not want to impregnate the girl because at 13 years, he was not ready to become a father, secondly, he chose not to have sex because he did not want to get HIV. Interestingly, the two motivations were discussed in the particular order of importance to him.

John also talked about his decision not to have sex at traditional dances as driven by internally-motivated actions.

John: Me, I go out at night all the time, I'm an all nighter too!
Facilitator: Is there anyone who forbids this?
John: No
Facilitator: Who do you stay with?

John: Alone

Facilitator: (To all boys) Does having someone to stop you from going out at night influence your behaviour (what you do or do not do)?

Stephan: Of course it does; it prevents you from making stupid decisions and engaging in risky behaviour.

John: But you know with HIV, you are the only person who can determine whether you get it or not. If you are into girls (as a womaniser) you are putting yourself at risk. If you go (to the traditional dances) like I do, just to dance and chat there's no way you can be at risk.

Facilitator: Is it possible to have good objectives in the beginning: today, you go and chat, tomorrow the same, the next day you start doing other things...?

John: That's why I say it's all about choices...

In this conversation, John claims to be fully aware of the risks associated with activities at night dances. He however claims that because of his clear objective, a clearly defined strategy of how to keep himself safe, he is determined not to engage in risky sexual behaviours.

John is a 15-year-old boy who frequents night dances, and proudly declares that he has no curfew as he does not have any guardian to impose it. As a teenager without a caregiver, John is responsible for the provision of most of his everyday basic necessities, such as food and shelter. Furthermore, John also bears a huge responsibility towards his own sexual and reproductive health. From the quotation above, John acknowledges his obligation and need to make good choices, claiming that both engaging in and preventing risky behaviour is simply a matter of personal choice. John presents himself as an agent in two ways in this quotation.; firstly, as an autonomous individual who leads his life according to his will as opposed to being in communion, where his actions and decisions could be influenced by others, such as guardians, friends or mentors; secondly, as someone who acts purposefully or intentionally, as against being controlled by external circumstances such as social class, gender, or historical period.

Fatalism

Some of the teens revealed that sometimes they did not want to 'think' about AIDS when they found themselves in sexual situations as elaborated by below:

McLeod: Rita, that's her name. She was older and voluptuous. I was young and naïve. She was my neighbour when I lived in the village. One evening, one thing led to another and it just happened, we had sex. That was my first time.

Facilitator: Did you use a condom?

McLeod: No. it's not that I didn't know about them [condoms]. I guess I
            wanted to 'do it' as much as she did and I thought *Za Edzi tiziona
            mawa man, wafa wafa*[9] (McLeod, 16)

In this encounter, McLeod claims that an opportunity to have sex presented
itself rather serendipitously, and so unwilling to lose out, he went along with it.
However, the question of condom use is something he consciously disregarded
by resigning himself to fate.

In this section, I have discussed how the participants narrated the forces that
drove their actions. The narratives underscored the importance of communion
in the lives of the participants. However, perhaps overlooking or unaware of
their nuanced 'acts of agency' in the narratives, participants often presented their
narratives as driven by externally motivated factors. In the next section, we see
how drama afforded flexibility to the narratives and how some other narratives
reproduced were driven by other forces. Most importantly, drama allowed for
alternative endings to the narratives. Participants examined what happens when
the 'self' in character has been stripped from the protective buffer provided by
serendipity and communion to confront their risky sexual situation alone; to face
their fears and to explore their dilemmas and anxieties in situations of risk.

'Acting out'

The process of devising and animating scenes allowed an indepth, embodied
discussion of participant's perceptions on issues that affected their lives. The scenes
were created based on the shared narratives of the participants. After generating
the narratives, drama provided an excellent 'live' laboratory for understanding
and interpreting their ideas and actions reflexively.

In this respect, Forum Theatre was employed to engage the participants in a
further discussion of issues, and searching for alternative solutions to the problem.
The main focus of the drama, however, was to critically analyse the protagonist's
agency. The facilitator therefore sought to uncover how the protagonist behaved
and why, what inhibited them from acting in certain ways, what the sources
of dilemma, fear or anxiety were and how the protagonist and the spect-actor
understood the notion of responsibility and constructed notions of agency[10].

In one of the dramas, participants enacted the most common narratives
involving sexual encounters at Mganda night dances. The play was fashioned from
Dziko's narrative.[11] In the enactment, Chikondi, a fictitious character, becomes
the protagonist, replacing Dziko, (the participant who narrated the story). In the
first scene, the character Chikondi links up with Chimwemwe, a girl he meets at
Mganda night dances. Chikondi and Chimwemwe go to the same school; they
know each other, but do not hang around the same circles. On this particular
night, the two get flirty and soon, they find a private corner where things get

heated up. Chikondi is not sure if he should have sex with her, yet he does not want to look like a baby.

In the original narrative, this moment is when the two persons are interrupted by another guy who had been following them. Dziko is consequently 'saved' from proceeding to sexual intercourse because of this distraction. However, in the enacted scene, the facilitator stops the action at this particular moment (before the outside intervention), to investigate the motivation underlying the choices Chikondi has made so far, independent of the serendipitous save. In particular, the facilitator pauses the action on stage to probe deeper into this moment in Chikondi's mind:

Facilitator: I would like to throw a question to Chikondi, the character you are playing, John. What's going on in your head Chikondi?

John: Ehm ehm! I like her and she's getting very tempting.

Facilitator: Why are you stalling then?

John: I don't know, I guess I'm not too sure about everything.

Facilitator: Everything like what?

John: Like going all the way and having sex.

Facilitator: Why?

John: I don't know, it's not like I had planned this, it just happened we met.

Facilitator: So if the other guy doesn't come, and there is no interruption, will Chikondi 'do it'?

John: [Pause and then smirk, other participants giggle excitedly] Yeah, I think so.

Facilitator: Why?

John: Come on, the girl is practically throwing herself at him!

Facilitator: (To the group). So what happens if girls throw themselves at 'you'?

Bilo: If you're a baby you run (laughter from the group). If you're cool, you give her what she wants (cheers from the group).

John: Besides, probably most of his friends are doing it, that's what they talk about.

Facilitator: Are 'your' friends doing it?

John: Yeah, some of them are doing it.

In analysing the protagonist Chikondi's actions and his thought pattern, it is clear that Chikondi would choose to have sex with Chimwemwe even though the idea makes him anxious in the beginning. Some of the reasons that would motivate his action are the fact that he is attracted to Chimwemwe, peer pressure, an opportune moment and Chimwemwe's flirting. The issue of responsibility was later addressed when the facilitator asked who was responsible if Chikondi had contracted HIV. The majority attributed responsibility to Chikondi on the grounds that he is accountable for his actions. However, others argued that Chimwemwe was to blame for fuelling the sexual encounter.

The conversation with the participants is also purposefully multi-layered, to highlight the different layers of self and perception of the participants. Note that from line 1 to 8 the facilitator addresses the 'character' on stage (Chikondi), while lines 9-12 is a conversation between the facilitator and the 'actor' (John), and lines 13-17 are addressed to the audience and all participants. The conversation demonstrates that despite being distinct, (for example, Chikondi, the character's thoughts and actions may differ from John the actor); the layers are in many ways interlinked because they stem from the similar lived experiences of the participants; sexual encounters at the night dances. In this respect, the protagonist's action/ inaction in the play functions as a window to investigate the participants' patterns of thought and action in real life situations that might be considered as risky sexual encounters.

As a way of generating alternative solutions to the play, a fictional ending was added to the original 'script' for performance. In the fictitious scene, Chikondi does go ahead to have sex with Chimwemwe. However, he regrets his decision and confronts his best friend about his fears of having contracted HIV. After the enactment, the facilitator engaged the participants in finding alternatives to the problem of risky sexual encounters of the protagonist.

Facilitator: How well do you think Chikondi handled the situation and the outcome?

Bilo: Personally, I do not think Chikondi handled the situation well at all; he shouldn't have done what he wasn't sure about.

Facilitator: So, if you were Chikondi, what would you do differently, to change the outcome?

               (Hands up from the participants)

Facilitator: Instead of telling us what you would do, why don't you take turns to come on stage and show us your ideas?

The first participant, as Chikondi on stage, uses his wit to flee from the scene, basically avoiding the sexual encounter; the second Chikondi takes a moralistic approach by reminding Chimwemwe of Christian values. However, the scene drags on as the actor playing Chimwemwe is not ready to back down (antagonists are instructed to be strong-willed so as to challenge the protagonists into finding solutions to the problem). The third Chikondi engages Chimwemwe in a conversation about condom use, after some resistance from Chimwemwe they agree to have sex only with a condom.

In a discussion on the most effective alternative, most participants agreed that the first alternative was best for someone who wished to totally avoid a sexual encounter. However, a few others did not opt for this strategy because it implied that Chikondi would have to avoid meeting Chimwemwe for the rest of the school term. The second alternative was acceptable for participants who believed a divine intervention was the best answer, though others argued that the strategy was incompatible with the context of Mganda night dances and therefore impractical. The third alternative was deemed most effective for those who thought that the sexual encounter was unavoidable for 'their Chikondi'. However, it was noted that finding condoms late in the night was improbable and that the risk of unprotected sex was high. The participants argued that Chikondi should have either chosen to take condoms to the night dances or avoid any sexual encounters while there.

From the enactment and discussions that followed, it became clear that there were gendered norms for sexual behaviour that influence the way participants respond to sexual encounters. Participants' response to the first and third alternatives were clearly working for and against the gender script which demands the Malawian male to demonstrate 'manhood' by showing assertiveness and dominance in sexual encounters. Avoiding the sexual encounter meant punitive consequences for 'Chikondi', since he might appear 'uncool' and also might have to avoid the girl for some time.

Conclusion

The project investigated how young people define, negotiate, and perform roles and identities in what they consider risky sexual situations in the context of HIV transmission. The narratives were crucial in exploring how the participants defined their roles and identities under those circumstances. While the narratives themselves only provided the content of the discussion and dramas, it is the 'narration' of the narratives that presented insights as to how the participants defined their identities in the situations they described. There were two major ways in which the participants defined their roles and identities. Participants either presented themselves as active agents that were internally motivated in their actions or as passive subjects dependent on external motivations. In narratives that were driven by agency and fatalism, the action was consciously decided upon and performed by the narrator, either with specific objectives to reach a certain outcome (agency), or the narrator later attributed the consequences of their action to fate or destiny (fatalism). In narratives that were driven by communion and serendipity, the action/inaction was determined by external forces, either by friends (communion) or other chance situations (serendipity).

Discussions that followed narratives that were driven by external factors often unveiled some nuanced acts of agency by the narrator. Participants often discovered that the outcome of their situation was not exclusively dependent upon external forces but that they themselves had made a series of choices that led to the situations and that also contributed to the outcome of their situation. These choices were further explored in the dramatic re-enactments of these situations. In some instances, the participants also discovered that serendipitous acts are not that random since sometimes the choice of friends in a social network could influence how often one gets into risky sexual situations, and whether an outside intervention takes place at all.

Communion proved to be an important aspect in the livelihood of the participants because most of the action/inaction in their narrations was determined by friends and relatives. Even amongst the members of the workshop itself, alignments were observed.   For example, there was a group of participants that accompanied each other at Mganda night dances and others who went to the same school. Most importantly, all participants of the workshop were united by being members of YONECO drop-in centre. Some of the members had been friends for years. Given that the participants clearly identified themselves in terms of communion, and also the fact that looking out for each other was one of their mechanisms when confronted with situations of sexual risk, sexual health interventions (in HIV prevention) that capitalise on communion would be more effective for them. Moreover, friendships in this case (of orphaned teen boys) are even more important because having minimal parental/adult protection or guidance forces the teenagers to rely on friendships for companionship, play and survival.

The enactment of the narratives provided a podium where participants could explore how they negotiate roles and identities in real life situations. The participants were engaged in a continual process of re-scripting the narratives, discovering alternative ways of negotiating situations of risk. Participants also demonstrated their awareness of the framed nature of drama in a workshop environment and how it is different from situations they meet in everyday life. Since the drama scenarios are induced, interventions would play out differently in real life situations which demand time and space bound responses. However, the participants were quick to identify the relevance of the drama intervention. They noted that with drama, they were able to analyse their own actions and explore alternative approaches of confronting situations of sexual risk.

The workshop made the most of the close relationship between the performance of roles on stage and the performance of roles in real life. By performing on stage, the participants interrogated how they perform their roles in life; why they behaved in certain ways, and what inhibits them from doing certain things. The stopping of the action on stage by the facilitator allowed the participants to get into the psyche of the protagonist to discover what made them behave in certain ways and how they constructed notions of personal responsibility for their actions. Participants discovered that most of their actions were motivated by peer pressure, opportune moments and attraction. Through the stage performance, participants also discovered and challenged how they performed their gender and age in real life situations. As a combination of participatory, performative and child-centred approach, the research endorsed self-representation by the youth, as an effective way of engaging young people in research, especially in HIV prevention.

Notes

1. Behaviour change communication attempts to bridge the gap between information, a person's knowledge, attitudes and subsequent behaviour. This approach addresses the knowledge, attitudes, practices and skills of individuals, families and communities as they relate to specific programme goals.
2. A spectator who takes on a dual role of spectating and acting.
3. The average age of the participants was 15years while the facilitator was 25 years. The participants were all male while the facilitator was female.
4. Only one participant was in secondary school. The academic background of the rest of the group ranged between Standard 4 and Standard 8 of primary school.
5. 'Work places' is used in quotes to denote the places where the participants engage in after-school activities for the generation of income.
6. All names that appear in this paper are not the real names of participants.
7. Mganda is a militaristic mimetic dance found in Malawi, Tanzania and Zambia. Although it is danced to the accompaniment of songs, the dominant part of the music comes from drums, whistles and gourds that are specially designed to play like trumpets.
8. A type of Hide and Seek.
9. Literal translation: 'I'll have to see about AIDS tomorrow, man, if I'm dead, I'm dead'
10. The term protagonist is used as a specific term for a participant who is the main character in a play. The terms, 'group' and 'boys' are also used elsewhere to describe the participants of the workshop. The terms 'researcher' and 'facilitator' have also been used to refer to the same person, highlighting the roles taken at various moments of the workshop.
11. Dziko's narrative is discussed in the previous section under serendipity.

References

Conrad, D., 2004, 'Exploring Risky Youth Experiences: Popular Theatre as a Participatory, Performative Research Method', *International Journal of Qualitative Methods*, Vol. 3, No. 1, pp. 1-24.

Corsaro, W.A., 2005, *The Sociology of Childhood*, London: Pine Forge Press.

Davidson, J.O., 2005, *Children in the Global Sex Trade*, Cambridge: Polity Press.

De Boeck, F. and Honwana, A., 2005, 'Children and Youth in Africa: Agency, Identity, and Place', in A. Honwana and F. De Boeck, eds., *Makers and Breakers: Children and Youth in Postcolonial Africa*, Oxford: James Currey.

Evans, R., 2010, '"We are Managing Our Own Lives..." Life Transitions and Care in Sibling-Headed Households Affected by AIDS in Tanzania and Uganda,' *Area*, Vol. 43, No. 4, pp. 384-396.

Fals-Borda, O. and Rahman, M., eds., 1991, *Action and Knowledge: Breaking the Monopoly with Participatory Action-Research,* New York: Apex Press.

Houston, V. and Hovorka, A., 2007, 'HIV/Aids Messages in Malawi and their Implications for Effective Responses', *African Journal of Aids Research,* Vol. 6, No. 3, pp. 205–214 (*wwwisis.unam.na/hivdocs/houston2007.pdf*), 8 August 2011.

James, A. and James, A.L., 2001, 'Childhood: Towards a Theory of Continuity and Change', *Annals of the American Academy of Political and Social Science,* Vol. 575, pp. 25 – 37.

Jones, A., 2007, 'Child-Centred Methodology: A Means to Understanding Children's Experiences of Family Separation Through Migration: The Case of Trinidad and Tobago', in *Focus on Children in Migration from a European Research and Method Perspective: A European Conference,* 20 – 21 March 2007, Warsaw, Poland. (http:// eprints.hud.ac.uk/4199/). 20 September 2011.

Lieblich, A., Zilber, T.B. and Tuval-Mashiach, R., 2008, 'Narrating Human Actions: The Subjective Experience of Agency, Structure, Communion, and Serendipity', *Qualitative Inquiry,* Vol. 14, No. 4, pp. 613-31.

Mann, G., 2005, 'Family Matters: The Care and Protection of Children Affected by HIV/ AIDS in Malawi,' *Save the Children Sweden,* (http://www.repository.forcedmigration. org/showmetadata.jsp?pid=fmo:3707), 13 August 2011.

Mwansa, D. and Bergman P., 2003, *Drama in HIV/Aids Prevention: Some Strengths and Weaknesses: A Study in Botswana, Tanzania, South Africa, Kenya, Ethiopia and Uganda.* (http://comminit.com/?q=edutain-africa/node/270296), 10 August 2011.

Mwale, M., 2008, 'Behavioural Change Vis-à-vis HIV/AIDS Knowledge Mismatch Among Adolescents: The Case of Some Selected Schools in Zomba', *Nordic Journal of African Studies,* Vol. 17, No. 4, pp. 288–299.

Mwalwanda, B.N., 2009, 'Towards the Use of Drama as a Therapeutic Tool to Enhance Emotional Rehabilitation for People Living with HIV/Aids: A Case Study Of Paradiso HIV/Aids Support Organisation'. *Dissertation, University of the Witwatersrand,* (http://www.hdl.handle.net/10539/7801), 9 August 2011.

Smette, I., Stefansen, K. and Mossige, S., 2009, 'Responsible Victims? Young People's Understandings of Agency and Responsibility in Sexual Situations involving Underage Girls', *Young,* Vol. 17, No. 4, pp. 351–73.

UNAIDS, 2008, Report on the Global AIDS Epidemic. (http://www.unaids.org/en/ dataanalysis/epidemiology/2008reportontheglobalaidsepidemic/). 10 August 2011.

UNAIDS, 2010, UNAIDS Report on the Global AIDS Epidemic, (*www.unaids.org/ documents/20101123_GlobalReport_em.pdf*). 10 August 2011.

7

Building Resilience in Child-headed Households: An Exploration of the Integrated Community Home-based Care Model in Maseru District, Lesotho

Ts'epang Florence Manyeli

Introduction

Lesotho's population is estimated at 1.8 million with a child component of 777,440 (Lesotho Bureau of Statistics 2007). The country is completely surrounded by the Republic of South Africa; hence, it has considerable influence on social and economic trends in the country. Lesotho is a mountainous country with a topography that has resulted in a fragile subsistence agricultural economy. According to the World Food Programme [WFP] (2008), Lesotho experienced a decline in its human development index over the last decade because of the negative synergy of poverty, food insecurity, unemployment, and HIV and AIDS.

According to the UN's General Assembly Special Session (2009), the estimated adult HIV prevalence rate in Lesotho is 23.6 per cent. The most recent estimates show that there are approximately 260,000 HIV-positive adults (15-49 years), and this ranks the country as the third highest in the world (UNICEF 2007). The HIV-related illnesses and AIDS have inevitably created a pool of orphaned children who account for 17 per cent of the total population (USAID, UNICEF and UNAIDS 2002). Unfortunately, the high HIV prevalence has resulted in chronically-ill people who are forced by their health and surrounding circumstances to prematurely leave the labour market in order to receive care at home. This situation does not only have a negative impact on the households' income but has also depleted household resources in general. Consequently,

UNICEF (2005) contends that about 17 per cent of children in the age group 5–14 years are child labourers who are often working to fill the vacuum created by the inability of adults to perform their natural care-taking responsibilities. While this is dismal, many children demonstrate considerable fortitude by assuming responsibility for their kith and kin, thus giving rise to adolescent and child-headed households.

In consideration of the plight of children generally, the Lesotho Government and other institutions have introduced measures aimed at providing protection and proper care to the minors. Accordingly, it has formulated legislations and policies such as the Children's Protection and Welfare Act, 2011; National Social Welfare Policy, 2002; Adolescent Health Policy, 2003; and the National Policy on Orphans and Vulnerable Children, 2005. It has also ratified and domesticated various international and regional instruments like the United Nations Convention on the Rights of the Child (UNCRC), 1989 and the African Charter on the Rights and Welfare of the Child (ACRWC). These policies are in line with what other governments in collaboration with various UN agencies, local and international Non-Governmental Organisations (NGOs), Community Based Organisations (CBOs) and Faith Based Organisations (FBOs) are doing in southern Africa and other parts of the continent to mitigate the challenges. These are meant to complement a wide range of longstanding caring patterns within traditional African societies, with the most common being the extended family structure, fosterage and community care. It is within this context that this contribution looks at children's effort through an exercise of their agency to assume responsibility for themselves and other family members in times of adversity brought by the death or incapacity of their parents.

Resilience in Child-headed Households

The most far reaching impact of HIV and AIDS on children is the premature loss of an adult member who would have provided for their wellbeing, maintain the household and hold the family together. According to Gilborn, Nyonyintono, Kabumbuli and Jagwe-Wadda (2002), children's setbacks begin before parental death when the parent is diagnosed as HIV-positive, becomes ill with any of the opportunistic diseases or develop a full-blown AIDS. Children in such households become witnesses to the debilitating illness and, over time, experience less and less care and responsibility from the parents. This tampers with the general functioning of the family unit as a household and may result in the displacement of children (Gow and Desmond 2002). As asserted by Wood, Chase and Aggleton (2006), children in such situations worry about the quality of care and social support networks around them, the physical and emotional impact on their loved ones, death and its aftermath, concerns about their own infection, as well as uncertainties about care and support.

Child-headed households are primarily confronted with the challenges of survival: generating incomes, securing food supplies to avert hunger and malnutrition, health and welfare services, and adult supervision (Kelly 2000; Foster and Williamson 2000; Beeka 2008). Townsend and Dawes (2004) also point out that many child-headed households face eviction from their homes, either through property grabbing by relatives upon the death of their parents, inability to sustain mortgage agreements or because they are too young to access housing subsidies.

According to Foster (2007), the few studies on impact and adjustment that have been conducted with African children suggest a tendency for children to reveal internalised signs of grief such as depression, withdrawal and failure to thrive, and in some cases, externalised ones such as anger, aggression, and behaviour considered unacceptable by adults. Orphaned children also report a higher frequency of physical symptoms such as headaches and stomach aches (Stein 2003), while UNICEF (2004) warns that children in child-headed households might also be victims of crime, drugs and alcohol abuse, exploitation, forced labour, begging, prostitution or early marriage, largely because of their vulnerability. In addition to these are psycho-social problems such as stigmatisation, discrimination, and social exclusion that can arise from their interaction with unsympathetic members of the public.

Though formal and informal mechanisms are being adopted to mitigate the impact of poverty, HIV/AIDS and other risks on vulnerable households during times of severe crises, Beeka (2008) contends that state-administered support is not commonly available throughout Africa. However some governments, for example those of South Africa and Lesotho, provide support to HIV/AIDS-affected households, especially those headed by children through formal safety nets. These include employment creation, free basic education and health care, community development programmes, feeding schemes and grants (Foster 2007). These community and social support systems are believed to enhance the ability of people, especially children, to thrive under such adversity. According to Beeka (2008), the positive intention of these safety nets is acknowledged but the processes through which the services reach people have been less effective.

In sub-Saharan Africa, the extended family (assisted by the community at large), is by far the most effective response for people facing household crises (Foster 2005), and continues to be the predominant caring unit for children orphaned through any form of death. It is believed that the extended kinship and community networks are able to provide better quality services to orphans than residential-based models of care (Loening-Voysey and Wilson 2001; Foster 2007). Traditionally, child care in the African culture has historically been viewed as a social task to be performed by the entire extended family and the community, rather than an individual household (Brink 1998). Therefore, it is believed that the care-giving efforts of extended families, kinship and community networks should be supported. Even though this approach is encouraged by governments and supported internationally, it is increasingly becoming a strained resource as the number of orphaned and vulnerable children continues to grow (Beeka 2008). In fact, the emergence of child-headed households in communities affected by AIDS is an indication that care and support offered to orphaned children under the traditional extended family system is reaching its saturation point.

An alternative model is the community home-based care which is regarded as an appropriate mechanism through which joint efforts and complementary roles can be played to respond holistically to the needs of children in need. Consequently, a wide range of community care models are being implemented, with the most popular ones being the community home-based care model and the integrated community care model. Despite the efforts, it is apparent that coverage through community care and support for orphans and vulnerable children (OVC) and child-headed households is very patchy, most often lacking in depth and quality, as many of these operate with very little external support and uncertain prospects of sustainability.

Notwithstanding the challenges confronting child-headed households, they still persevere in restoring balance and harmony and, in fact in the extant literature, these children are considered as resilient (Boyden and Gillian 2005). They are not merely passive observers of the imperatives of their lives and the societies in which they live; rather they assert themselves, and seek to adapt in ways that challenge notions of children as generally incompetent under such circumstances. As Schaffer (1996:89) notes, "whatever stresses an individual may have encountered in early years, he or she needs not forever more be at the mercy of the past ... children's resilience must be acknowledged every bit as much as their vulnerability". Resilience in this sense is attributed to three kinds of phenomena: good outcomes despite high-risk status, sustained competence under threat, and recovery from trauma (Masten, Best and Garmezy 1990). Evidently, different writers have noted that in as much as there are multiple definitions of resilience, they have common themes. As Beeka (2008:11) puts it, "resilience emerges in the face of challenge; it carries the property of buoyancy (the individual has the ability to bounce back) and is described in terms of wellness rather than pathology". The understanding of resilience has evolved to include the interplay of risk and protective processes over time, which involves individuals, family and socio-cultural influences. Resilience is also viewed as essential in child development (Garmezy 1991).

However, Walsh (1996) argues that in discussing resilience, much focus tends to be placed on the individual rather than the family. He states that family resilience differs from individual resilience in that the unit of analysis is the family as a whole rather than the individual. Resilience is also considered as a dynamic, emergent, multidimensional process that unfolds over time (Walsh

2003). They further assert that the concept of resilience is embedded in the studies of children who functioned competently despite exposure to risk. Some studies have attempted to explore the notion of resilience and recommended ways in which it can be nurtured in children affected by HIV/AIDS to help them cope with the cumulative stressors which usually begin long before the death of a parent. Mallmann (2002) for example, suggests building children's capacity and developing their ability to express emotions, maintain a family and autobiographical memory, experience a sense of belonging within a community, cope with daily life, have a sense of control over their current and future lives, and protect themselves from the negative effects of different forms of material and emotional vulnerability. They also require external resources, like secure and supportive relationships with their caregivers, extended family members, and other key adults like teachers, and community workers. It is in this regard that Gilborn et al. (2002) argue that in order to enhance children's resilience, the capacity for adult-to-child communication, especially about difficult issues such as sex education, parental illness and parental death, should be strengthened. They further argue that it is important to respond to this demand because the psycho-social needs of the children are often overlooked.

Silence can also be problematic, and so, breach children's resilience. For example, cultural silence emerges as a risk factor that increases children's vulnerability by undermining both closeness and competence, while disclosure and openness – the breaching of cultural silence – are revealed as protective factors that may enhance resilience among children. According to Walsh (2003), despite the apparently devastating odds, not all children exposed to risks and adversities develop problems later on in life.

Resilience depends both on the individual and group strengths and can be highly influenced by supportive elements in the wider environment like community care programmes. It is still questionable if all models of community care followed in Lesotho recognise the element of resilience. As Beeka (2008) points out, many communities in Africa have developed innovative mutual support initiatives as responses to the epidemic through the utilisation of a range of strategies and models. Since community safety nets are not new, an important question is how much of it have been used as a response to the problems affecting child-headed households, and to what extent have they enhanced resilience amongst children. Programmes helping vulnerable children tend to focus on material needs, followed by education and children's skills, but very few adequately address the social and psychological needs of affected children. For instance, long term solutions need to be crafted for the children because the impact of HIV and AIDS will linger for decades, even after the epidemic wanes.

Greater understanding of the impact of HIV/AIDS on children's resilience is important in the design and evaluation of programmes to support children living in difficult circumstances. It is against this backdrop that this study examined the extent to which the integrated community care model enhances competence in child-headed households. It further determined the degree to which the community care models have been successful in protecting children and their contribution towards the forging of resilience in them. Furthermore, it established the additional services that are required in community care models for children to grow in a caring family environment. In short, the study sheds light on how the implementation of community care models can be improved for the benefit of children.

The Research Process

The study was undertaken in an Orphans and Vulnerable Children (OVC) child care community-based project in Thaba-Bosiu, Maseru District of Lesotho. The project is coordinated by the Lesotho Red Cross Society (LRCS), a local NGO in a rural community that is still immersed in the Basotho traditions and lifestyles. The primary target group was children and youth living in child-headed households; that is, orphaned and abandoned or deserted children and young people who are living on their own. They were aged between 7 and 18 years. A purposive sampling technique was used to select four households which consisted of a total of twenty children and youth, inclusive of the household heads. Twelve were females while eight were males. Amongst them, 9 were in primary school, 8 were in secondary and high schools, while 3 were in tertiary institutions.

A qualitative research, based on qualitative methods of in-depth interviews and observations, was adopted to enable the exploration of general and specific questions relating to changes child-headed households have been experiencing over time, problems encountered, and adjustment to their new settings. Furthermore, issues relating to responsibilities, family chores and relations with their extended family were also raised for discussion in the interviews. Since a central aspect of the research was children's agency in times of adversity wrought upon them by the untimely deaths of their parents and other significant adults, the issue of resilience was also addressed in detail. In this respect, particular inquiries were made about their understanding of resilience, the sources of and influences on their resilient behaviours, psycho-social and cultural factors that impinge on their resilience, the contribution of the Lesotho Red Cross Society (LRCS) programme, as well as suggestions on what the programme should do to improve their capacity to manage and withstand challenges in their households and personal lives. Lastly, their sources of support, the impact of their parents' death and factors that have a bearing on their childhood since the loss of their parent, were also probed.

Access to households and individuals was gained through the community leaders and LRCS. Interviews were conducted in Sesotho, tape-recorded with the permission of informants, and subsequently transcribed into English. Prior to the eventual deployment of the instruments, they were pre-tested following which necessary changes were made. In seeking the permission of participants, they were informed in advance of the study and the objectives it intended to achieve, so as to first facilitate their effective participation and second, make them aware of their right to participate and withdraw anytime they wished. Considering that discussions about HIV and AIDS-instigated deaths and the resulting loss of parents are highly emotional topics, especially where the subjects of the research are children and young people, it was imperative that they were accorded the necessary protection of their views and opinions. This privacy was achieved through anonymity and confidentiality assurances, through the application of the "opt-in" and "opt-out" principle in order to avoid any degree of "forced compliance" (Luttrell 2010:226) on the participants of the study.

The resulting data was analysed qualitatively through the process of coding and categorisation of major themes that emerged from the discussions. This provided a structure to the data based on the purpose and objectives of the study. However, because a purposive sampling strategy was used to select a small sample, the outcome of the study could not be considered as representative of the general population. Nonetheless, the depth of information and discussions makes up for the unrepresentative nature of the sample.

Assuming Adult Roles and Responsibilities

What was evident right from the beginning of the interviews and observations was that the participants of the study had more responsibilities to shoulder than previously. However, although all the participants were from child-headed households, they were not completely left to their own devices as they still had very close contacts with other members of the extended family. They continued to regard the extended family members as their custodians, even in cases where they were not receiving any assistance from them. As Thabo, one of the heads of households indicated:

> Even though my parents are both dead, at least my uncle is still there and keeps checking on us regularly. I live with my two sisters and youngest brother and I am happy that we are still in my parents' house.... Since I am the eldest, I know that I have to look after them. It is my responsibility.... I know, however, the Red Cross project officer and the care facilitators are there for us too. They too come to my house so often that we feel they are starting to be part of the family too. They are so caring [Thabo, male, 17 years]

Thabo demonstrates an awareness of the situation – death, the aftermath, consequences – and the responsibility that goes with being the leader of the family. It appears that Thabo and his household are not completely left to their own fate; his uncle's regular checks occasionally yield a much needed bag of provisions, however meagre, while his presence offers some degree of emotional support and opportunity for guidance and counsel when there is the need for advice about one thing or the other. Neo, a 15-year-old girl, also noted that they started to assume immediate responsibility for themselves as soon as their parent fell seriously ill. According to her:

> As the eldest in my family, I had to look after my mother when she became sick. It was very hard for me as I had never nursed anyone before. I was always stressed and cried all the time. I didn't know how to help her, especially because she was HIV-positive. The care facilitators helped us a lot and gave us guidance but what I wanted was for her to get well and take care of us.....I had to help her bath, clean the house, cook and feed her. At the same time, I had to go to school and do my school work when I got home, help my siblings with their homework and look after my mother as well. I had no time to rest [Neo, female, 15 years].

An important aspect of Neo's account is her concurrent experience of vulnerability and agency. She had to assume responsibilities she was not initially prepared for as evident in the phrase, "I didn't know how to help her..." But beneath the pragmatic support of bathing her mother, cooking and feeding her and assuming the responsibilities of an adult was emotional insecurity such that she wanted "her to get well..." so that she would "... take care of us". In effect, she wanted to be liberated from those adult roles through her mother's recovery so that she could be a 'little' girl again. Clearly, the complexities inherent in the performance of such a responsibility are evident in the emotional stress she had to undergo. Like Thabo, although she received some support from the facilitators and they apparently filled a vacuum in their lives, it is obvious that at that stage she did not rate that as comparable to what her mother would have offered if she were capable.

The children's responses generally revealed the emotional and psychological trauma of witnessing the deaths of parents. Words like 'anger', 'sorrow' and 'grief' were frequently used. For example, 15-year-old Lerato (female) stated that "...I was never happy seeing how much pain my father was going through; he suffered and had no rest at all...I was always sad...I couldn't play. I wouldn't want to see anyone closest to me suffering like that ever again". Some indicated that they experienced these emotions even before their parents' death, as they witnessed their pain and deteriorating physical and mental health. Some of them even had to live under suspicions of being HIV-positive from the community. For example, according to Mpho, an 18-year-old girl who attends a local vocational school, "The villagers thought my mother was HIV-positive and after her death they said I was also infected because I had been nursing her." While there is evidence that the community is usually supportive of children in such adverse situations, Mpho's case symbolises some degree of rejection and stigmatisation by a section of the same community. Such actions however deepen their trauma and the emotional scars they sustained from the illnesses and death of their parents.

They also noted that they generally experienced financial problems, shortage of food and clothing. This is unexpected since, as children and young people, they had no employment and regular sources of income and therefore had to depend on the generosity of others and more importantly, their own ingenuity. Thus, although six of them obtained a monthly child support grant of US$42, it was grossly insufficient, considering the size of their households. However, all participants of the study indicated that they obtained assistance in form of food parcels, health services, educational materials, household items and clothing from LRCS, while some of them received financial support from their relatives as well. But the lessons and experiences propelled them to act in ways that protected their interest and helped to improve their quality of life. For example, they initiated personal actions such as selling of vegetables and basic items like matches, candles, and snacks to generate extra income to complement what they were receiving from others. However, as a result of the paucity of those resources, they noted the need for self-denial in order to cover their priority needs, such as food. Lebohang, an 18-year-old female indicated: "... with the child support grant, we have to buy all the basics and food and it lasts us a month... maybe that is so because we don't buy some things like vegetables but grow them in our garden". It is evident that the minimal or lack of direction from adults in their households, and assurances of having a mother or father in the background has sharpened their sense of awareness and ingrained skills of survival and economy, such that they exhibited extra care in the use of resources. They were therefore more adaptive to situations and willing to take up additional responsibilities that would lead to an improvement of their household economy.

Community care was also evident through family support, with some relatives occasionally offering them material support in form of food supplies and other essential household items. Lereko, a 15-year-old male, noted that their grandfather who is an old-age pensioner receives only US$50, but buys them some groceries like soap, salt, tea, paraffin and candles. Over and above these, he shares his agricultural yields like maize, sorghum, beans and peas with them all the time. The essence of extended family comes to the fore here as we encounter evidence of support from family members like grandparents who feel an obligation to support them financially and materially. This is a good indication of empathy, care and direct communication amongst family members – behaviours that are essential in boosting the children's and their households' resilience.

The eldest members who often assumed the status and responsibility of parents or significant 'adult' in the households talked about how caring and protective they were of their siblings. According to Lereko, he had "... to make sure that they are happy". He noted further:

> "I don't want them to be subjected to any form of abuse or harm. I have got to know everything that is happening in their lives, especially because some people may take advantage of the fact that they are orphans". (Male, 15 years)

Such responses show individual effort on the part of the relatively older ones to assume the key responsibility of being heads of the households and so ensure security and protection of their siblings. The role of the community in shoring up the confidence and resilience of the participants is therefore ambivalent. On one hand, some members of the community offer emotional and material support but, on the other hand, the plight of the children are worsened in some cases by the insensitive way in which they are treated and accepted in the larger society.

The Role of Lesotho Red Cross Society (LRCS)

The LRCS, the national version of the International Red Cross one of the leading global organisations in the provision of care and support in times of adversity and need, has been instrumental in the community-based effort to support child-headed households. Inquiries about their contribution from the children showed that their activities bolster their resilience. They noted that as members of the community youth clubs organised by the LRCS, they are empowered in a number of ways to cope with challenges and adapt to changes in life. Some noted that the clubs helped them regain their self-esteem. According to Mphonyana (female, 15 years), "this is where we share our problems openly with peers. We have a lot in common in the club, so no one laughs at the other. The LRCS provides us with counselling as well". A forum where they could interact with people with similar concerns and discuss everyday experiences had a therapeutic effect; they could voice their frustrations, learn from others, as well as benefit from the professional expertise of the counsellors from LRCS. In this respect, many of the participants of the study indicated that their ability to cope was closely connected to the support, aid and care the facilitators readily provided whenever they were faced with challenges that exceeded their individual or collective capacity as a household.

As part of their strategies to fortify them psychologically, the LRCS had also introduced them to the memory work concept which is an initiative that helps them to cope with the emotional and psychological problems of losing their parents. In stressing the relevance of this to their lives, Relebohile, an 18-year-old female noted that, "… this is where we keep all the memories about our parents and any valuable items like photos, books about their lives and any other special items that remind us of them. They help us maintain the connection with our parents". The memory work concept has been used in many other situations in the country and has proved to be an effective way of dealing with emotional and psychological problems, as it guided the participants to focus their minds on useful and relevant memories and information while suppressing the harmful and irrelevant ones. For example, images of terminally-ill parents could leave children and young people in distress whenever they are reminded of them or they choose to relive those experiences. But while remembrance may be important for their personal healing, it could also be destructive if too much emphasis is placed on the heart-rending scenes from the past.

Additionally, the LRCS provides all the OVC in the community with psycho-social support under which all the eleven participants at secondary, high school and tertiary institutions receive payments for their annual school fees and school uniforms, medical services as the need arises as well as clothes, especially warm clothes and blankets in the winter. In this respect, there have been two special cases whereby shelter had been provided to destitute children, some of whom were in that position because of the loss of primary care from their parents or extended family. In order to meet this challenge, the LRCS has established five support groups/youth clubs for OVC in the target area, with the intention of giving them life skills and also ensuring food security for their families. The clubs are trained on issues relating to HIV/AIDS, children's rights, approaches to helping children who require protection, the memory work concept, resilience, and general life skills. They meet every weekend under the guidance of peer mentors. They also engage in sporting activities and cultural plays and games. The care facilitators and guardians as well as older siblings also have the responsibility of ensuring access to paediatric art and other health care services as the need arises. As a way of securing the future supply of food items for the benefit of such children, the LRCS has secured land to produce wheat, beans and vegetables, while other support groups have introduced poultry and piggery projects. The management of the projects is the responsibility of the guardians, OVC, chiefs and the care facilitators. The respondents confirmed that they benefit directly from all these initiatives. In addition to that, the care facilitators visit them at least three times a week to counsel them, see how they are coping and also link them with structures that can help them deal with any distinct problems. The project officer also follows up closely on individual child cases to ensure that they are handled accordingly.

Conclusion

The aim of the research was to explore the contribution of the OVC community care programmes in building resilience in child-headed households. The study has revealed that some of the children experienced the trauma of caring for their ailing parents, looking after siblings and eventually losing their parents. Resultantly, they experienced financial, social and emotional/psychological problems from the premature death of their parents.

There appeared to be a high sense of family bond amongst the children and, in many cases, with the extended family members. There was a strong sense of belonging, sharing, support and protection among siblings and sometimes with some extended family members. The results also portrayed a strong belief in religion and traditional caring practices. Family adaptability was clearly spelt out as they all lived in their parents' houses and continued with their normal household chores, similar to what they had to do before the death of their parents. Notably, the respondents also managed to take care of the family within the tight budget in the absence of the adult member. This illustrated the flexibility of the family as referred to in the Family Resilience Framework (Beeka 2008). It was also observed that they communicate and relate closely, and also share roles, usually under the guidance of the eldest member. Generally, the study found that the integrated community care model followed by the LRCS is emphatic on holistic approach to care for OVC. Respondents indicated that they do not only receive social assistance but also psychological support from the programme.

These support services are however complemented by traditional social support structures like the extended family. It has been established that OVC community care programmes appreciate the key supportive roles that are played by the community leaders as well as social and religious structures like the church and its support mechanisms. Notably, the LRCS contributed immensely in developing the competence of OVC by initiating the formation of youth clubs, by imbuing them with valuable skills of life, paying home visits to the families, offering material, educational, financial and psycho-social support. The main reason for offering such assistance was to ensure that the OVC can cope with all the identified challenges, even in the absence of their parents. Even though most of them appreciate the support of their extended families, there are situations where they do not get adequate support from them; and so, they have to fend for themselves. In such instances, there is the need for strong intervention from other structures like the chieftaincy and the community at large. However, considering the levels of household poverty, the communities sometimes are unable to help, even though their desire to do so may be palpable. It can be concluded that these child-headed households show considerable levels of resilience in the face of adversity.

References

Beeka, H. A., 2008, 'Resilience in HIV/AIDS Adolescent Headed Families', unpublished MA thesis, Port Elizabeth: Nelson Mandela Metropolitan University.

Boyden, J., and Gillian, M., 2005, 'Children's Risk, Resilience and Coping in Extreme Situations', in M. Ungar, ed., *Handbook for Working with Children and Youth: Pathways to Resilience across Cultures and Contexts*, London: Sage Publications.

Brink, P., 1998, *Adoption Practice in the AIDS Era: A Southern African Perspective.* (http://www.togan.co.za/cindi/papers/paper1.htmBrittain & Minty), 17 August 2011.

Foster, G. and Williamson, J., 2000, 'A Review of Current Literature on the Impact of HIV/AIDS on Children in Sub-Saharan Africa', *AIDS 2000*, Vol. 14, No. 3, pp. 275–284.

Foster, G., 2005, *Under the Radar-Community Safety Nets for Children Affected by HIV/AIDS in Poor Households in Sub-Saharan Africa,* Harare: UNRISD.

Foster, G., 2007, 'Under the Radar: Community Safety Nets for AIDS Affected Households in Sub-Saharan Africa', *AIDS Care*, Vol. 19, No. 1, pp. 54-63.

Garmezy, N., 1991, 'Resiliency and Vulnerability to Adverse Developmental Outcomes Associated with Poverty', *American Behavioral Scientist*, Vol. 34, No.4, pp. 416-430.

Gilborn, L. Z., Nyonyintono, R., Kabumbuli, R. and Jagwe-Wadda, G., 2002, *Making a Difference for Children Affected by AIDS in Uganda*, Washington DC: Population Council.

Gow, J. C. and Desmond, C.J., 2002, *Impacts and Interventions: The HIV/AIDS Epidemic and the Children of South Africa*, Pietermaritzburg: University of Natal Press.

Kelly, M., 2000, *HIV/AIDS and Education in Eastern and Southern Africa: The Leadership Challenge and the Way Forward*, Addis Ababa: UNECA.

Lesotho Bureau of Statistics, 2006, *Lesotho Census Results*, Maseru: Lesotho Government.

Loening-Voysey, H. and Wilson, T., 2001, *Approaches to Caring for Children Orphaned by AIDS and Other Vulnerable Children: Essential Elements for a Quality Service*, New York: UNICEF.

Luttrell, W., 2010, 'A Camera is a Big Responsibility: A Lens for Analysing Children's Visual Voices', Visual Studies, Vol. 25, No. 3, December 2010, pp. 224-237.

Mallmann, S., 2002, *Building Resilience among Children Affected by HIV/AIDS*, Windhoek: Catholic Relief Services.

Masten, A., Best, K. and Garmezy, N., 1990, 'Resilience and Development: Contributions from the Study of Children who Overcome Adversity', *Development and Psychopathology*, Vol 2, No.1, pp. 425–444.

Nyamukapa, C., Foster, G. and Gregson, S., 2003, 'Orphans' Household Circumstances and Access to Education in a Maturing HIV Epidemic in Eastern Zimbabwe', *Journal of Social Development in Africa*, Vol. 18, No. 2, pp. 7–32.

Schaffer, H. R., 1996, *Social Development*, Oxford: Blackwell.

Stein, J., 2003, *Sorrow makes Children of Us All: A Literature Review On The Psychosocial Impact of HIV/AIDS on Children*, Cape Town: University of Cape Town.

Townsend, L., and Dawes, A., 2004, 'Willingness to Care for Children Orphaned by HIV/AIDS: A Study of Foster and Adoptive Parents', *African Journal of AIDS Research*, Vol.3, No.1, pp. 69–80.

UNICEF, 2004, *HIV and ADIS in Lesotho*, Maseru: United Nations.

UNICEF, 2005, *Humanitarian Action, Lesotho*, Maseru: United Nations.

UNICEF, 2007, *HIV and AIDS in Lesotho*, Maseru: United Nations.

United Nations General Assembly Special Session, 2009, *UN Status of the National Response to the 2001 Declaration of Commitment on HIV and AIDS*, Maseru: National AIDS Commission.

USAID, UNICEF and UNAIDS, 2002, *Children on the Brink: A Joint Report on Orphan Estimates and Program Strategies,* Washington DC: TvT Associates.

Walsh, F., 1996, 'The Concept of Family Resilience: Crisis and Challenge', *Family Process*, Vol. 35, No.3, pp. 261-281.

Walsh, F., 2003, 'Family Resilience: A Framework for Clinical Practice', *Family Process*, Vol. 42, No.1, pp. 1– 18.

Wood, K., Chase, E., and Angletton, P., 2006, 'Telling the Truth is The Best Thing: Teenage Orphans' Experience of Parental AIDS-Related Illness and Bereavement in Zimbabwe', *Social Science & Medicine*, Vol. 63, No. 1, pp. 1923–1933.

World Food Programme, 2008, *Lesotho Food Security Monitoring System Bulletin*, Maseru: Disaster Management Authority.

8

Children's Perceptions of the Images of Kenya's Principal Political Leaders

Mokua Ombati

Introduction

In the twentieth century, research on children's political awareness was stimulated largely by Piaget and Inhelder (1969) who argued that adult mental structures, to some extent, are the product of the individuals' early cognitive and affective development. Since then, a   number of studies have investigated the process of children's socialisation in the West (e.g. Coles 1986; Moore, Lare and Wagner 1985; Stevens 1982).

Childhood is considered a particularly critical or the most formative period for political socialisation (Sears 1975), since learning mainly takes place at a non-conscious level through imitation and identification (Greenstein 1965). According to Sears and Levy (2003), individuals are particularly impressionable during their childhood years because they are just awakening to the political and social world. This formative stage could have enduring predispositions and attitudinal effects on the generation that experienced them as children (Miller and Shanks 1996). According to Jennings and Markus (1984), this period witnesses a surge in the crystallisation of a variety of socio-political attitudes, with the crystallisation increasing with age as children move from childhood to adulthood. Learning that begins in childhood obviously continues into adulthood as individuals adjust to internal psychological changes as well as external changes in their social and political environment (Sears and Levy 2003). Thus, inherited dispositions and social experiences interact to advance political learning. As noted by Smith (1999), there is evidence that civic identities developed during childhood may strongly persist to shape adult citizenship profiles and behaviours. This approach, known as the persistence model, rests on the assumption that political lessons learned early in life will endure throughout adulthood to structure the adult's attitudes (Jennings and Markus 1977).

In spite of the extensive studies and extant literature on the subject in the West, there is a scarcity of studies on Kenyan children's political knowledge, attitudes and behaviour; hence the motivation for this study. In order to achieve the primary objective of the study, a framework situated in the theory of political socialisation was adopted. Political socialisation is the development process by which children become oriented towards the beliefs, cognitions, attitudes, values, knowledge, opinions, norms, behaviour, civic identities and participation patterns related to their society's political culture, social institutions, systems and practices (Atkin 1981). In the view of Shah (2010), it is the process through which a society's members become orientated and so engage themselves in political activities. This could be expressed through political interest and knowledge, discussion, participation, and engagement. As this is undertaken, they acquire information about political leaders and eventually get to know them. In the case of children, as they acquire political attitudes and information, they use it intelligently to further their understanding of politics and connect with others in a desired way (McDevitt and Chaffee 2002). In this 'trickle-up' approach, children are not merely receptive to civic development but they proactively socialise with other agents to take a more proactive role in the political environment, even affecting adults' political information seeking, opinion formation and stimulation.

Although in general, children on their own do not search for political information, they live in a general environment saturated with politics; hence, the process of political socialisation seems to be unavoidable. Children's concept of authority and political information stems from a variety of sources (Howard and Gill 2000), including exposure to peers, media channels, (television, radio, internet and newspapers), political parties and the current government's civic activities and policies. The fact that each generation is socialised according to a historical period, in which norms, activities and attitudes towards political participation are formed, is also critical to the development of children's political awareness. Sapiro (2004:11) contends that, 'in societies that undergo dramatic political changes, children's political experiences are more strongly affected than in politically stable countries'. Family habits are undoubtedly a factor as McDevitt and Chaffee (2002: 281) argue, '[I]ntrinsic forces of family adaptation make the home a powerful incubator of citizenship'. Parents are centrally involved in political socialisation, for the more parents know and the more they encourage their children to discuss politics, express their opinions and be politically involved, the more politically socialised the children will be (McIntosh, Hart and Youniss 2007). As argued by McDevitt (2005), schooling not only provides a strong flow of information, but also fosters the development of cognitive tools that facilitate this information to help nurture a political ideological identity into the schemata of the individual.

Children's attitude towards political authority is one of the elements in their development (Coles 1986), while an appreciation of their political inclinations provides a means for projecting their political future. As Greenstein (1965:56) has pointed out, the 'favourable' feelings towards political leaders acquired early in childhood seem to have a more substantial effect on the individuals' adult political behaviour than do the various negative orientations towards politicians which emerge later in life'. It is in the light of this that the study scanned Kenyan children's political engagement by registering their views, opinions and attitudes as to how they perceive Kenya's foremost political leaders, President Emilio Stanley Mwai Kibaki and Prime Minister Raila Amollo Odinga. Kibaki emerged the winner over Raila in the 2007 presidential election that was marked by accusations of fraud and irregularities. There was a major breakdown of law and order, as the situation threatened to disintegrate the whole country, but was saved by the power-sharing peace agreement between Kibaki who remained as President and Raila who took up the re-created position of Prime Minister.

The motivation for the study was the need to move away from a focus on the persistence of childhood learning as a predictor of specific electorally focused attitudes and voting behaviours, towards a focus on the socialisation of children as citizens and members of the civic community. It is necessary to recognise the fact that although children are not voters, they are citizens, and that the process of political learning may well structure the types of citizens they will become later in life (Conover and Searing 1994). As Greenstein (1965:1) argues, children develop 'awareness of most conspicuous features of the adult political arena' years before they comprehend factual political information. Importantly, children's political socialisation begins with the tendency to idealise key political figures. Coles (1986:23) maintains that, for politicians to stay in power, 'political authority needs to become an object of belief, if not faith'. In this respect, children have been found to 'consistently' define authority as respected, superior and powerful, and identify the President as 'the boss of the country', the authority who 'runs the country', and as the authority who 'makes the laws' (Moore, Lare and Wagner 1985:223).

As noted by Gill (2006), national leaders may symbolise strong nationalism or hegemonic leadership and the populace may accept this type of leadership as desirable. In this regard, it may be argued that the values, beliefs and ideology of a nation's leadership represent the country's political culture. In discerning children's perspective of the Kenyan political landscape, this study sought to understand what kind of conspicuous images, in terms of leadership patterns, behaviour, traits, styles, features, mannerisms, designs, qualities and characteristics, the two foremost Kenyan leaders evoke in the minds of children. The aim was to capture the conscience of Kenya's political masses as treasured and embedded in the mindsets, attitudes, opinions and perceptions of children.

Research Process

A qualitative design was envisaged as the best approach to obtain an in-depth description of children's perspectives, experiences, understanding, perceptions and interpretations of Kenya's political environment. The researcher, therefore, purposively selected a Municipal Primary School in Eldoret town, and thirty-six of its lower primary pupils aged between 7 and 10 years for the study. On account of their ethnicity, enrolled class, residence, age, gender and knowledge of the subject of study, nine pupils from each class from Standards I to IV were selected (see Table 1). These children were selected for the investigation because they are in a formative period.

Table 1: Background of Respondents

No. of Participants	Class	Gender		Years
		Male	Female	
9	1	6	3	7
9	2	5	4	8
9	3	4	5	9
9	4	3	6	10
Total: 36		18	18	

A semi-structured interview schedule that allowed children to organise the nature and extent of their responses was the main tool of data collection. Individual conversational interviews or dialogues, which are considered a more equal two-way process, were conducted, lasting no more than ten minutes. To activate the children's imagination, the study employed a specialised form of projective or associative methodology known as 'play of associations' which, as described by Catterall and Ibbotson (2000), are unstructured tests that rely on the respondents' interpretation of stimuli and report on what particular associations they bring to mind. Because of the leeway provided by the tests, respondents project their own personalities onto the stimulus, thus often revealing personal conflicts, motivations, coping styles and other characteristics.

The children were asked to associate their foremost national political leaders, Raila Odinga and Mwai Kibaki, with a car, tree, building and an animal. Prior to the actual interviews, the investigator ensured rapport and built trust with the children by spending time in the school, observing and communicating with them in groups and individually on various topics without asking them questions related to the study. The best interests of children, with especial regard to ethical standards and moral requirements, concerns for their protection, confidentiality and anonymity were considered when they were engaged in the research. Data drawn from transcribed verbatim audio-tape recordings and field notes were subjected to qualitative analysis and data reduction. Answers were coded, depending on connotations as defined by Kenyan culture, particularly on perceptions of beauty, value and mythological beliefs.

Results

All the participants of the study knew who the Kenyan President is by names such as "Mwai Kibaki", "Baba Jimmy", and "Emilio Mwai Kibaki". The tendency to mention the President's patronymic/baptismal names, Emilio Stanley, was especially evident in the children's answers. Also, all the thirty-six children knew who the Prime Minister is by the names of "Agwambo", "Tinga Tinga" or "Raila Odinga". The fact that all the children knew the various names and/or nicknames of the President and Prime Minister is attributable to the attention the school curricula gives to civics and social education in socialising and educating children on good citizenship. It could also be explained by the high level of media penetration, especially radio and television. As one 10-year-old girl confirmed, "We have a TV and a radio in our home. Both systems work the whole day when we guys [children] are at home, and we devote many hours watching TV and listening to radio while mommy and daddy are at work". Another 9-year-old girl enrolled in Standard III commented, "Raila with his vitendawili (riddles) and parables is akin to a political celebrity or legend. TV and radio news without him is not news". The children revealed that although politics was not made a special topic of conversations with parents, they could overhear their comments on political events and issues when they watched television or listened to news, particularly evening news, together.

Children's Perceptions of President Kibaki

On the balance, the majority of children who participated in the study had positive perceptions of the images of the Kenyan President, Mwai Kibaki. While answering the question, "If Kibaki were a car, what kind of car would he be?" Twenty-two respondents came up with a list of concrete manufacturer's names. Some respondents (fourteen) associated Kibaki with "the most prestigious car, Limo"; two others named such cars as Jeep; two named Mercedes; two saw him as a foreign car; one saw him as a Ferrari; another saw him as a Bentley; while one each saw him as Toyota and Audi. Fourteen others used perceived properties of a car such as "big and cool", "colourful and rich", "a little bit strict", "armoured and speedy", "big and gorgeous", "big and smart", "white, big and speedy", "a car robot", "a dark blue car", "a foreign car", and "a black foreign car". A 9-year-old boy said, "comfortable, cozy, warm and with a stereo system". An 8-year-old girl identified Kibaki with the presidential motorcade: "many cars and motorcycles speeding on both lanes of the road with a blaring siren". Importantly, majority of the respondents (twenty-four) associated the President with foreign (imported) cars. This was particularly significant in a nation where foreign items are highly revered and esteemed, as articles of value and quality that symbolise success and prosperity. A 7-year-old girl summed up her response thus: "The car is white because a white colour is associated with purity".

Twenty-five respondents named a concrete tree while answering the question, "If Kibaki were a tree, what kind of tree would he be?" The most popular tree mentioned by the respondents (ten) was a fig tree. This was not a surprise because of the symbolic value of the fig tree in Kenya. In fact, President Kibaki had compared the strength of the former ruling party, Kenya African National Union(KANU), to a fig tree, by declaring that attempts to dislodge KANU from power was like "trying to cut down a fig (mogumo) tree with a razor blade" (Walsh January 4, 2003). An 8-year-old standard two boy in reaction to the question noted "Kibaki would be a beautiful fig tree; it's mighty". Asked by the interviewer if a fig tree could be mighty, he responded confidently, "Yes, it's strong".

An oak, which is mentioned in some Kenyan folktales, was named nine times. An 8-year-old girl described Kibaki as a tree by saying, "He would be an oak. It is strong, big, and beautiful; it stands in the centre of the forest and it is the tallest tree. Its leaves do not fall down". Other respondents provided descriptions of the qualities, features and properties of trees in their associations. Respondents used descriptions such as "Big and thick, many branches", "Big and beautiful", "With big fruits", "A very green tree", "The most prominent tree", "Tall, a lot of leaves, and beautiful", and "Tall and strong" to describe Kibaki as a tree.

A leitmotiv of a high object in associations related to the Kenyan President was evident in respondents' answers to the question, "If Kibaki were a building, what kind of building would he be?" Particularly, twelve respondents came up with images of a "skyscraper", "tall building" or "multi-storied building". Ten respondents specifically named the KVDA (Kerio Valley Development Authority) building, which is the tallest in Eldoret town, while five respondents saw Kibaki as the Zion Mall (the most recent and prestigious building in Eldoret town). Kibaki as a skyscraper/tall building, the KVDA or Zion Mall was extremely positive, also meaning, "Kibaki is our hope". A 10-year-old girl associated Kibaki with a house painted in white with "tables, chairs, and fireplaces made by famous companies for famous people". Another 10-year-old boy said that Kibaki as a building would be a "big house with slot machines and pool tables". Perceptions of the President as the official who is "at the crest of the wave" while he is making important decisions was manifested in such responses as "A building in which something important is going on", "A movie theatre because something interesting is going on there" and "A drama theatre because it is interesting there".

Sixteen respondents associated Kibaki with predators such as lion, leopard, tiger, and cheetah while answering the question, "If Kibaki were an animal, what kind of animal would he be?" As one 9-year-old girl argued, "Kibaki is a snow leopard because it's a rare animal, which lives on the highest mountain peaks". A 7-year-old-boy joined respondents who provided descriptions without naming a concrete animal, saying: "Big and powerful, fast, beautiful, smart; it has sharp hearing and it is a good runner". Two respondents associated Kibaki with a dog because "a dog is smart and it easily grasps everything". Furthermore, two respondents saw Kibaki as a bull, while one each saw him as a boa, wolf, monkey/gorilla, bear, and an elephant. According to an 8-year-old girl, Kibaki would be an elephant because the "elephant is the king of animals", whereas a 9-year-old girl said that the president would be a "kind of animal which always fights for justice".

Although perceptions in general were favourable, as associations depicted the President as strong, powerful and a source of hope, some associations, nevertheless, revealed mixed perceptions, since images such as wolf and monkey/gorilla were also attributed. For example, a 7-year-old boy, thinking aloud said, "He is evil... He is a wolf!" Descriptions relating to specific qualities, features and properties included black, dull colours, and Russian- manufactured cars, like a "government black Volga" which symbolises the Soviet Union's communist past. The President was also associated with "old times, Kenya's past", with "awkwardness or backwardness", thus depicting him as old-fashioned and old, as noted by the description of him as a car that "moves at the speed of 20 kilometres per hour".

Children's Perceptions of Prime Minister Raila

The respondents' associations were less favourable towards Prime Minister Raila, than they were towards President Kibaki. While associating Raila with a car, some respondents drew pictures similar to descriptions of Kibaki as a car: "Big and cool", "Colourful and rich, and a little bit strict", and a "robot". However, there were five negative perceptions of Raila as a car. As an example, Raila was seen as a "black Zhiguli of the early centuries with flat tires, broken windows and headlights, and smashed bumper". Two respondents said that Raila would be a truck, which is associated with awkwardness in Kenya. As for positive associations, the Prime Minister was perceived by eight respondents as a Jeep; three as a Limo; three each as a Mercedes and Ferrari; and one each as a BMW, Hummer and Mazda. However, as an 8-year-old girl intimated, "Raila is a foreign car but not as cool as Kibaki".

The perception of Raila as a less favourable figure was evident in respondents' associations of the Prime Minister with a tree. For instance, a 7-year-old Standard I one girl, noted that he was a "big tree but not tall". However, twenty respondents either equated the two principal political leaders by saying, "Raila is a tree that is equal to Kibaki" or provided such favourable associations as "Raila is a tall tree and sweets are hanging on it". They also saw the Prime Minister as a pine (four);

fig (two), maple (two), and spruce (two). All these associations were positive. Nine respondents associated Raila with an oak. However, as respondents' comments showed, not all oak-associations were positive. A Standard IV 10-year-old boy said, "Raila would be an oak. He is not like our President. Raila makes many unserious decisions". The respondent may have been referring to the fact that Raila had, immediately before this study, unilaterally suspended a prominent cabinet minister who also happens to be the legislator from the area of study. Though the President reversed the decision, the minister was later dismissed in fraud-related scandals. An 8-year-old girl drew an even more negative picture by saying, "Raila is an oak. It would fall down all the time, worms would eat it; the core would fall down".

As for associations with a building, seven respondents pictured Raila as a skyscraper or a multi-storied building, while two saw him as a bank. Two others perceived him as a prestigious school and university; this could be explained in terms of the *vitendawili* (riddles), parables and other metaphorical speeches that Raila is best known for. One association had a straight link to the premiership – "the prime minister's office". An attempt to compare the Prime Minister and the President was evident in answers like "Raila is a big building but smaller than Kibaki". Although perceptions of the Prime Minister as a building were favourable in general (a "glamorous hotel", an "armoured tall building"), negative associations were also articulated: "It has broken windows, the roof is leaking; it's being destroyed and decayed". These explanations could be linked and related to the kind of turmoil and bickering going on in the party headed by Raila, where groups of disgruntled former allied legislators, mainly from the Rift Valley region (the area of study) are leading a rebellion.

Associations of the Prime Minister as an animal were not unidirectional either. Eight respondents saw Raila as a powerful predator like lion, leopard or tiger. Two 10-year-old girls registered in Standard IV associated him with a unicorn, with one of them commenting:

> Raila would be a unicorn because in the cartoon series, a unicorn fights for freedom of the other animals, and Raila fights for freedom in Kenya and Ivory Coast. Ivory Coast troopers are terrorists, they capture people but Raila's troops free them.

This was in reference to Raila's African Union mediation role in the electoral dispute between the two presidential contenders, Alassane Ouattara and Laurent Gbagbo in the Ivory Coast. The participants erroneously regarded the African Union forces which were maintaining peace, as Raila's soldiers.

Some respondents built their associations by contrasting the two leaders in their reference to the massive protests that led to mayhem, terror and destruction, as the police struggled to contain and maintain law and order. While Kibaki as an animal was "big and beautiful; he would rescue people", Raila was "big and evil;

he would kill everyone". While both were perceived as big, the point of departure was in what they would do with that power. With regard to electoral competition, a 9-year-old boy said, "Raila would be a rhinoceros because he is forcing his way and doesn't listen to Kenyans', while an 8-year-old girl in Standard II perceived the Prime Minister as a snake because "Raila is dangerous for Kenya". Associations of Raila with a dog, ostrich and hare were considered positive, whereas reference to such animals as a porcupine, hamster and wolf might be taken as relatively negative. In general, associations with animals might be considered the most hostile among the four associations – a car, building, tree, and an animal – for the Prime Minister. This may be to attributable to the fact that an "animal" association provided the participants with a wider scale to express their perceptions of the Prime Minister, compared to the other three categories.

Discussion

The respondents were a little more hostile towards Prime Minister Raila than they were towards President Kibaki. Respondent's answers like "He [Raila] is a good Prime Minister" might indicate that children perceived Raila through the image of Kibaki, though both as conversations and interactions showed, could be their role models. There was some evidence that Raila is perceived as a less important figure compared to Kibaki, who for example, was a "foreign car", whereas Raila was a "foreign car but not so cool"; or Kibaki was a "big building" whereas Raila was a "big building but smaller than Kibaki".

The sentence construction, "Raila is also (Limo, tiger) but he is (not so great, weaker) compared to Kibaki", was commonly used by the respondents. Presumably, the respondents perceived Kibaki and Raila exclusively as President and Prime Minister, individuals who are operating in conjunction with each other. In other words, the children's judgment was based on their perception of the presidency and premier's office and on the basis of the perceived images of Kibaki and Raila as President and Prime Minister respectively.

Though the participants did not reveal political judgments in some of the associations, they showed themselves as individuals who were familiar with some of the policies and internal politics of the two leaders. They manifested their disapproval of the 2007/2008 post-election violence through such images as "The Pentagon," (the highest decision-making organ of Raila's Orange Democratic Movement Party (ODM)). "Raila is a hospital because of too many victims of the post-election violence", "a burnt church and destroyed houses and buildings" and "Lily as a symbol of aggression". Continuing the topic of the post-election violence, it should be underlined that children interpreted the same phenomenon in opposite ways. Particularly, it was evident in their perception of Raila as a mythological unicorn (a TV cartoon character) that fights for freedom in a "stolen victory".

Descriptiveness and vagueness in the children's responses, "big and cool" (Kibaki and Raila as cars) or "big, thick and rich" (Raila as a tree), might be explained by the participants' inclination to associate a person, not with a concrete but with a mythological or imagined entity. As in Stevens's (1982) study, children in the present study used fantasy to describe ideal personal attributes (e.g. strong, powerful, or beautiful). The participants did not provide more diverse, sophisticated, and concrete associations with objects existent in reality. Moreover, they appeared to be less enthusiastic about commenting on their responses, however when they did, they succinctly and manifestly captured the Kenyan political terrain. For example, a 10-year old girl said, "Kibaki as an animal is undoubtedly a lion, the chief of animals". And in a second, she added, "Kenya has always had and loved chiefs".

In general, participants were consistent in their associations. If they had a positive attitude towards the President, then all four associations would be positive. For example, there was no discrepancy between the perception of Kibaki as a car (Limo) and the perception of him as an animal (Lion) for the children. Colour was found to be more important in the respondent's descriptions; colours such as white and green had positive connotations when the associations related to Kibaki, while dark colours (black and dark) expressed either negative or positive connotations in their perceptions of both leaders. Interestingly, the children associated Raila with infamous Russian made-cars (Zaporozhects and Zhiguli), but associated Kibaki with the State House. In other words, they attributed items that have a negative reputation to Raila and one of the most famous Kenyan symbols to Kibaki. Associations of Kibaki to a foreign-made and imported car suggest that respondents regarded the President as having prestige and power, because in Kenya foreign items are perceived to be of high quality, compared to the local ones.

Although interviews showed that the majority of participants were enthusiastic about Kibaki's presidency, negative associations were also present in their responses. For example, even though Kibaki's economic and investment policies were seen positively through the perceptions of him as an armoured car or fortress, the politics of governance and territorial integrity in relation to immigration, territorial sovereignty, food security and the social distance between citizens and the centre were seen negatively. As one 7-year-old girl commented, "Kibaki is a carriage that goes through a crowd of people" which indicates that he is indifferent and out of touch with the concerns of the populace. These associations showed Kibaki as a person who is "rather alone" up there. As for an association of Kibaki with a boa (a large, heavy-bodied non-venomous snake), and "a symbol of wisdom", that wisdom did not prevent him from squashing his enemies and subverting democracy. In 2007, Kibaki, previously regarded as a mild-mannered and gentle leader, showed his steely core by furtively swearing himself in as president after controversially emerging victor over Raila, in an election denounced as fraudulent. This action sparked mass action and revenge protests. Even as the violence degenerated, threatening to collapse the whole country into cataclysmic disintegration, he defiantly appealed for the "verdict of the people" to be respected.

It may be hypothesised that the purported failures and the reported feelings of a failed coalition government, together with a growing anti-Railaism in the Rift Valley, generated negative associations about him. It should be noted that there are concerted campaigns by Raila's erstwhile allies from the Rift Valley to paint him as an ungrateful beneficiary of their magnanimity; as a person who has now turned against the people who overwhelmingly voted for him. The study shows that the mass media dominated as the source of political knowledge and served to arouse interest, curiosity and information about political affairs for the children. For some children, evening television and radio news was almost always listened to. Children with different backgrounds appeared to acquire varying amounts of political knowledge from the media programmes, thereby becoming more informed about political matters.

The study also shows that an association might mislead the investigator's interpretation if the respondent did not provide an explanation, since words and colours such as, 'oak', 'wolf' 'snake' and 'green' might have double meanings. In Kenya, an 'oak', used to describe a person, might indicate either his strength or stupidity. 'Wolf', might mean strong and independent or greedy, cruel and evil. Green may indicate 'bountiful, lavish and philanthropic' or 'stubborn, firm, steely, stained and dominant'. The association of Kibaki with a boa ought to be understood in this perspective. A 'snake' can be construed as 'cunning, devious, conniving, conspiratorial, treacherous, deceitful, lethal, malicious' or 'wise, clever, intelligent, portent of good tokens, and omen of beneficial mystical powers'.

One of the most striking results of the study was the respondents' perception of the President and Prime Minister as rich individuals. Today in Kenya, as in many parts of Africa and even the distant world, political power is linked to financial prosperity. Noting the prominence of oligarchs and tycoons, respondents equated political power with wealth, saying for example, "Kibaki is a 'Limo' because the rich drive limos" or "Kibaki is a mansion, the President is rich." An 8-year-old boy responded thus: "Kibaki is a money tree. Put money under the tree, and your dream comes true". A 7-year-old girl opined; "Kibaki has a lot of money, he spoils his grand-daughters so that they think he is the best grandpa in the world". As in the association of Raila as "a tall tree and sweets are hanging on it", the money theme was continued in two respondents' association of Raila with a bank, without providing descriptions of the qualities, features and properties of the bank in their associations.

Another important observation was the children's construction of their own environments through play. Observation of the children in the days before the interviews revealed that girls, using play cards, asked questions like, "Will I be a celebrity?", "Will my husband be mtu wa nguvu (an oligarch)?", "Will we have a palatial home?". A 10-year-old girl, commenting on such a focus said that girls in her class read "glossy" magazines for women and dreamed about a prosperous life "just like it is depicted in the magazines". In this light, girls' consumerism as a reflection of such a terminal value as a prosperous life (Corsaro 2011), might be a special feature in their political perceptions.

In general, the findings of the study are consistent with studies that have found that children tend to have favourable attitudes towards the foremost national political leaders. The findings also suggest that children's political attitudes affect and are affected by the prevailing political culture, mood and temperature of the moment. Investigations are, however, needed to see whether psychological mechanisms (e.g. the feeling of powerlessness before authority), which might determine a child's attitude towards political authority, are shared by children regardless of their geographical region (county), ethnicity, religious affiliation, race and age.

Conclusion

Past political learning surveys rarely measured children's attitudes and beliefs because of their assumption that children unreliably report on these concepts. This study set out to fill this void by documenting the first-hand political experiences, awareness, outlook, orientation and socialisation of Kenyan children, by giving their visions, perspectives and worldview a forum to be shared. The findings have shown that children are not mere victims of the political process and civic events in their country; they are not politically passive, irrational, incompetent, and dependent beings. They have reasonably shown their political agency, competency, rationality and activity as citizens. They have shown that they are more politically active, aware, judgmental, complex, clever, smart, knowledgeable and participative individuals. Secondly, understanding the role that children play in the political environment has a significant normative and practical application for the study of childhood and for the design of education-based civics curricula that capitalises on the assets of the 'political child'. This study is an example of how a play of associations, which appears to be non-serious entertainment at first glance, might provoke children to come up with different kinds of political generalisations.

References

Atkin, C., 1981, 'Communication and Political Socialization', in D. Nimmo and K. Sanders eds., *Handbook of Political Communication,* Beverly Hills, CA: Sage, pp. 299-328.

Coles, R., 1986, *The Political Life of Children,* Boston/New York: The Atlantic Monthly Press.

Conover, P.J. and Searing, D.D., 1994, 'Democracy, Citizenship and the Study of Political Socialization', in I. Budge and D. McKay, eds., *Developing Democracy,* London: Sage. pp. 24-55.

Corsaro A.W., 2011, *The Sociology of Childhood,* London: Pine Forge Press/Sage Publications

Gill, G., 2006, 'A New Authoritarian Rule in Russia?', *Democratization,* Vol. 13, pp. 58-77.

Greenstein, F., 1965, *Children and Politics,* New Haven: Yale University Press.

Howard, S. and Gill, J., 2000, 'The Pebble in the Pond: Children's Construction of Power, Politics and Democratic Citizenship', *Cambridge Journal of Education,* Vol. 30, pp. 357-378.

Jennings, M.K. and Markus, G.B., 1977, 'The Effects of Military Service on Political Attitudes: A panel Study,' *American Political Science Review,* Vol. 71, pp. 131-147.

Jennings, M.K. and Markus, G.B., 1984, 'Partisan Orientations Over the Long Haul: Results from the Three-Wave Political Socialization Panel Study,' *American Political Science Review,* Vol. 78, pp.1000-1018.

McDevitt, M., 2005, 'The Partisan Child: Developmental Provocation as a Model of Political Socialization', *International Journal of Public Opinion Research,* Vol. 18, No. 1, pp. 67-88.

McDevitt, M. and Chaffee, S., 2002, 'From Top-Down to Trickle-up Influence: Revisiting Assumptions About the Family in Political Socialization', *Political Communication,* Vol. 19, pp. 281-301.

McIntosh, H., Hart, D. and Youniss, J., 2007, 'The Influence of Family Political Discussion on Youth Civic Development: Which Parent Qualities Matter?' *Political Science and Politics,* pp. 495-499.

Miller, W.E. and Shanks, J.M., 1996, *The New American Voter,* Cambridge: Harvard University Press.

Moore, S., Lare, J. and Wagner, K.A., 1985, *The Child's Political World,* New York: Praeger Publishers.

Piaget, J. and Inhelder, B., 1969, *The Psychology of the Child,* New York: Basic Books.

Sapiro, V., 2004, 'Not Your Parents' Political Socialization: Introduction for a new Generation', *Annual Review of Political Science,* Vol. 7, pp.1-23.

Sears, D.O. and Levy, S., 2003, 'Childhood and Adult Political Development', in D. O. Sears, L. Huddy, and R. Jervis, eds., *Oxford Handbook of Political Psychology,* New York: Oxford University Press, pp. 60-109.

Shah, D., 2010, 'Political Socialization Through the Media', in W. Donsbach, ed., *International Encyclopedia of Communication,* Malden, MA: Blackwell.

Smith, E. R., 1999, 'Affective and Cognitive Implications of Group Membership Becoming Part of the Self: New Models of Prejudice and of the Self-Concept', in D. Abrams and M. Hogg, eds., *Social Identity and Social Cognition,* Oxford: Blackwell Publishers, pp183-196.

Stevens, O., 1982, *Children Talking Politics: Political Learning in Childhood,* Oxford, UK: Martin Robertson.

Walsh, D., 2003 'Nairobi's Corruption- busting New Leader Tries to Undo Moi's Years of Misrule', *The Independent,* (London), Available online at http://www.independent.co.uk/ news /world/africa/nairobis-corruption-busting-new-leader-tries-to-undo-mois-years-of-misrule-602580.html. Retrieved October 10, 2011.

Appendices

Appendix 1: Children's Associations of Kibaki and Raila as Cars

	Car	Number of Children	
		Kibaki	**Raila**
1	Limo	14	3
2	Jeep	2	8
3	Mercedes	2	3
4	Foreign car	2	1
5	Ferrari	1	3
6	Bentley	1	0
7	Toyota	1	0
8	Audi	1	0
9	BMW	0	1
10	Hummer	0	1
11	Mazda	0	1
12	Truck	0	2
13	Zhiguli	0	2
14	Zaporozhects	0	2
Total		**24**	**27**

Appendix 2: Children's Associations of Kibaki and Raila as Trees

	Trees	Number of Children	
		Kibaki	**Raila**
1	Fig tree	10	2
2	Oak	9	9
3	Pine tree	2	4
4	Aspen	1	1
5	Chestnut	1	0
6	Birch tree	1	0
7	Red tree	1	0
8	Maple tree	0	2
9	Spruce	0	2
Total		**25**	**20**

Appendix 3: Children's Associations of Kibaki and Raila as Buildings

	Buildings	Number of Children	
		Kibaki	Raila
1	Skyscraper/ Tall building	12	7
2	State House	6	0
3	Movie Theatre	3	2
4	D.C's Government Building	2	0
5	Complex	2	2
6	Mall/supermarket	3	1
7	Mansion	1	0
8	Bank	2	2
9	School/university	1	2
10	Hotel	1	1
11	Castle	3	1
12	Premier's Office	0	1
13	Big Ben	0	1
Total		36	20

Appendix 4: Children's associations of Kibaki and Raila as Animals

	Animals	Number of Children	
		Kibaki	Raila
1	Lion/leopard/tiger/panther/cheetah	16	8
2	Dog	2	1
3	Wolf	1	1
4	Bull	2	0
5	Bear	1	1
6	Monkey/gorilla	1	1
7	Elephant	1	0
8	Rhinoceros	0	2
9	Unicorn	0	2
10	Hamster	0	1
11	Cat	0	1
12	Ostrich	0	1
13	Porcupine	0	1
14	Snake/boa	1	1
15	Hare	0	1
Total		25	22

9

A Study of Children's Participation in School Management in Cameroon

Tete Jesinta Lebsonga

Introduction

Socio-anthropological orthodoxy has for a long time presented children as passive and sometimes irrational social beings and, for that matter, cannot be granted full autonomy in their lives. In the Cameroonian society, and possibly many other African societies, the status and place occupied by a child is determined by his or her age, but against a background of relative incompetence. As a result, typical traditional education in Cameroon places greater emphasis on the transmission of knowledge and experience from the old to the young. Similar trends are discernible in formal education in the country, with adults acting as teachers and decision-makers in virtually all matters. In both cases, children's education valorises group cohesion, since the child is trained and encouraged to develop the group's identity, community spirit and a sense of responsibility towards others.

As a result of developments that date back to the global adoption of United Nations Convention on the Rights of the Child (UNCRC), Africa's enactment of a Charter on the Rights and Welfare of the Child (ACRWC) and in Cameroon, the domestication of many of those articles into its national laws, children today occupy a fundamental place in both formal and informal education and are in fact viewed as capable of making significant contributions to the process. Thus, in line with contemporary pedagogic interventions and reforms in the country, children are offered more opportunity to participate in decisions and issues that concern them in their schools. The conceptual basis of this recognition can be partially located in the so-called new social studies of childhood which places considerable emphasis upon children as 'beings' rather than 'becoming', and demands that children's lives be studied in the here and now, rather than in terms of what they may or may not become in the future (Prout and James 1990;

Ansell 2005). In this context, children are considered as active participants and producers of social action. Childhood is not a mere biological marvel but what it constitutes is 'socially constructed' with children being 'actively involved in the construction of their own social lives' (Prout and James 1990: 8-9).

In line with this thinking, an initiative for children's participation in school management themed the Children's Goverment has been created under the framework of Child-friendly School (CFS) in almost all Cameroonian schools. The CFS initiative is a conceptual whole made up of interdependent actions, which aim at laying foundations for the total fulfilment of the child in the physical environment through a simulative pedagogic method which permits the full participation of the child as a receiver as well as a co-actor in the learning process (Saint 2002). Consequently, the CFS, or more specifically any school in which Children's Goverment is practised, operates within the framework of quality education that ensures an integration of all children in the education process, irrespective of their age, gender, social or economic background. The CFS's primary aim therefore is to prepare boys and girls to take up roles that empower them to make decisions and to make their own choices. Considering the traditional belief, especially amongst teachers and school administrators, that school management is a professional activity best left to those with the requisite education and experience to undertake, this study seeks to examine the extent of children's participation and the impact of that experience on their childhoods.

The School as a Framework for Change in Children's Social Position

Education is an important instrument for the construction of collective and personal identities. Seen from any of the two predominant perspectives in Africa, Western/Christian or Islamic, it is a decisive factor of personal emancipation because it empowers the individual to take control of his or her destiny. Furthermore, education generally brings about social integration because it promotes, incubates and nurtures habits that are critical to the development and progress of a society (Durkheim 1922). It is a factor of social cohesion because it prepares individuals to live together, thereby promoting a community life based on rights and responsibilities. This therefore is one of the major objectives of the education of children and young people in African societies, as is the case in other communities around the world. While this appears to be a laudable objective, there have also been reservations about the adoption of Western-style education, as many people believe it has rather led to the production of people who are mentally enslaved to Western ideas (Ndlovu-Gatsheni 2013). An extreme reaction to this claim is the tacit rejection of Western education and the senseless campaign of violence being waged in some parts of Nigeria by the radical group, Boko Haram. Nevertheless education, regardless of the philosophical underpinnings, continues to be the most effective way of grooming children in African societies to take over from the older generations. In this respect, an environment where children are allowed to participate in decision making at early stages and are offered greater opportunities to challenge the status quo as is envisioned under the CFS can address some of the shortcomings of the present system in the country.

In the majority of African societies, the status and place occupied by a child is determined by the social age, and for that reason the degree of social and economic capability (Mungala 1982; Bayart 1985). Traditional education in this context is in form of family-based transmission of knowledge and skills and/or apprenticeships that are steeped in socialisation processes under which children learn adult tasks such as child care, land cultivation, livestock tending and so on, through direct or indirect involvement, depending on their age. Although this set of activities is not essentially guided by chronological age, it culminates in cohorts of children that are categorised according to social age and social grades. Their participation in family and public discourses follows this trend and the scope allowed a child depends on his or her perceived ability to interact with adults and others.

According to Mbaiosso (1990), in most Central and West African cultures, because the child is considered as a common property, he is subject to the educative action of all; he can be sent on errands, advised, corrected or punished by any elderly person in the village. It is generally accepted that the child's informal education and upbringing is a collective responsibility of all well-meaning adults in the community. Consequently, the child receives diverse influences, but the results are convergent because of the cohesive nature of the social group since externally disruptive influences are usually at their minimum. What is significant here is the social role that each adult, regardless of familial relations, has to play and the need for conformity. As such, children's upbringing and informal education aims at teaching them to situate themselves in the group, respect rules and values so that they can effectively conform and perform roles assigned to them in the group. It is the group's continuity that is mostly valorised and not necessarily the personal fulfilment of the individual child's ambition or aspirations. The child is encouraged to develop the group's identity, community spirit, and sense of responsibility towards others; hence, although competition is not discouraged, it is expected to be in the collective interest of everybody (ibid). However, while this collective approach to a child's upbringing and informal education can be effective in a traditional environment united by common culture and language, and in fact has served many African communities very well, it is much less relevant or effective in the culturally divergent and heterogeneous urban environments where different factors interplay in the training of a child.

The interplay of various factors is quite evident in formal education systems of many African countries that generally envision children as largely passive and benign actors in a dynamic social environment akin to Parsons' (1937) 'social pond'. As a learner, the growing child is inducted into the social and cultural world of adults through, first the family and then schools and other institutions to shape him or her in such a way that the values and rules of adult society are internalised. However, this situation has greatly evolved, especially with the economic and social transformation of the world, partly due to the 'universalisation' of the school as a place for secondary socialisation and globalisation (Mvesso 1998). Modernisation and rural-urban migration have brought children more and more into the public domain, especially informal working environments such as streets and markets of many African cities and towns. As such, children have over the years become more and more involved in non-traditional socio-economic activities which in turn have shaped them in a variety of ways. All these are at variance with the traditional upbringing of children in small culturally-resilient communities, thus leading to the emergence of different childhoods that, as Frones (1993) argues, are at the intersection of different cultural, social and economic systems and environments.

In the 1980s, a growing number of European and American scholars called attention to the relative absence of children in the knowledge of the social sciences. They argued that children should be studied in their own right, as full social actors, rather than being framed primarily as adults-in-training or as problems for the adult social order to rectify to the preferred level of normality. In an early critique, Enid Schildkrout (2002) observed that children rarely entered descriptions of social systems and proposed that they should be understood as children rather than as the next generation of adults. This perspective is fundamental to the 'new sociology of childhood' which emphasises children's agency; their capacity to help shape the circumstances in which they live and also those of others through their actions that largely promote their self-interest.

Against this background, there is a general tendency towards the recognition of children as not just learners but also people with a role to play in the dissemination of knowledge. This conception is grounded in the aspirations of the child rights movements which promote children's participation and support pedagogic interventions and reforms that aim at improving the quality of education (Archambault and Chouinard 1996). It also promotes the inclusion of children's ideas and actions in the organisation and management of school activities. However, within the context of the UNCRC and ACRWC, it is arguable that considerable limitation is still placed on children's ability to participate in decisions that relate to them in schools. This is not surprising because the traditional assumption by teachers is that children under education are not yet cognitively and socially developed. This however raises challenges in the implementation of the core principle of 'best interest of the child' and the participation rights under the UNCRC because many teachers, considering themselves as competent individuals mandated to train children in formal education settings, are disinclined to consult children in the education process, especially in the management of schools. This is clearly at odds with the contemporary idea of the child as a capable being with the capacity to shape his or her social world, as variously shown by Mayall (2002), Liebel (2003), Corsaro (2005), Mizen and Ofosu-Kusi (2013) and others.

In order to address this challenge and reinforce children's participation in the primary school milieu, the Cameroon Government and UNICEF signed a programme of cooperation for the period 2008-2012. The aim of the programme was to 'contribute in reducing poverty by promoting an environment where children's rights to livelihood, development, protection and participation are realised in a sustainable manner by 2012' (République du Cameroun and UNICEF 2007:8). Under the component 'Quality Education', the programme among other objectives aimed to develop a favourable environment for learning because a baseline study of children's plight in 2008 revealed that inappropriate school environment was a major reason for the low demand for education in those communities. This was the context in which the project *'Ecole Amie des Enfants, Amie des Filles'* (EAEAF), also known as the 'Child-Friendly School' (CFS) programme was initiated, so that children's participation in the management of the schools will be enhanced (MINEDUB 2002; 2003).

The CFS initiative in projecting children's participation in the educational system fulfils the tenets of the UNCRC and ACRWC. The first evaluation done in the schools showed that children have the capacity to be assertive as well as dynamic both at home and in their communities and therefore could improve their livelihood and auto-conservation instincts (Forum Camerounais de Psychologie 2005:2008). It is in this regard that, with the support of UNICEF, the Ministry of Basic Education (MINEDUB) decided to extend Children's Government to all primary schools in the country in order to reinforce the capacities of all actors, especially children.

The Children's Government affords children the opportunity to organise, express themselves and participate in the running of their schools and communities. It is an information channel which is not parallel to the school system, but complements its decision-making structures. It aims to improve and/or change the conditions of the school environment, the attitudes and behaviours of pupils, teachers, parents and the community. Even though the children involved can seek advice and collaborate with adults (who assist them from a distance), their first commitment is to their government as they make their own decisions, exercise real responsibilities and are called upon to behave like real citizens. This activity requires competence which is gradually constructed from the problems solved by the children, with the help of the knowledge accumulated in and out of school.

It is for these reasons that emphasis is placed on the competence, capacities and creativity that children have and how they can take part in the world around them and manipulate it to their advantage. Competence leads to effective action and engenders the ability to organise the necessary knowledge and capacity at a given time to identify and resolve real problems (Saint-Onge 2006). The initiative emphasises the notion of participation implicitly referred to by the UNCRC and ratified by Cameroon in 1993. It is operated fully by children and, just like a real government, the children create ministries for health, education, justice, environment and so on, according to the needs of a particular school. These ministries, headed by ministers democratically elected by the pupils themselves, make appropriate and relevant decisions, sometimes in consultation with adults. It is this recognition of the potential of children to grapple with matters concerning them that the study focuses on.

Methodology

The study's primary inquiry was how Children's Goverment help in reinforcing children's capacity to act through a socially constructed childhood in which the child is an active participant. It therefore examined children's capacity to take action through participation in the educational process under the framework of the CFS initiative in selected public and private schools in Yaoundé 3 District of the Mfoundi Division in the Central Province, the institutional headquarters of Cameroon.

In order to provide an interactive opportunity for children involved in the study and also pay particular attention to their points of view, qualitative tools of in-depth interviews and focus-group discussions were primarily used to collect data in 2011 and early part of 2014. Yaoundé was conveniently selected as the study centre for the sake of proximity and the advanced state of CFS in the community. A purposive sample of twenty-five was selected from fifteen public and ten private schools in the research area. This consisted of 7 boys and 9 girls aged between 9 and 12 years, all of whom were members of the Children's Goverments in their schools. The adults' component of the sample consisted of 9 resource persons with considerable knowledge about Children's Goverment in the district. They were aged between 27 and 40 years, with a gender distribution of 5 men and 4 women; variously as head teacher, school consultant, representative of the Ministry of Basic Education, school inspector, and parent of pupils in the schools under study. Members of the Children's Governments in these schools were then interviewed individually and collectively. In addition to this, participants from different schools were interviewed in groups to generate cross-school views and information about their activities and functioning of their specific school governments so as to cross-check and balance the information from the variety of sources. The adults were interviewed individually.

Participation, Engagement and Self-esteem

The experimental concept of Children's Government in schools has the primary objective of nurturing initiative and skills of decision-making amongst primary school children. As noted earlier, children aged 9–12 years are not usually vested with opportunities to decide matters concerning them, regardless of the geographic region or cultural context. However, the inception of the African Charter and UNCRC has brought the potential and agency of children to the fore, especially in Cameroon. In this regard, the Children's Government adequately prepares children, given that they learn to act by marshalling their knowledge and resources. Against this background, the children reported that they have benefited considerably from the creation of the Children's Government in their schools since it has affected their daily personal as well as school lives. In Catholic School Mvog Ada, Carine attested to this in the following way:

> The Children's Government has brought effectiveness and respect. It has also encouraged me in all I do. And now everybody respects me and I have a lot of advantages, like I have the possibility to see the head teacher any time that I want. We have seminars where we learn life skills, how to become good citizens. We also learn about the rights and obligations of children. Some people came to train us on democracy but the school year was already getting to an end (Carine, 10 years, female, Minister of Health).

The Children's Government therefore creates a sense of responsibility among primary school children and helps them to develop the requisite skills for the prevention and management of conflicts as they learn 'about the rights and responsibilities' of others. The experiences gained by the children therefore boost their confidence and belief in themselves. They also learn, through trial and error, the management of power and the public space, the balance of power and responsibility between boys and girls. For example, the pupils acquire the notion of sexual equality, even though tasks are accomplished in an unequal manner. Children in the programme therefore gradually construct their personalities through the exposure to problems in their social environment, and problem-solving skills acquired at seminars. Such changes are also visible at home, as noted by a parent:

> I am particularly impressed by the Children's Government initiative which has helped my son, the Prime Minister of his school, to bring out a talent of governance that was hidden in him. He is called up to school each time for this or that and that is very encouraging. These young people have developed a lot of competence in management that can help to change things in our country (Amed, Parent, 29 years).

Once elected as ministers, these young people become conscious of the fact that they have to be more responsible and disciplined. As such, they work hard to maintain their academic and ministerial positions while non-ministers follow their examples. In this regard, the children are active in the construction of their own social lives, as well as the lives of those around them and the societies in which they live. They are, as appropriately noted by Prout and James (1997:8), 'not just the passive subjects of social structures and processes'. However, they are given the opportunity to play a role in governance which in turn helps them express their ability to manipulate and manage power. The Children's Goverment gives them the opportunity to acquire new capabilities and skills, such as self-esteem, commitment, team spirit, gender sensitivity, citizenship and democratic values, assertiveness and invigorated survival and self-preservation instincts. This development does not undermine their status as children; rather, it nurtures their potential in the quest to become responsible adults in future. A school supervisor confirmed the essence of the programme in the following words:

> For example, the Prime Minister in our institution was a lady and this girl developed a lot of skills. I will start with the aspect of responsibility in her class with her mates: she was able to control the situation, and made sure that students respected the school rules and regulations. You would never find her with some of the common problems that children always face; she would not make noise in class, or get involved in a fight or gossip. On the contrary, some of her classmates, especially the junior ones, sometimes got into trouble (Supervisor, Ecole de la Gendamarie Mobile, Group 'A').

A sense of responsibility is ingrained in them as they become role models in their classes and schools, hence they do "not make noise in class" or get "into trouble". Moreover, the children develop leadership and communication skills and so are able to express themselves better before authorities and make insightful decisions and also are able to speak in front of adults and their classmates. This was attested to by Amed, whose son was enrolled at Ecole Publique de la Gendarmerie Mobile in these words:

> At first, my son could not express himself in public because he was shy. I could not imagine him taking decisions and discussing with his friends about school matters. Also, there were some subjects that were a problem to him but because he intends to maintain his post as Prime Minister, he tries as much as possible to be excellent in all his subjects. And what is impressing here is that these children are responsible, they organise their work without anybody telling them what to do (Amed, 29 years).

Here, we see initiative and dedication to responsibility, as the children align their behaviour with expectation. Their capacity to do what they consider appropriate and right is evident in the claims of Bouba, for example:

> My school is better now than before because, at first, pupils were not involved in decision-making; we were silent. The teachers could not believe that we could contribute anything in school, that we could have ideas about certain things in life. We keep our latrines clean by washing them every day and our school compound is kept clean. We have planted trees that will always remind us of something (Bouba, 11yrs, Minister of Women's Affairs, Ecole Publique de la Gendarmerie Mobile).

It is apparent that the pupils gradually develop the ability to organise themselves and discuss issues concerning their schools and their daily lives (management of portable water, washing of hands, children's rights, etc.). Each minister encourages the pupils to participate in the school's activities, thereby learning to work with their communities and assuming responsibilities. While they recognise the need to compete for the best possible results in their examinations, and to win when there are elections for the Children's Goverment, they also realise the need for mutuality and cooperative existence in order to achieve the objectives of their school governments. These are critical lessons for the development of competent citizens for the nation.

The concept of children's agency has been used in various ways, given that current research on children's everyday lives emphasise their capacities as subjects capable of autonomous actions and exerting some influence on social and cultural practices. The responses given by the pupils reveal that the duties of these little ministers go from organisation to execution, as each of them executes a project depending on the needs of the school. The number of ministers in each school also varies, depending on the priority of the school and the capacity of children to identify their priorities. The pupils collaborate with one another by organising themselves with the aid of self-designed schedules in order to create a congenial school environment. This is exemplified by the pupils' Prime Minister when he notes that:

> I have to make efforts to work with my collaborators who are the Ministers of Justice, Hygiene and Environment, and Education. We organise ourselves; draw a work programme for each week. The Minister of Environment takes care of the environment, the flower beds and the cleaning of classrooms; the Minister of Cultures ensures that there is regeneration of culture in the school by teaching various cultural dances and traditional things. Despite all these, we have some difficulties which disturb our activities like the lack of materials and object (Daouda, 10 years, Ecole Privé Bilingue Laïc les Bambis).

The level of cooperation and motivation is obvious, since distinct lines of work and responsibility are drawn up through the children's own initiative and actions. The Minister of Environment also elaborated this point by commenting on his responsibilities and the cooperative manner in which they all discharge their functions:

> I ensure the cleanliness of the school. I have a time table with the day's task and which class has to do it. Together with other pupils, we weed the flower beds and pick papers around the school compound. Together with the Minister of Health, we go round and check that there is clean water in the classes and that the classes are clean; those who do not sweep their class are punished. If somebody is sick, we take him to the sick bay. We always sit with the others and discuss how the school has to look. It has to be clean and welcoming (Abo'o, 9 years, Ecole Privé Bilingue Laïc les Bambis).

This approach, contrary to traditional pedagogy, illustrates the dynamic nature of children and young people's potential when they are allowed to take the initiative and assume responsibility. At the same time, it shows that in the actual context of the child-friendly school, children's engagement and participation is placed at the centre of the functioning of the school system. They proceed through a social division of labour that responds to their priorities, but also invests in the school's livelihood through these new forms of school activities. The Children's Goverment therefore becomes a social framework where children take initiatives through participative management. It reveals the roles that children play as masters of their future, as strategists and proactive citizens of their socio-cultural and political environments. As such, the organisation and progress depend on the children's awareness and school needs and the definition of a schedule which helps them tackle the challenges they are confronted with at school. Through their engagement with the structures, children establish the mechanisms and strategies necessary to overcome challenges so that they become actors of their own history. In this sense, ' it allows children a more direct voice and participation' (James and Prout 1997:8) in matters concerning them because childhood is not conceived as a stage of ignorance and constancy. It becomes one of social awareness and dynamism. In reaction to a question on decision-making, one of the adult-respondents, a head teacher related that:

> Our aim is to train children on decision making. Most often, we try as much as possible not to interfere when there is a problem. They solve the problem except if it is a complex situation that they cannot handle, and then the Prime Minister will come and report the problem to us. They always give us reports and we provide absolute counselling. If there is a need for punishment, we do that and at the end of the month the Children's Goverment is briefed on how to manage such situations. So, we allow them to explore their talents but if we are always there, it means that we have given them the responsibility but have not given them the space to implement. We equally let the pupils in school know that they do not bring problems directly to the teachers but, instead, problems should be directed to the pupils' government and if they cannot solve them, then they take them to the teachers (Rudolf, 37 years, Head teacher)

This portrays an implicit trust in children's ability to assume responsibility and also to discharge them to the best of their abilities by keeping a distance, refraining from interference and allowing their talents to blossom. Rudolf's reaction therefore questions the dogmatic view of children as incompetents in need of training and instruction. Instead, it elevates children as active and sensible constructors of their lived experiences, if they are allowed to explore, initiate and construct meanings and reactions according to the demands of the time. This is confirmed by Bouba, as follows:

We make decisions like those concerning pupils who do not respect the ministers and we equally make decisions to solve problems identified in school. We make decisions together with our supervisor (Bouba, 11yrs, female, Minister of Women's Affairs).

Rudolph, the 37-year-old head teacher and supervisor of the Children's Goverment of Parents National Educational Union (PNEU) added, the Children's Goverment "is a body or forum where children can sit and talk about situations concerning them; it is also a situation whereby we are impacting leadership into the children".

The nomination of pupils for elections in some schools is done by the teachers, depending on the pupil's academic performance, their interactions with other clubs to which they belong and their human capacity, regardless of their sex, religious or ethnic background. Nominated candidates are presented to the pupils for voting. According to the Prime Minister for Ecole Publique du Camp Genie:

To become a minister, the teacher wrote our names and took it to the head teacher, we were all gathered in one class, our names were read out to the pupils and then the head teacher asked for those who wanted Meningui to be Prime Minister. Many pupils' hands were lifted up and I became the Prime Minister (Meningui, 11years, female, Prime Minister).

The practice generates a sense of recognition through the initial nomination, and a perceptive appreciation of the abilities of the nominee by the other school children before they exercise their right to vote. Elsewhere, the nomination is done by the pupils, followed by campaigns under the supervision of the teachers and head teachers. Doauda, a 10-year-old Muslim of Mbororo origin, and Prime Minister of Ecole Premiere de la Gendarmerie Mobile enthusiastically explained how he was selected:

We were informed that there would be the election of a Prime Minister and ministers in our school and that those who thought that they could occupy the posts should give their names to the teachers. After that, we started the campaigns by telling the pupils the types of changes that we wanted in our school and even though some people were saying that I could not become a Prime Minister because I am small, I was voted as such. Thank God for that (Doauda, 10 years, Prime Minister, Ecole Premiere de la Gendarmerie Mobile).

Apparently, a democratic and participatory process is followed in the cases cited above. The capacity of children to determine and select the right people to steer some of the affairs concerning them are left to their judgement. However, the criteria for the nomination of the 'little' ministers in some schools reveal the creation of a new class of elites. Pupils are nominated for elections, depending on their academic performance as the first criterion which might indeed encourage others to work hard but on the other hand create frustrations amongst others, thereby posing the problem of representativeness. However, on the positive side, the way members of the government are designated portrays recognition by the teachers that the children are competent, self-controlled human agents capable of ensuring order and initiating some degree of change.

Conclusion

In Cameroon, Children's Goverments abound in many schools, thus giving children a voice through participation as active members of the society. The UNCRC in its participation articles implies that children are social agents and meaning-makers of their own lives and those of others in the wider society. As such, the child is not only a receiver that has to be protected but he or she is also a constructive co-actor in the development process. They are therefore entitled to some degree of self-determination. While the experiences may not instantly transform the lives of all children, they leave a mark on their personality and might be oriented towards the more preferred types of citizens. Thus, a child who has had the opportunity of making a decision, the opportunity of carrying out a project, or discussing issues of common interests in the group, has already acquired different kinds of experience that are not easy to acquire, even for many adults. The experience therefore helps children to become more responsible and independent.

Parents are impressed by the impact of the initiative on their children because it helps them to better organise themselves and to project things in a more constructive manner. Such children behave according to norms shared by the group as opposed to the defeatist and nonchalant attitude often evident in expressions like "what else can we do". Faced with a problem, a child who has experienced the Children's Goverment would organise himself or herself better in accordance with his/her abilities and aptitudes. The Children's Goverment therefore stands out as an effective way of actively involving children in matters concerning them.

In spite of the benefits, the education community is not sufficiently informed through the school curricular to reinforce the learning and practical competence of children, thereby weakening the dynamic partnership between children and their community. Children constitute part of the educational community and so a regular consultation with them will enhance the cooperative social existence. To this effect, teachers have to try as much as possible to facilitate the learning process by providing useful and child-based lessons that recognise the potential of children as agents of social change. This could be achieved through continuous in-service training for school personnel under the framework of New Pedagogical Approach and Competence-based Approach in child-friendly schools.

References

Ansell, N., 2005, *Children, Youth and Development,* New York: Routledge.

Archambault, J. and Chouinard, R., 1996, *Vers une gestion éducative de la classe,* Boucherville: Gaëtan Morin.

Bayart, J.F., 1985, L'Etat au Cameroun, Paris : Presse de la Fondation Nationale des Sciences Politiques.

Corsaro, W.A., 2005, *The Sociology of Childhood,* London: Sage Publications.

Durkheim, E., 1922, *Education et sociologie,* Paris: PUF.

Erny, P., 1972, L'enfant et son milieu en Afrique noire, Essai sur l'éducation traditionnelle, Paris : Payot.

Frones, I., 1993, 'Changing Childhood', *Childhood,* Vol. 1, No. 1, pp. 1-2.

FOCAP/UNICEF, 2005, Etude diagnostique sur les pratiques des enseignants et la vie scolaire : le cas des « *Ecoles Amies des Enfants, Amies des filles* ».

FOCAP/UNICEF, 2008, Etude sur les Gouvernements d'Enfants « *Ecoles Amies des Enfants, Amies des Filles* » au Cameroun.

Lloreda, M., 2003, Apprendre la démocratie et la vivre à l'école, Paris, cahiers pédagogiques.

Liebel, M., 2003, 'Working Children as Social Subjects: The Contribution of Working Children's Organisations to Social Transformations', *Childhood,* Vol. 10, No.3, pp. 265-285.

Mayall, B., 2002, *Towards a Sociology for Childhood: Thinking From Children's Lives,* Buckingham: Open University Press.

Mbaiosso. A., 1990, L'éducation au Tchad : Bilan, problèmes et perspectives, Paris : Karthala.

Ministère de l'éducation, 2002, *À chacune son rêve pour favoriser la réussite : l'approche orientant.* Québec : Gouvernement du Québec, 54 p.

Ministère de l'éducation, 2002, *Les services éducatifs complémentaires : essentiels à la réussite.* Québec : gouvernement du Québec, 59 p.

Ministère de l'éducation, 2003 *Le plan d'intervention… au service de la réussite de l'élève.* Québec : gouvernement du Québec, 68 p.

Mizen, P. and Ofosu-Kusi, Y., 2013, 'Agency as Vulnerability: Accounting for Children's Movements to the Streets of Accra', *The Sociological Review,* Vol. 61, No. 2, pp. 363-382.

Mungala, A.S., 1982, 'L'éducation traditionnelle en Afrique et ses valeurs fondamentales', *Ethiopiques* Revue socialiste de culture négro-africaine, numéro 29.

Mvesso, A., 1998, *L'école malgré tout,* Yaoundé, Presses Universitaires de Yaoundé.

Parsons, E. T., 1937, *The Structure of Social Action,* New York: The Free Press.

Ndlovu-Gatsheni, S.J., 2013, *Coloniality of Power in Postcolonial Africa: Myths of Decolonization,* Dakar: CODESRIA.

Prout, A. and James, A., 1990, 'A New Paradigm for the Sociology of Childhood? Provenance, Promise and Problems', in A. James and A. Prout, eds., *Constructing and Reconstructing Childhood: Contemporary Issues in the Sociological Study of Childhood,* New York: Routledge Falmer, pp.7-34.

République du Cameroun and UNICEF, 2007, Plan d'Action du programme de Pays entre le Gouvernement de la République du Cameroun et le Fonds des Nations Unies pour l'Enfance, Yaoundé.

Saint-Laurent, L., 2002, *Enseigner aux élèves à risque et en difficulté au primaire*, Boucherville: Gaëtan Morin.

Schildkrout, E., 2002, 'Age and Gender in Hausa Society: Socio-economic Roles of Children in Urban Kano', *Childhood*, Vol. 9, No. 3, pp. 344-368.

10

Children's Assembly as a Strategy for Children's Active Participation in Kenyan Society

Pamela M. Y. Ngugi

Introduction

Of late, the concept of children's participation and inclusion in society has been heightened in national and international policy agenda in different countries (Mokwena 2003). The new perspective requires child-focused development organisations to fundamentally re-assess their assumptions and re-think their approaches. The aim of these efforts has been to improve the understanding of children's lives, their interest, capacities and needs (Theis 1998:81). Boyden and Ennew (1997:39) provide an idea of children's active participation when they note that children must at least '... be informed about and consulted in actions taken for their welfare, and may be involved in planning, implementation and evaluating these actions'. McNeill (1998:31) points out clearly that participation should not be seen as a token involvement of children but an incorporation of their specific needs and views into the decision-making process, within the context of what is possible institutionally and culturally. This is based on the recognition that children are capable communicators, who can effectively engage in decision-making in their own lives, in their families, schools, in respect of their own healthcare, in courts, in local communities and in political forum (Lansdown 2005; James and Prout 1997).

Indeed, the concept of participation has been central to current thinking and implementation of the United Nations Convention on the Rights of the Child (UNCRC) (McNeill 1998). For instance, Article 12(1) affirms the right of the child to 'express his or her own views freely in all matters affecting the child with the views of the child being given due weight in accordance with the age and maturity of the child'. It adds in Article 13(1) that: 'The child shall have the right to freedom of expression; this right shall include freedom to seek, receive and impart information and ideas of all kinds, regardless of frontiers, either orally, in writing or in print, in the form of art, or through any other media of the child's choice'. Moreover, the African Charter on the Rights and Welfare of the Child (ACRWC) also concedes these social changes and the resultant capacity of children to be self-determining in many regards. What is clear here is that these international conventions have fostered significant achievements in children's welfare by making states parties both directly and indirectly responsible for them. This has added to children's belief in themselves and their capacity to be more assertive and proactive in homes and communities, as well as invigorated their survival and self-preservation instincts.

Children's Agency and Participation

One important consequence of the focus on active participation of children has been a growing concern with the agency of children, since it is an acknowledged fact that children have agency and are socially competent beings. Giddens (1984) cited in Honwana (2005) considers agency to be the capability of doing something rather than the intention of doing something. In essence, agency concerns events of which an individual is the perpetrator, in the sense that the individual involved could, at any phase in a given sequence of conduct, have acted differently. Whatever happened would not have happened if that individual had not intervened since agency implies a transformative capacity to intervene or refrain from intervention. In that sense then, Honwana (2005) points out that agency is intrinsically connected to power. To be able to act otherwise, the individual must exercise some sort of power. This means that people have the ability to act on their own behalf and also to influence others out of their own volitions. Children's agency therefore refers to their capacity to help shape the circumstances in which they live, by for example, successfully claiming agency within the contours of the family (Jans 2004). This is what du Bois-Raymond (2001) cited in Jans (2004:28) speaks of as 'negotiation' within families. This aspect is also reflected outside the sphere of influence of the family, where children grasp the opportunity to show themselves as individuals.

Promoting children's agency and social interaction requires their self-expression being facilitated in their interaction with adults. In view of this, young people must be given the opportunity to learn through participation in decisions that affect their lives and through performing significant services that affect others. Expression of views is not restricted to formal language only, but also through emotions, drawing, painting, singing and drama. According to Rejani (2000) cited in Lansdown (2005:17), children build competence and confidence through direct experience, since participation leads to greater levels of competence, which in turn enhances the quality of participation.

Hart (1992:5) describes the term 'participation' as the process of sharing decisions which affect one's life and the life of the community in which one lives. It is the foundations upon which democracy is built and the standard against which democratic credentials are evaluated, since participation is a fundamental right of citizens. In the view of Smith (1998), participation of children should mean a radical change in the approach towards children. It means taking children seriously, trying to look at things from their perspective and treating them as 'subjects in' instead of 'objects of' research and intervention. It requires information sharing and dialogue between children and adults, which is based on mutual respect and power sharing. Genuine participation gives children the power to shape both the process and the outcome.

As rightly observed by Hart (1992), there are a multitude of examples of children who organise themselves successfully without adult help. For instance, most adults can probably remember building a play house with friends at seven or eight years of age, unknown to adults, or perhaps selling refreshments from a small stand in front of their home. Such examples from adults' memory are the most powerful evidence of young people's competence. The principle behind such involvement is motivation; young people can design and manage complex projects together if they feel some sense of ownership in them. If young people do not at least partially design the goals of the project themselves, they are unlikely to demonstrate the great competence they possess. Involvement fosters motivation, which fosters competence, which in turn fosters motivation for further projects.

Young people's community participation is a complex issue which varies not only with a child's developing motivations and capacities, but also according to the particular family and cultural context. In cultures where adults themselves have little opportunity to influence community decisions, young people can become the initiating force for change.

Various perspectives on children's participation abound. For example, according to White and Choudhury (2010), participation of children in international development centres on efficiency, efficacy and justice. The first, efficiency, requires the involvement of beneficiaries in order for appropriate and sustainable projects to be designed. The second, efficacy, relates to the fact that when children speak for themselves in national and international meetings, the impact is much greater than if the same arguments were made by an adult on their behalf. Thus, the most effective preparation for a sense of self-efficacy is to achieve a goal for oneself and not merely to observe someone else achieving that goal. The third, justice, ensures that people have a right to speak on and to be represented in matters concerning them as stipulated in the UNCRC, Article 12.

Other useful typologies have been developed to help in recognising the way in which participation is a process rather than a product. For example, Sherry Arnstein's 1969 Ladder of Citizen participation has been taken up and adopted by others such as Hart (1992), who draws on Arnstein's well-known conceptualisation to create a child-specific ladder. He points out that, in order for a project to be truly labelled as participatory, it must adhere to the following four requirements: first, participants must understand the intentions of the project; second, they need to know who made decisions concerning their involvement and why they were made; third, they must have a meaningful rather than a 'decorative role'; and fourth, they must volunteer rather than be coerced into participation. Similarly, Boyden and Ennew (1997) argue that in order for children to participate meaningfully, they must be provided with information about the reasons and consequences of what they are doing.

It is in reaction to this new perspective on childhood that the Children's Assembly was created in Kenya as a way of facilitating children and young people's social participation. It affords them the opportunity to become more assertive in advocating for their rights and articulating their issues before the rest of the community. Mukasa and Grift-Wanyoto (1998) advise that if properly handled and facilitated at their own pace, children open up to new ideas and contribute to the fulfilment of their rights and responsibilities as embedded in the UNCRC, the African Charter and the Children's Acts of various African countries. This chapter contributes to the discourse on children's agency and participation in society by presenting the findings of a research that evaluated the progress of the Children's Assembly in Kenya. In particular, the research examines the functions of the Children's Assembly, how it has impacted on the general implementation of children's rights in Kenya and how it engages children in contributing in meaningful ways to discussions of issues affecting them.

Children's Assembly in Kenya

In 1990, Kenya became the twentieth country to deposit her instruments of ratification with the United Nations General Assembly, thus enabling the UNCRC to come to force (The Hansard 2001). The UNCRC programmes in Kenya operate under the Ministry of Gender, Children and Social Development. The Department of Children's Services currently draws its mandate from the Children's Act 2001 as well as the Constitution of Kenya, 2010, under Children's Act, Article 53. This is an Act of Parliament that makes provision for parental responsibility, fostering, adoption, custody, maintenance, guardianship, care and protection of children. It also makes provision for the administration of children's institutions and gives effect to the principle of the UNCRC and other related purposes. It provides for leadership in co-ordination, supervision and provision of services, towards promoting the rights and welfare of all children in Kenya. It is the children's officers in this Ministry who organise and oversee the election of the various categories of members of the Children's Assembly, such as the Governor, Deputy Governor, Speaker and Delegates at various stages of representation.

The Department of Children's Services has come up with operational guidelines as a strategy that will enhance the Children's Assembly to reach all children, even the most marginalised groups of children, by involving them in public debates, networking and skills development at local and national levels (Department of Children's Services 2011). The specific objectives of the Children Assembly are to:

- Empower children with knowledge and skills on children's rights and responsibilities;
- Involve children in policy formulation, planning, implementation, monitoring and evaluation;
- Provide a forum to promote children's participation in local, national and international events;
- Facilitate networking among children and other relevant organisations and institutions; and
- Promote nationhood among Kenyan children.

The leadership structure of the Children's Assembly is modelled on the Kenyan Constitution of 2010, with a decentralised system of governance that is represented by counties in the country. Based on this structure, there is the County Children's Assembly, the Regional Children's Assembly and the National Children's Assembly. In order to obtain the national delegates, several stages of selection are followed until the group has reached the required number that is agreeable to all. This is done in order to ensure a balanced representation.

The Research Process

In order to properly take account of children's views in social science research, many researchers adopt ethnographic methods, such as participant observation, interviews, focus group discussion and other participatory activities as well as experimental procedures. This affords children higher levels of participation in the research process than pure surveys, for example. Thus, considering the interactive potential of focus group discussion, it was used as the primary research method, and for that reason afforded children and young people the opportunity to raise and discuss both local and national issues that are of interest and importance to them. The participants of the study were forty-seven in number. This consisted of twenty-three girls and twenty-four boys, aged between 8 and 17 years who were drawn from the forty-seven counties of the country. This therefore was the National Children's Assembly and so included the President, Deputy President, Cabinet Secretaries, the National Speaker, Clerk and County Delegates. The composition of the officials was a reflection of the cultural diversity – urban, semi-urban and rural mix of the national population.

With the support of the Children's Officer, the participants were informed of the research objectives, the purpose of the interview and what the information generated would be used for. The children were also informed of their right to withdraw from the research or decline an interview any time they felt like doing so. This is in line with the ethical requirements for undertaking   participatory research with children, as described by Hart (1992). The research was conducted in the middle of November, 2011 at the Railways Club, Nairobi where children had converged for the 10th Annual Forum of the Children's Assembly under the theme 'Reading for Fun'. The interview questions followed a brief explanation of the role of the Children's Assembly in Kenya before embarking on the discussion of other issues that affect children from different locations of the country.

Participants' Perceptions and Experience of Children's Assembly

In order to gauge their understanding and appreciation of the concept of Children's Assembly, inquiries were made about the role the Assembly plays in the country. According to Peter, a 16-year-old speaker of the Children's Assembly:

> We as children gather every year to discuss and come up with solutions to various issues that affect us as children and also those that touch on our rights. These include rights to education, shelter, association among other issues. During such meetings, our organisers make sure that all the forty-seven counties in the country are represented.

Interviewer: As the speaker of the Children's Assembly and a representative of children in Kenya, would you say that the assembly has benefited the Kenyan child?

Peter: I would say that it has made a positive impact since many children now know their rights. For example, as far as the rights to education are concerned, I can say that at the moment there are many children who are going to school. But we know that there are still some children who are not going to school in some areas. We get this information from the county representatives during our meetings, such as this one. In a sense, I can say that children in Kenya will no longer be looked at as passive recipients of decisions made about their lives.

Interviewer: So, in situations where children do not go to school, how does the assembly help such children?

Peter: During our last meeting, we agreed that we should write letters to our Members of Parliament to help us get these children go to school. By the end of this session, we will know how many of us wrote the letters.

Apparently, the influence of the Assembly is obvious, since the children are using their right to participate in decisions and discussions to raise issues that affect their lives. Clearly, such actions show the potential of children and give substance to the participation rights embedded in the UNCRC, particularly Article 12, which imposes a responsibility on states parties to assure children the right to express their views on all matters that affect them.

At that particular meeting, the leaders had solicited various publishing houses to display samples of their children's books so as to expose the participants and other children to books in order to encourage them to develop the habit of reading. Peter succinctly explained the rationale this way:

> This time, we wanted to encourage the children to read. We have noted that many children read to pass examinations and few read for leisure. Like today, we are organised into small groups to discuss various issues regarding the theme of today. Later, we will come together and present our findings. The findings will be given to the Officers to forward them to the various schools for action.

The children's action shows a tactical coup in projecting reading as a major cognitive developmental activity. Indeed, it is true that when one cultivates the habit of reading, it contributes to the development of skills, such as analysis, questioning, comprehension and rationality. By possessing these qualities, children would be more appreciative of the complexities of society and so be able to articulate their views and concerns better. In a bid to collate information on their collective activities, the researcher encouraged them to talk about their group activities. Peter began by noting that they discussed factors that "prevent children from developing an interest in reading' in his group.

Interviewer: Tell me about these issues.

Peter: One member in my group, who is from the nomadic group said that in his community, people keep moving from one place to another with their families in search of pasture and sometimes they don't carry any books with them. So these children have nothing to read.

Ohana: In my group, we noted that lack of libraries in slum areas and other settlement areas is a big setback to the reading culture among children living in these areas

(Female, 14 years).

Kabiru: In my group, we noted that we have no role models. We do not see our teachers reading nor do they encourage us to read. We do not see our parents and even our siblings reading. We also discovered that the TV is a big distraction for most of us children, especially for those who live in town (Male, 15 years).

Through participation, the children are able to raise critical issues relating to their future, especially the difficulties of nomadic life, lack of books, and the distractions of television. We learn from the children that, despite the government's effort to provide story books for children in all the government schools, there is still a problem of accessibility and usability. Thus, while they recognise the efforts of those close to them – teachers, government officials, and parents – they are also conversant with the limitations. When inquiries were made about the suggestions the various groups came up with, discussants in one of the focus groups noted:

Peter: We requested the government to provide these children with books so that they can carry with them and read them as they look after their cows. We also proposed that mobile libraries be made available in such areas.

Ohana: We proposed that letters should be written to the big organisations and the big people in society to donate books to schools in slum areas (Female, 14 years).

Wafula: In our group, we suggested that parents should spare some money and buy us books. For example, when they go to shop they can buy one book, then we share the books even with our neighbours at home. We also suggested that schools that refuse to lend out story books to the children should stop that habit (Male, 15 years).

Nyambura: The problem is that we do not have time for extra reading, especially for us children from the rural areas. This is because after school we are engaged in a lot of housework. We are only left with little time to do homework so we cannot even think about reading storybooks. We suggested that parents should create some time for their children to allow them time off to read their books (Female, 16 years).

Chebet: We suggested that the government should build child-friendly libraries in all counties (Female, 15 years).

The significance of the children's suggestions lies in their simplicity. Adult decision-makers know more than this but they have not always been very successful in devising and implementing policies in the interest of children. This is based on the traditional notion of children's incapability in making reasoned analysis to propose solutions to their problems, especially those of complex nature. Again, what we discern from their suggestions is that there is a reasonable need for revision in the traditional ways in which books are supplied to children. Their claim to involvement in decisions on the supply of books is a valid one, as their suggestions point to how school libraries can be managed to the advantage of children as end-users, rather than adults who are the mere providers of those educational materials. On the quality and accessibility of schools, Wambugu, a 15-year-old boy noted that:

> In Laikipia county, some children did not go to school because their parents worked in ranches and that only a few ranches had schools and therefore majority of children did not attend school due to lack of schools. For those children who

were in school, the schools are miles away from home and therefore the children have to walk long distances. In such a case, the young children cannot also attend school. Again in my county, one finds a big number of children who have dropped out of school, some in primary and others in secondary schools, most of them have joined their parents to work in the ranches leading to cases of child labour.

Another 14-year-old female participant, Waithera, raised the issue of girls' right to education in her country:

> I represent Kirinyaga County, and I want to talk about three major issues that I would like to see addressed because they affect in a big way most of the children I represent. One of the issues is the rights of the girl-child. The girls in my county continue to suffer educational disadvantage in terms of not being allowed to attend school and, for some, when they do attend they are forced to repeat class when they do not perform well.

Evidently, as pointed out by Wambugu and Waithera, both boys and girls face difficulties that arise from accessibility to educational facilities, class repetition as a result of poor performance and the likelihood of dropping out of school. But these are not peculiar to them alone, as children in many other parts of Kenya, especially those in the rural areas, are also confronted with similar problems of education every day. The consequence of this is often truancy and dropping out which for some children is an opportunity to engage in casual work, sometimes with debilitating effects on their development, as a means to survive and minimise the burden of economic insecurities on themselves and sometimes their families.

In addition, socio-cultural practices, such as female genital mutilation (FGM) and other rites of passage as well as early marriages and teenage pregnancies, cause girls to drop out of school. These represent some of the problems that bother children, yet they are accorded little status in decisions that border on such critical issues for them. This issue, for example, was raised by Halima, the 15-year-old Governor from Garissa County where cultural activities such as female circumcisions are still practised and rampant. Once a girl has been circumcised, she is considered old enough by the community to be married and start her own home, thus curtailing her education considerably.

Other issues relating to children were also discussed at the assembly. For example, Jacob, a 16-year-old boy reported that his group discussed the issue of orphaned and disadvantaged children. He observed that some children from his county did not attend school in the first place because of this problem and were forced by circumstances to engage in child labour. He noted:

> It moves my heart when I walk the streets and see destitute children who are supposed to be in school, suffering with no one to take care of them. My heart bleeds when I see them being harassed. It pains me when some parents refuse to educate their children and, instead, force them into child labour.

Peter, the Speaker of the Children's Assembly, also commented about the large number of children who work and are often found on the streets, "Nowadays you cannot miss seeing a street child even in the small towns. I think the problem has become so big. We only wish that the government can build homes for these children so that they can be taken care of". On what could be done to solve the problem, a number of suggestions were raised by participants like Rose and Ambasa:

Rose: The government can build good homes for the children so that they are all taken there (Female, 12 years).

Ambasa: I think families can be encouraged to adopt these children. In my county, one of the leaders told me that the Constituency Development Fund Committee gives some money to those parents who are fostering orphaned children. Maybe other counties can learn from my county (Male, 13 years).

The problem of orphaned children and street children is still an issue that has not been completely tackled by the government. In addition, child labour still thrives in many families, despite the fact that the children involved are expected to be in school. Of course, some aspects of child labour are integral to socialisation in many African societies and so cannot be wholly condemned. However, when children irregularly attend school or abandon schooling to work in order to survive, then every effort must be made to redress the situation. Due to policies such as elimination of school fees, the primary education sub-sector has experienced a fast growth in the rate of enrolment. However, marginalised children seem to be at a disadvantage, as observed by the children themselves who feel that some leaders are not doing enough to help these children. When pressed to talk more about the problems confronting children, the problem of disability facing children was extensively discussed by Wambulwa, a disabled 12-year-old participant of the study:

> Let me talk about the disabled children from my county – Kakamega. As you can see, I am physically disabled but this, as I tell other children, is no reason for me not to work hard in school. My parents support me very much. But there are children who do not go to school because, one, their friends laugh at their disabilities, and two, their parents don't support them. For some, they are so disabled that they cannot move without the support of machines. Their parents cannot afford to buy the machines for them. I have pledged for the construction of more public physiotherapy clinics, counselling centres and schools for children with disabilities. You find that in the country, most physiotherapy clinics and schools for children with disabilities are privately owned and most parents cannot afford their services. This denies disabled children from poor families education and physiotherapy services that are necessary for their wellbeing.

We see, in Wanbulwa's narrative, his own problems of disability vis-a-vis a quest for education, support from parents in the face of economic inability and inklings of neo-liberal policies that often discriminate against the poor because access and participation depends on market principles and economic ability, rather than compassion. Perhaps, the more disturbing part of the account is the persistence of discriminatory practices whereby the society in general continues to carry negative and deficit models of disability which results in the devaluation and, to some degree, social oppression of disabled children. What seems to come out from this statement is that, although there is the introduction of inclusive education in many schools in the country, the able children and society at large have not been prepared to accept children with disability problems. In addition, most disabled people, including children, continue to suffer because there are no supportive facilities in most parts of the country. Most importantly, we see agency, however limited, at work, as in this particular case a disabled child attempts, through participation and a discursive process, to expose the expectations and fears of children in his situation. While this could have been done in other ways, the Children's Assembly presents a unique and acceptable forum for such expressions to take place.

The perennial problem of child abuse, often via corporal punishment, was also raised by Mary who acts as the Deputy Speaker of the Children's Assembly. She noted that:

> Another problem that we would like to see addressed is the issue of child abuse, such as corporal punishment in school and even at home. The children are beaten by their parents and teachers, some to the point of death. We would like this to stop. Our teachers and parents are hurting us (Female, 14 years).

This abuse can best be contextualised in terms of physical, emotional and sexual abuse and, generally, neglect on the part of parents and even by extension the local and central government. As observed by Taylor (2009), abuse can be linked more closely to rights and be interpreted as any act of omission or commission by individuals, institutions or society as a whole which prevents children from reaching their potential or denies them equal rights. Indeed, the Government of Kenya through the Ministry of Education prohibits corporal punishment in schools, but there are many reported incidences of corporal punishment both in some schools and homes. Such cases can only be heard if the children themselves speak out about what goes on in their schools and homes so that stringent measures can be taken to protect the affected children. And in this respect, children can mitigate their plight by exercising their right to voice out abusive practices in their society. When both parties discern a lack of fear or willingness on the part of children to raise such issues, they might exercise more caution in their relationships with children.

The views expressed by the participants show that they are active agents who are making appeals concerning educational provisions on behalf of their colleagues who cannot access reading materials due to the difficult situations that affect them. The agency of their constituents lies in the fact that they exercise their right to vote in order to select representatives who can participate in a forum to discuss issues relating to children. They can use the same opportunity to effect change, albeit in a small way, by changing the representatives if they consider them to be incompetent.

Conclusion

The outcome of the discussions with children from the different counties show that they live under challenging circumstances. Some of the challenges arise because of the failure of adults to exercise their parental and care-taking responsibilities properly. There may therefore not be any serious incentives for the same people in some cases to be the champion of children's causes. So, it is a good argument for children to have their own assembly where issues of utmost importance to them could be broached and discussed. In this regard, solutions that are based on their own wishes and expectations could be put on the table for adults to implement on their behalf. It is also evident from the study that children in Kenya will like to see a range of issues, from accessibility to education, child labour, children with disabilities, and orphanhood to abolition of corporal punishment both at home and in school.

Clearly, the children demonstrate their agency in their everyday lives and through the issues raised in their discussions. There is evidence of children exercising their capacities as experiencing subjects capable of autonomous actions, not just to shape their own lives but also to influence other people's thinking and behaviour towards them as children. It is also obvious that when children are given a platform for participation, they show maturity, depth in their thinking and demonstrate a greater sense of responsibility. If the children seize these fora and understand the values their voices bring and the contributions they can effect, they can increase their own learning and develop leadership abilities. In addition, through active participation, the children expose themselves to new and creative ideas that will be of service to their families, community and country as a whole. As rightly pointed out by Ehlers and Frank (2008), children's participation contributes to their development of individual identity, competence and a sense of responsibility. Secondly, children's involvement in debate constitutes an important area for social democratisation because it represents the extension of some democratic rights to a disenfranchised group. Finally, the contribution of children gives us access to essential information that we could get from no other source.

References

Boyden, J., and Ennew, J., 1997, *Children in Focus: A Manual for Participatory Research with Children*, Stockholm: Rädda Barnen.

Ehlers, L., and Frank, C., 2008, 'Child Participation in Africa', in J.S. Nielsen, ed., *Children's Rights in Africa: A legal Perspective*, London: Ashgate Publishing House, pp. 111-127.

Hart, R., 1992, 'Children's Participation: From Tokenism to Citizenship', Innocenti Essay, No 4, Rome: UNICEF.

Honwana, A., 2005, 'Innocent and Guilty: Child Soldiers as Interstitial and Tactical Agents', in Á. Honwana and F. De Boek, eds., *Makers and Breakers: Children and Youth in Post Colonial Africa*, Oxford: James Carey Ltd. pp.31-52.

Jans, M., 2004, 'Children as Citizens: Towards a Contemporary Notion of Chid Participation', *A Global Journal of Child Research*. No. 1, pp. 27-44.

Kenya National Assembly Official Record (Hansard), 2001, *Children's Bill 200*, Nairobi: Government of Kenya.

Lansdown, G., 2005, *The Evolving Capacities of the Child, Florence*: Innocenti Research Centre, Rome, UNICEF.

McNeil, S., 1998, 'Child Participation: Ethical Values and the Impact of Mass Media', in V. Johnson, et al, eds., *Stepping Forward: Children and Young people's Participation in the Development Process*, London: Intermediate Technology Publications, pp. 31-33.

Ministry of Social Services, 2011, *Department of Children's Services*, Nairobi: Republic of Kenya.

Mokwana, S., 2003, 'Youth Participation: Taking the Idea to the Next Level: A Challenge to Youth Ministers', *Journal of Commonwealth Youth and Development*, Vol, 1. No 2, pp.87-107.

Mukasa, G. and Der Grift-Wanyoto, V., 1998, 'Giving Children Voices', in V. Johnson, et al, eds., *Stepping Forward: Children and Young people's Participation in the Development Process*, London: Intermediate Technology Publications, pp. 278-280.

Prout, A. and James, A., 1997, 'Introduction', in A. James and A. Prout, eds., *Constructing and Reconstructing Childhood: Contemporary Issues in the Sociological Study of Childhood*, London and New York: Routledge Falmer, pp.1-6.

Republic of Kenya, 2010, *The New Constitution of Kenya*, Nairobi: Government Printers.

Smith, E.I., 1998, 'Introduction to Children's Participation', in V. Johnson, et al, eds., *Stepping Forward: Children and Young people's Participation in the Development Process*, London: Intermediate Technology Publications, pp.259-262.

Taylor, A.S., 2009, 'The UN Convention on the Rights of the Child: Giving Children a Voice', in A. Lewis and G. Lindsay, eds., Researching Children's Perspectives, Berkshire: Open University Press, pp. 21- 33.

Theis, J., 1998, 'Participatory Research on Child Labour in Vietnam,' in, V. Johnson, et al, eds., *Stepping Forward: Children and Young People's Participation in the Development Process*, London: Intermediate Technology Publications, pp. 81-85.

White, S.C. and Choudhury, S.A., 2010, 'Children's Participation in Bangladesh: Issues of Agency and Structure of Violence,' in B.P. Smith and N. Thomas, eds., *A Handbook of Children and Young Peoples Participation Perspectives from Theory and Practice*, (www.fairplayforchildren.org/pdf/11289572187.pdf.oera.) 3 August 2011.

11

Étude comparative de la formation du schéma corporel à travers le conflit sociocognitif chez des « Enfants du monde de diamant » de Banalia et des « Enfants gardiens de la forêt » de Mambasa en RDC

Edmond Mokuinema Bomfie

La capacité d'agir des enfants dépend largement des représentations que ces derniers se font d'eux-mêmes au cours de leur développement. À cet égard, l'incidence de l'environnement social immédiat est déterminante. L'enfant devient pour ainsi dire le reflet de son milieu social direct. La formation de sa personnalité est tributaire de l'acquisition du schéma corporel à travers les différents conflits d'intérêts de son milieu ambiant. Ce qui renforce l'idée selon laquelle n'y a pas une mais des enfances en milieux africains.

Comment se développent les enfants ?

La tradition scientifique admet que les interactions entre l'enfant et le monde des objets et des autres humains lui permettent d'acquérir progressivement une représentation de soi ou encore de construire son moi corporel, lequel est un déterminant capital pour le développement et l'activité de l'enfant dans son environnement.

Considéré comme une représentation consciente du corps en activité, le schéma corporel (complexe de représentations et de significations symboliques relatives à la représentation du réel mettant en jeu la personnalité d'un individu) procède de l'intégration des informations sensorielles (extéroceptives, par le toucher, l'audition, la vision, et proprioceptive : musculaires, articulaires, vestibulaires).

La notion de schéma corporel revêt deux dimensions : celle du sensible (somato-esthésique : un paquet de chair et d'os) et celle du conscient (conscience de soi)[1].

Du point de vue constructiviste, qui soutient que l'individu est en quête d'adaptation à son milieu ambiant à travers l'assimilation et l'accommodation, le schéma corporel est le résultat d'une expérience purement individuelle d'apprentissage social, c'est-à-dire de socialisation majorante ou minorante. Mais la notion de construction sociale de l'intelligence par l'enfant accorde un rôle privilégié aux interactions sociales dans la construction de l'intelligence et l'action. Dans cette approche socioconstructiviste de l'intelligence, l'acquisition du schéma corporel est comprise comme un processus de socialisation de l'enfant, car celui-ci n'existe dans un système social que dans la mesure où il y est intégré. Les interactions continuelles entre les déterminants personnels, comportementaux et environnementaux fondent le processus d'apprentissage social (Bandura) au cours duquel l'individu se fixe des standards de comportements qu'il découvre chez l'individu modèle. L'enfant devient dès lors producteur de l'interaction sociale et construit en même temps les représentations mentales des conséquences futures de son action.

Notion de conflit sociocognitif

Pour l'approche socioconstructiviste, le conflit entraîne la coordination de centrations opposées. Dans le contexte social, un conflit sociocognitif est une interaction sociale à travers laquelle le sujet découvre des centrations opposées (actions, standing de vie, etc.) en même temps qu'il découvre la sienne. Il s'agit des rapports sociaux dans lesquels l'individu se découvre et découvre l'autre – depuis le contexte familial jusqu'au contexte social global.

L'enfant est contraint d'imiter, d'assimiler, ou de s'accommoder aux alternatives qu'il découvre. La théorie de l'apprentissage social aboutit ainsi à celle du modelage de comportement, qui consiste en une transmission des standards comportementaux sous l'effet de l'influence des modèles. Il s'agit des situations par lesquelles l'interaction sociale conduit l'enfant à un dépassement de ses capacités cognitives individuelles. Dans ce cas, on parle d'un conflit majorant.

Dans cette étude, il sera question de savoir comment se construit le schéma corporel chez les enfants dans les zones d'exploitation minière d'une part et d'exploitation forestière d'autre part. Ces zones, très captives pour les enfants, sont représentées par le « monde de diamant » de Banalia et celui de la « garde de la forêt » de Mambasa en Ituri.

Nous chercherons à comprendre quels types de conflits sociocognitifs déterminent leur capacité d'agir sur leur environnement.

Dans le contexte de Banalia, la présence d'un nombre impressionnant d'engins qui parcourent la forêt transforme profondément la physionomie et le mode de vie des populations riveraines. Bon nombre de parents abandonnent non seulement leur occupation habituelle dans les champs, mais aussi leur famille, pour résider en forêt dans les carrières.

Dans la mesure où les enfants acquièrent des dispositions cognitives en interagissant autour de problèmes à résoudre avec des partenaires adultes ou enfants comme eux, différentes situations de leur contexte social font éclore le conflit sociocognitif. Toutes ces situations créent chez l'enfant un conflit d'intérêts et de centrations.

Ces situations sont notamment :

- l'arrivée des acheteurs, libanais pour la plupart, dans leurs villages, avec des sacs pleins de dollars ;
- l'abandon de service par ses enseignants pour les carrières.

L'enfant se découvre impuissant devant une telle exhibition de puissance financière. L'exemple des enseignants suscite chez l'enfant une préférence envers le « monde de diamant » – au détriment des études.

Le conflit oppose alors principalement pauvreté et richesse ; école et carrière de diamant.

Dans cette recherche, nous avons recouru au dessin et au bonhomme auprès de vingt enfants par site ; mais plutôt que de leur proposer des modèles préfabriqués à observer et à reproduire, nous leur avons demandé de nous proposer des dessins de bonshommes auxquels ils s'identifient ainsi que des objets les plus marquants de leur milieu. Dans les deux cas, nous avons également recouru à l'entretien avec chaque enfant ciblé, pour un bref commentaire sur son dessin ou bonhomme. Puis à un entretien avec d'autres enfants non ciblés, mais qui tenaient à être écoutés. C'était une bonne occasion pour vérifier (par saturation) s'ils avaient les mêmes représentations que les autres. La photographie nous a servi à capturer ce qui ne peut être exprimé ni par dessin ni par entretien (conditions de vie, habitat).

Chez les enfants de Banalia, les dessins les plus repris représentent les négociants et les creuseurs de matières précieuses, le diamant, les motos, les comptoirs d'achat de diamant, qui sont des objets et des lieux en rapport avec cette activité. Dans ce contexte, les dessins en rapport avec l'école sont peu représentés. Cela confirme que les enfants du milieu se construisent une identité allant vers les activités minières où ils trouvent des modèles, plutôt que vers l'école, que désertent même les enseignants au profit de la première activité.

Par contre, chez les enfants Mbuti de Mambasa, les dessins et le bonhomme des enfants représentent des effets liés à la chasse, à la pêche et à la garde de l'immense forêt qui constitue leur habitat naturel. Quelques personnalités Mbuti, réfractaires à la modernité et à la scolarisation, constituent les modèles qu'ils représentent. Il faut cependant souligner qu'à côté des éléments susmentionnés, certains reproduisent quelques figures géométriques vues en classe pendant leur court passage[2] à l'école.

Le développement des enfants dans le « monde du diamant » congolais

Ce point aborde à travers quelques cas la manière dont les enfants habitant les carrières d'exploitation artisanale de diamant autour de la ville de Kisangani construisent leur moi corporel à travers les expériences et les interactions avec leur monde ambiant, dominé par le capitalisme minier. Car dès l'âge le plus tendre, les enfants s'emploient à être partie prenante du « monde du diamant ».

En effet, le territoire de Banalia est une circonscription politico-administrative qui commence à une vingtaine de kilomètres de la ville de Kisangani, et son chef-lieu est à 128 km. Essentiellement agricole au départ, ce territoire va connaître un tournant de son histoire à partir des années 1985 avec l'exploitation artisanale de diamant. On observe alors un mouvement intense d'exode urbain. Des vagues d'adultes, de femmes et d'enfants vont rejoindre celles du milieu rural pour cette exploitation. La forêt, qui compose l'essentiel des écosystèmes environnants, va subir une destruction sans précédent. De nouvelles catégories sociales et professionnelles vont apparaître dans ce milieu rural : les négociants, les plongeurs, les acheteurs, les « boulonneurs », et les encadreurs de carrière. De nouvelles catégories d'infrastructures et d'équipements vont faire leur entrée : motos, comptoirs d'achat de diamant, balance, moto-pompe, scaphandre, bière, etc.

Tableau 11.1 : Dessins et bonshommes des enfants de Banalia

N°	Personnes représentées	F	Objets représentés	F
1	Pikolo	7	Diamant	7
2	Sheriff	3	Moto Senke	5
3	Boulonneur	3	Comptoir d'achat	2
4	Libanais	7	Billet de dollar	4
5	-	-	Maison « en dur »	2

Ce tableau indique que les enfants se situent par rapport aux personnalités bien connues de leur milieu : Pikolo est l'encadreur des carrières les plus actives de la région et compte plusieurs biens à Banalia ; Shériff, son frère, est aussi bien connu du milieu. Les Libanais constituent la catégorie d'acheteurs (boss) les plus actifs – avec démonstration de puissance de capital financier. Les boulonneurs, qui sont de jeunes creuseurs d'or et de diamant, constituent également une référence pour les enfants. Ces personnalités de référence sont certainement des modèles d'élite trouvés dans le milieu social marqué par l'activité diamantifère.

« *Moi, je veux devenir comme le Président Pikolo, il ne manque de rien : femmes, argent, diamant. Quand on fait le diamant, on devient très vite nouveau patron* », dit Jeannot (8 ans).

Blanchard (7 ans) a un tout autre centre d'intérêt : « *maintenant, je suis* « *un pomba sans paquet* ». *Quand je serai boulonneur, j'aurai de gros biceps. Regarde comment ça se passe…* » (Il imite la démarche des boulonneurs avec démonstration de force musculaire).

Quant aux objets représentés par les enfants, leurs préférences gravitent autour du dessin de pierre de diamant, de moto Senke, du billet dollar et de la maison à niveau. Ces objets font la popularité et l'estime de ceux qui en possèdent dans leur milieu.

Mon père était enseignant à l'école primaire du village. Il était pauvre et s'est divorcé de ma mère qui m'a amenée l'aider à faire des remises ici à la carrière. Maintenant ma mère a beaucoup d'argent, elle vient d'acheter une moto bodaboda. Moi, j'aimerais aussi avoir la mienne. Mon père a abandonné l'enseignement, j'ai appris qu'il est parti vers la carrière de Kondolole. (Albertine, 8 ans).

La capacité d'agir des enfants Mbuti (Pygmées) de Mambasa

Le territoire de Mambasa est l'œuvre de l'autorité coloniale. À l'époque, d'Ituri à Avakubi (deux grands centres d'administration coloniale), il n'y avait pas de villages. Au niveau de l'actuel Nyangwe (un des trois groupements qui constituent la chefferie arabisée de Mambasa) vivait un groupe de Pygmées sous la conduite du chef Deke, un anthropophage qui semait la terreur chez les porteurs et agents coloniaux. L'autorité coloniale décida alors de faire déplacer les arabisés de Mawambi à Nyangwe pour lutter contre ce chef mbuti et fournir aux porteurs et agents coloniaux une escale sûre.

En 1915, le chef-lieu du territoire était transféré à Penge. En 1922, il dépendait d'Irumu, qui était le grand centre de l'administration coloniale. En vertu de l'ordonnance n° 426/AIMO du 22 décembre 1947, l'autorité coloniale créa le territoire de Mambasa le 1er janvier 1948.

En dépit de sa vaste étendue, il est le moins peuplé des territoires à cause de l'impénétrabilité de la forêt. Cette situation s'observe tant dans la zone de la Réserve de faune à Okapi que dans les landscapes. Sa population est estimée à 245 605 habitants (dont 245 596 nationaux et 9 étrangers).

Les Mbuti représentent 21 pour cent de la population totale de territoire de Mambasa. Cependant, les résultats du recensement des Pygmées de Mambasa réalisé d'avril 2010 au février 2011 par l'Organisation d'accompagnement et d'appui aux Pygmées, OSAPY, présentent un effectif de 16 762 de Pygmées[3] répartis comme suit :

– 6 585 sur l'axe Mambasa-Lolwa ;

– 3 146 sur l'axe Mambasa-Nduye ;

– 5 200 sur l'axe Mambasa-Teturi ;

– 1 831 sur l'axe Mambasa-Kisangani.

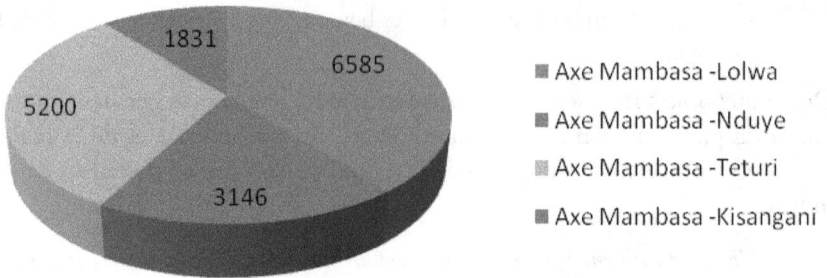

Figure 11.1 : Répartition des Mbuti sur les axes routiers du territoire de Mambasa.

La lecture de cette figure montre que la plus grande partie des Mbuti se trouve sur l'axe Mambasa-Lolwa, suivi de l'axe Mambasa-Teturi, Mambasa-Nduye et enfin Mambasa-Kisangani. Cette répartition serait due au passé historique et au degré de cohabitation avec leurs voisins directs.

La question mbuti

Le territoire de Mambasa est caractérisé par une biodiversité humaine. Avant l'indépendance, il était occupé par quatre tribus autochtones : les Mbuti, les Bila, les Lese (Dese et Karo) et les Ndaka[4].

Le groupe Ngwana, qui se compose de Balengola venus d'Ubundu, de Kumu venus d'Angumu et d'autres comme Zinga et Bakwange venus de Kasongo, de Barumbi de Bafwasende, Rega de Pangi et de Shabunda sont venus juste après l'indépendance. Les autres tribus à la recherche de terres fertiles y arrivent tardivement, notamment les Nande, les Budu, et les Alur.

Il convient de signaler que le groupe « Ngwana[5] » domine toutes les tribus de territoire de Mambasa. Cette domination n'est pas due à l'importance numérique mais à la position sociale, économique et politique. La considération dont ils sont l'objet leur a permis de maîtriser l'ensemble du système qui concourt à la vie du territoire. Ce groupe ethnique représente une majorité des élites politiques, économiques et scientifiques qui occupent les postes de commandement dans tous les domaines du territoire. C'est un groupe de référence. Le groupe autochtone Mbuti est quant à lui une minorité sociale et numérique marginalisée.

Le territoire de Mambasa est couvert d'une vaste forêt dont une grande partie est classée pour sa Réserve de faune à okapi (RFO) gérée par l'Institut congolais pour la conservation de la nature (ICCN). Cette forêt constitue l'habitat naturel des Mbuti qui l'occupent en plusieurs bandes. Mais avec la pression des groupes ethniques envahisseurs, les Mbuti ont perdu leur hégémonie et se sont enfoncés dans les profondeurs de la forêt. Les enfants Mbuti reproduisent le comportement des parents et restent indifférents à tout ce qui appartient à la modernité autour d'eux (route nationale, véhicules, hôpital, école). Mais ils sont précocement très entreprenants pour les activités liées à la forêt, leur environnement immédiat.

En effet, contrairement à ceux de Banalia, les dessins des enfants mbuti des zones d'exploitation aurifère et forestière de Mambassa représentent ce qui suit : le hameau, l'arbre, un gibier (okapi), un homme armé de lance ou de flèches, une femme au travail, et quelques personnalités Mbuti célèbres.

L'enquête menée sur l'axe Mambasa-Epulu, précisément au campement Banana – à 28 km de Mambasa – situé le long de la route Kisangani-Bunia a révélé que plusieurs services sociaux ont été ébauchés (école, hôpital) autour du site de capture d'okapi d'Epulu, en vue de la sédentarisation et de l'intégration des Mbuti. Mais la plupart des actions sont vouées à l'échec, car ces derniers ne semblent pas s'accrocher aux valeurs proposées.

Quand vient la période de chasse[6], de pêche communautaire, de récolte de miel, ou même du « Kumbi[7] », les enfants mbuti désertent l'école pour accompagner leurs parents et prennent une part importante à ces activités. Le même constat a été fait par le Père Pierrot chez les Mbuti de l'axe Mambasa-Beni à Biakato.

Mais comment, pour reprendre notre question, acquièrent-ils leur schéma corporel ? Les personnes et objets repris dans leurs dessins sont parlants.

Tableau 11.2 : Présentation des dessins des enfants Mbuti

N°	Personnes représentées	f	Objets représentés	f
1	Wisky	8	Gibier (okapi)	4
2	Mombi	5	Arbre	4
3	Une femme au travail	3	Hameau	4
4	Padri (Père Pierrot)	1	Poisson	3
5	Chasseur	3	Piège	5

Comme les enfants de Banalia, les enfants mbuti éprouvent des conflits sociocognitifs dans leur environnement et se représentent en fonction de cela. Mais, alors que dans le premier cas le conflit est majorant, dans ce second cas il est minorant. En effet, dans le tableau ci-dessus, Wisky et Mombi8 sont des Mbuti très populaires dans leur milieu car ils représentent deux échantillons de Pygmées que le régime politique avait mis à part pour la socialisation dans les allées du pouvoir, en vue de servir de modèles à leurs congénères. Mais revenus en congé dans leur milieu naturel, ils ont renoncé aux avantages reçus pour revenir à leurs coutumes.

Une femme au travail et un chasseur représentent la division du travail selon le sexe assigné par la coutume mbuti. Le Père Pierrot est un prêtre qui milite pour la promotion des Mbuti, mais qui est très souvent désigné par ces derniers comme le destructeur de leur patrimoine culturel et naturel, tentant de les déposséder de la forêt par une vaste campagne de sédentarisation. Aucun d'entre ces personnages représentés ne constitue un modèle majorant.

Quant aux objets représentés, il ne s'agit que de ceux qu'ils manipulent dans leurs activités de chaque jour dans leur milieu familial où l'on est d'abord Mbuti avant d'être citoyen congolais. Bien qu'ils se disent « premiers citoyens du Congo », à vrai dire les Mbuti se reconnaissent comme les premiers occupants de la forêt qui est menacée par les migrants envahisseurs privés et publics. La réserve de faune à Okapi et les forêts aux alentours sont des écosystèmes ambiants d'où ils tirent leur subsistance en qualité de populations riveraines et surtout d'autochtones.

Si les objets représentés sont en rapport direct avec leur activité quotidienne, le facteur culturel a une incidence non moins déterminante :

> *« L'école et les véhicules, c'est pour vous qui habitez les cités. Notre ancêtre, lui, était un excellent chasseur et habitait la forêt. Pendant le « Kumbi », j'ai appris que nous (les Mbuti) sommes les gardiens de la forêt »*, dit Matchozi (10 ans).

Ce propos reprend le contenu mythique des cosmogonies mbuti selon lesquelles leur ancêtre patriarche avait deux fils ; à sa mort l'aîné était à la chasse et le cadet se trouvait à son chevet. Ainsi donna-t-il les cités (univers à problèmes) en héritage à celui qui se trouvait au village et la forêt (univers de bienfaisance) à celui qui restait à la chasse. Les Mbuti se disent des descendants de ce dernier et résistent à tous les mécanismes de sédentarisation et de scolarisation. L'éducation traditionnelle (Kumbi) éveille avec précocité les enfants Mbuti aux activités liées à cet héritage.

Comparés aux enfants de même âge des autres groupes ethniques et du même environnement, les enfants Mbuti affichent une précocité inégalable dans les secteurs liés à la forêt. Entre cinq et neuf ans, ils sont actifs, notamment dans la maîtrise de la pharmacopée mbuti, la sélection de certaines essences forestières, la chasse, la pêche, la récolte de miel, le piégeage et l'entretien d'exploitation agricole

Le chef Petro nous rapporte :

> Nos enfants doivent apprendre nos valeurs en bas âge. Ils nous accompagnent dans toutes nos activités en forêt. Chacun apprend une spécialité. Comme celui-ci (Sweri, garçon, 6 ans), il soigne bien les maladies courantes, quand je suis fatigué, il entre en forêt chercher les essences de notre pharmacopée. Il sera un bon guérisseur.

> Mbotika (fille, 7 ans) s'interpose : *« moi, je vends près de dix variétés de feuilles à l'ICCN pour nourrir les Okapis domestiqués à la RFO. Je les cueille dans la forêt, ma mère n'y va plus. Je fais cela seule ou avec les autres enfants ».*

En effet, cette activité est la spécialité des Mbuti qui observent le régime alimentaire des Okapis pendant la chasse ou le ramassage dans la forêt. Ils ont pu aider les chercheurs de la RFO à sélectionner une gamme d'essences comestibles par cette espèce animale.

Mwapili (garçon, 9 ans) a déjà à son actif capturé des gibiers par piégeage. Les jeunes filles de 5 à 9 ans affirment pratiquer la pêche seules dans leurs rivières. Les garçons assurent journalièrement l'entretien des champs des exploitants agricoles, souvent à l'insu de leurs parents. C'est le phénomène appelé « par jour ».

Un tel conflit n'est pas pour autant (entièrement) minorant. Nous avons notamment constaté des gains obtenus par quelques enfants Mbuti : certains savent lire et écrire leur nom, et d'autres ont représenté les objets comme un véhicule, un carré, un triangle, fruit de la scolarisation.

Ce que l'on peut retenir de ces deux analyses, c'est que l'apprentissage social peut s'opérer à travers une socialisation inconsciente, où l'enfant acquiert des codes de conduites d'un groupe social sans s'en rendre compte, ou bien par l'identification consciente de l'enfant à un héros ou un modèle qu'il copie (habillement, démarche, goûts, parler).

Dans le contexte d'un capitalisme dominé par les matières premières, les enfants de la région de Banalia entrent en interactions et en activités dans une *zone proximale de développement* (pour reprendre les intentions de Vygotsky) dont les conflits sociocognitifs sont du type majorant. Les enfants se représentent le « monde dominant du diamant » et modèlent leur comportement en fonction des modèles qu'ils trouvent dans cet univers. Dans un tout autre environnement, dominé par le capital « tradition », les enfants mbuti connaissent des conflits minorants.

L'étude approfondie des deux cas susmentionnés est un signal d'alarme pour le développement harmonieux des enfants africains et leur comportement écologique vis-à-vis de la préservation de la forêt.

Les problématiques de socialisation relatives à l'accès à l'éducation (adaptation de calendrier scolaire), à l'accès à la santé et à l'utilisation des ressources naturelles, sans oublier la question de la participation à la vie nationale des peuples autochtones, ou celle des croyances rebelles au changement sont également convoquées.

L'État et les communautés concernées sont ainsi appelés à prendre en compte ces catégories d'enfants marginalisés pour mettre en place un système d'éducation de masse adapté à leur environnement (minier ou forestier) afin qu'il rencontre leurs aspirations. La nécessité d'un cadre multidisciplinaire et d'un espace public appropriés à leur développement semble urgente.

Notes

1. Cette double dimension est illustrée par le cas des enfants qui se disent « Pomba sans paquet » et se comportent comme des « boulonneurs ».
2. Dans les campements mbuti enquêtés, la situation générale de décrochage scolaire se présente comme suit : 15/22 enfants à Banana II ; 7/12 à Banana I; et 12/15 à Mabokulu.
3. Les populations dans la forêt profonde n'ont pas été atteintes par ce recensement.

4. Information recueillie lors de nos préenquêtes au mois d'août 2011.
5. Les arabisés qui maintiennent leur domination sur les Mbuti qui demeurent minoritaires.
6. Rapport du groupe de travail de la Commission africaine sur les populations/ communautés autochtones. Visite de recherche et d'information en RCA, 15-28 janvier 2007, 50-51.
7. Initiation traditionnelle à caractère obligatoire où les adultes transmettent les valeurs fondamentales aux enfants dès le bas âge. Elle se passe en forêt pendant plusieurs mois.
8. Mombi a remis à l'administration de territoire le véhicule qu'il avait rapporté de Kinshasa, il le trouvait encombrant, il a repris le chemin de la forêt

Références

Bandura, A., 1977, *Social learning theory*, Englewood Cliffs, NJ.
Doise, W. & G. Mugny, 1981, *Développement social de l'intelligence*, Inter Éditions, Paris.
Mead, M., 1973, *Une éducation en Nouvelle-Guinée*, Payot, Paris.
Moscovici, S., 1979, *Psychologie des minorités actives*, PUF, Paris.
Royer, J., 2005, *Que nous disent les dessins des enfants*, 2e éd., Journal des Psychologues, Paris.
Vygotsky, L., 1985, *Le problème de l'enseignement et du développement mental à l'âge préscolaire*, Delachaux, Neuchâtel.
Wallon, H., 1959, *Kinesthésie et image visuelle du corps chez l'enfant*, Enfance, Paris.

12

Les enjeux théoriques et sociaux de la modélisation du comportement environnemental à travers l'éducation relative à l'environnement : cas de l'élève du primaire en Côte d'Ivoire

Kabran Aristide Djane

Si nous portons ici l'accent sur la modélisation, c'est qu'elle nous semble au cœur de l'actualité scientifique elle-même. [...] La modélisation est ce processus par lequel le chercheur va transmuer un phénomène en un objet scientifique, en lui imposant une structure explicite et en le rendant manipulable. Pascal Bressoux, *Modélisation statistique appliquée aux sciences sociales*, p. 13.

Introduction

Comme le rapporte Bressoux, Passeron a distingué « le statut épistémologique de deux types de modèles : les modèles purs (universels) et les modèles à déictiques (qui ne peuvent être exemptés de significations singulières) [...]. Selon lui les premiers sont réservés aux sciences de la nature, tandis que les seconds seraient caractéristiques des sciences sociales » (Bressoux 2010:21). Or le comportement pro-environnemental, défini par Kollmuss et Agyeman comme « un comportement adopté par un individu qui décide, de façon consciente, de minimiser ses impacts négatifs sur les milieux naturel et construit » (« *by « pro-environmental behavior »* *we simply mean behavior that consciously seeks to minimize the negative impact of* *one's actions on the natural and built world* », 2002:240), est à la croisée de ces deux dimensions.

Cette production vise dès lors à concilier les caractéristiques épistémologiques des sciences de la nature et celles des sciences sociales. Il s'y agira d'un fait social et scientifique qui lorsqu'il est appliqué à l'élève du primaire participe de la résolution pérenne de la crise environnementale. En effet, cette crise est reléguée au second plan par les décideurs ivoiriens depuis le déclenchement de la crise sociopolitique que connaît la Côte d'Ivoire en 2002. Notre problématique invite à rechercher les solutions concrètes et construites du côté des plus jeunes membres de la société ivoirienne, chez qui une Éducation relative à l'environnement (ErE) a davantage d'effets que sur les adultes.

Le but de ce travail est d'exposer la logique qui conduit à l'adoption du comportement (pro-)environnemental par l'élève du primaire à partir de l'ErE, en vue de la structurer (modéliser). Cette optique se veut socioconstructiviste et positiviste à la fois, puisqu'elle interroge la problématique épistémique et empirique du comportement environnemental de l'élève, à la croisée des sciences de la nature (majoritairement positivistes) et des sciences sociales (majoritairement socio-construites).

Afin d'étayer cet argumentaire, des entretiens avec deux personnes-ressources de l'Éducation nationale en Côte d'Ivoire (DESAC[1], DPFC[2]) et huit enseignants du primaire ont été menés. Des études de terrain (156 élèves pour le questionnaire distribué et 192 pour le *focus group* scindé en des *mini groups* de huit élèves) ont également été conduites. Ces élèves ont en outre participé au remplissage d'une grille qui leur a été distribuée, sur les déterminants du comportement environnemental de l'élève. Les résultats de cette étude ont été traités par les logiciels Sphinx et WeftQDA. Le type d'échantillonnage adopté pour l'unité d'enquête élève est un sondage aléatoire simple, extrait de la série des échantillonnages probabilistes. Chaque élève rencontré dans la classe avait la même probabilité d'être tiré au sort aux fins de l'enquête.

Prenant appui sur le paradigme positiviste et le paradigme socioconstructiviste décrits par Robottom et Hart en 1993, un modèle structurant le comportement environnemental de l'élève en contexte ivoirien, fondé sur l'ErE, a été construit.

Justification d'un modèle du comportement environnemental de l'élève du primaire

Justification sociale et empirique

La construction d'un modèle concernant le comportement environnemental trouve sa source de justification dans les commentaires des répondants à cette étude. Leurs aspirations, qui à notre avis, devraient être approfondies et scientifiquement construites, vont du jeune élève aux administrateurs institutionnels en passant par les enseignants. S'effectue alors, comme l'évoque Essane, « un passage des aspirations latentes aux aspirations manifestes, qui se recompose finalement en revendications » (Essane 1997:21).

Ainsi, selon les enquêtés, pour que les élèves adoptent un comportement positif envers l'environnement, « *...l'accent doit être mis sur l'éducation à l'environnement...* »

Dans la mesure où la majorité des élèves ne sont pas suffisamment éduqués aux questions environnementales, il faut selon eux leur apprendre le respect de l'environnement ; c'est l'opinion de cet élève de CM1 à l'EPP Lagune 1 qui déclare que : « *les enfants qui le font sont mal éduqués, ils n'ont pas été bien éduqués* », il faut d'après lui les amener à « *respecter la nature comme on respecte les parents* » ; « *le problème de l'environnement, c'est une question d'éducation* » énonce encore un enseignant à l'EPP Arras 3. En outre, des sanctions sont parfois nécessaires pour amener les acteurs de l'école au respect de l'environnement : « *je pense qu'on doit les punir parce qu'ils gâtent l'environnement, ce qui n'est pas une bonne chose* », dit un élève de CM1 à l'EPP Arras 3.

À ce sujet, les responsables de la DESAC pensent qu'il « *faut accentuer cette éducation et assurer le suivi des activités entreprises, sensibiliser et former les individus afin de les rendre responsables du cadre actuel de l'environnement* ».

Pour la direction de la pédagogie : « *il faut inculquer des valeurs telles que l'assainissement, la préservation de l'eau, les pratiques d'hygiène adéquates, l'amour du prochain, la non-violence, le partage, le respect d'autrui et au-delà de la sensibilisation, inculquer des comportements aux élèves et individus* ».

En somme, les acteurs de l'école trouvent nécessaire de construire une éducation relative à l'environnement au niveau scolaire structurant le comportement environnemental de l'élève.

Justification et appui théorique du modèle

La justification de ce modèle prend tout son sens à partir du paradigme positiviste et de la position théorique adoptée par Robbotom et Hart en 1993. En effet, toute approche éducative doit pouvoir unir le social à la définition d'une démarche scientifique et éducative, qui elle-même prend sa source dans le social et, finalement, penche vers ce que les deux auteurs appellent le *socio-critique*. Cependant, ce modèle ne saurait revêtir uniquement une dimension socio-constructiviste ; il doit également intégrer une dimension positiviste relayée par les sciences exactes.

Ainsi que l'expose Carine Villemagne, dont nous reprenons ici *in extenso* la présentation du courant *socio-critique* :

> L'éducation socialement critique est associée au changement visant l'émancipation des personnes et de leur groupe social à travers un processus de réflexion critique et d'action qui concerne leur réalité sociale, et où le langage joue un rôle crucial. Une telle éducation, selon Robottom (1987) refuse tout consensus quant aux concepts qui lui sont associés. Pour lui, il n'y a pas de consensus possible pour

plusieurs raisons : les concepts associés à l'éducation sont socialement construits, historiquement situés et influencés par un ensemble de présupposés propres à un groupe social ou une communauté. L'atteinte d'un consensus peut donc conduire à instrumentaliser les concepts en jeu ; toute contestation est alors une activité saine qui amorce le changement.

Ainsi, toute proposition ou programme en éducation est construit à partir d'un ensemble de concepts contestés ou contestables, ce qui est évidemment le cas pour l'éducation relative à l'environnement. Par exemple, on dénombre plusieurs interprétations possibles de l'Éducation Relative à l'Environnement qui se manifestent à travers une éducation à/au sujet de, pour, dans/par et relative à l'environnement. Cette pluralité n'a rien de pathologique selon Robottom (1987) mais plutôt ouvre le débat et suscite le changement en Éducation Relative à l'Environnement. Elle offre un contexte favorable aux praticiens de développer et de théoriser leur propre vision de l'Éducation Relative à l'Environnement.

L'Éducation Relative à l'Environnement socialement critique repose alors sur un ensemble de principes que nous avons rassemblés ci-dessous (Robottom 1987 ; Robottom 1989 ; Robottom & Hart 1993 ; Sauvé 1997 ; Robottom 2003).

- les questions d'environnement sont contextualisées, historiquement situées et socialement construites ;

- les valeurs, les intérêts, les fondements et les présupposés sous-jacents à diverses problématiques socio-environnementales (les relations d'exploitation, par exemple) sont clarifiés et explicités ;

- le processus d'investigation de ces problématiques est fondé sur des situations particulières, vécues par les individus et leur communauté de manière réflexive, critique, éthique et métacognitive ;

- le processus d'investigation est orienté vers l'action personnelle et collective ; elle poursuit des changements sociaux et environnementaux, en particulier la construction d'un nouveau système de valeurs, d'une nouvelle relation à l'environnement, l'émancipation des personnes et l'amélioration de l'environnement ;

- l'éducation relative à l'environnement est doublement idiosyncrasique ; les problèmes d'environnement sont situés dans le temps et dans l'espace ; ils font l'objet de solutions spécifiques ; toute proposition ou modèle d'éducation relative à l'environnement qui préfigure la pensée ou prescrit une démarche est alors limitatif ;l'éducation relative à l'environnement est ancrée dans la communauté, son organisation, sa culture, son histoire naturelle et humaine ;

- l'éducation relative à l'environnement est fondée sur un processus collaboratif faisant appel à la participation de tous les membres et les acteurs de la communauté ;

Ces principes dits socioconstructifs sont donc exclusifs. En ce sens, qu'ils rejettent la modélisation et le caractère positiviste qu'il implique. Or le comportement environnemental est lui-même socio-construit mais intègre un principe du positivisme, extrait des Sciences Exactes, qu'il importe de relever par la modélisation.

Les paradigmes socioconstructiviste et positiviste dans lesquels s'inscrit cette approche de théorisation du comportement environnemental de l'élève en contexte ivoirien nous conduisent à nous imprégner de cette perspective croisée de principes théoriques qui doivent mener à l'élaboration des variables de ce modèle. (Villemagne 2008:58-59)

Les variables du comportement environnemental de l'élève fondé sur l'Éducation relative à l'environnement (ERE)

Dans le champ de l'ErE, nombreux sont les auteurs qui ont produit des modèles.

Pauline Côté et Mireille Picard rapportent ainsi les résultats antérieurs de Mireille Picard qui en 1995, a proposé des modèles basés sur les représentations des enseignants. Voici ce qu'elles en concluent :

Deux modèles d'intervention éducative avaient émergé de leurs discours. Le modèle culturaliste utilisé aujourd'hui encore par la majorité des enseignants, vise à transmettre des connaissances et à prescrire des comportements. Un autre modèle adopté par un petit nombre d'enseignantes et d'enseignants, vise le développement de l'émotivité, de la créativité et de certaines habiletés en action dans le milieu. Il se rapporte au paradigme humaniste puisque l'environnement est perçu non seulement comme un Objet mais aussi comme un Milieu d'apprentissage. (Côté & Picard 2003)

Leur modèle ultérieur s'inspire des représentations des élèves, il :

rejoint le paradigme inventif de Bertrand et Valois (1992) où l'environnement est perçu comme un objet, un milieu d'apprentissage et surtout comme un Lieu d'action. Dans d'autres contextes, d'autres auteurs ont développé des modèles qui conduisent à l'adoption du comportement environnemental en milieu scolaire. (ibid.)

Olivier Meunier dans les *Dossiers de la veille* (dossier consacré à l'ErE) en rappelle quelques autres, et nous lui empruntons cet exposé :

Banks […] propose, quant à lui, un modèle d'enquête réflexive relatif aux valeurs en vue de résoudre des problèmes. L'enseignant aide alors les élèves (primaire ou secondaire) à repérer les données ou les comportements du problème qui relèvent des valeurs, à identifier celles qui sont incompatibles les unes des autres, et enfin à choisir des valeurs plus appropriées tout en justifiant le choix en regard aux conséquences envisageables. […] Le modèle d'action environnementale de Cox et Stapp (1979) vise l'éveil et l'appréciation de l'environnement pour les élèves du primaire et l'identification et la résolution de problèmes pour ceux du secondaire. L'enseignant propose aux élèves des activités de contact avec l'environnement afin non seulement de développer le respect de l'environnement, mais aussi leurs capacités à résoudre les problèmes dont l'analyse et la clarification des valeurs.

Dans le cadre d'un projet d'action, les élèves vont être amenés à définir le problème, recueillir les informations, identifier des solutions, les évaluer, élaborer un plan d'action, le mettre en œuvre et évaluer l'action [...] Dehan et Oberlinkels dans le cadre d'une approche constructiviste et pluridisciplinaire, proposent une relation dialectique entre le milieu et l'élève prenant en compte l'ensemble des composantes du milieu de vie à la fois comme source, moyen et but de l'acquisition de connaissances. Il s'agit d'explorer un milieu de vie afin d'en construire une représentation, de penser, d'élaborer, de communiquer et d'évaluer ce projet. La représentation obtenue est alors enrichie si nécessaire par la mise en place d'un nouveau projet. [...] Vaquette considère que l'éveil sensoriel et conceptuel de l'élève (du primaire) à l'environnement naturel est la première étape de l'éducation à l'environnement global. Dans le cadre, d'une sortie ou d'un voyage imaginaire, l'élève est sollicité à entrer en contact avec la nature et à explorer par le biais de jeux sensoriels et écologiques ; puis les élèves formulent sous la direction de l'enseignant les connaissances qui en résultent. (Meunier 2004:18-21)

Au travers de ces différents modèles, l'on observe divers types d'approches affectives, pragmatiques, morales, expérientielles, coopératives et réflexives. Ils relèvent d'une approche socioconstruite et éliminent le caractère positiviste qu'ils recoupent dans leur principe. Cependant, aucun de ces modèles ne visite l'approche spiritualiste, également socio-construite, que Sauvé (1992) définit comme étant « le développement d'un rapport de type spirituel avec la nature, le milieu de vie, l'environnement » (Meunier 2004:19).

Or cette approche s'affirme dans les discours des élèves. Au regard des discussions et résultats en contexte ivoirien, le modèle construit obéit davantage à cet acquis social : d'où une socio-construction culturaliste inspirée du paradigme positiviste dans son élaboration.

Ce modèle invite à concevoir l'ErE à partir de la dimension (*dans* et *pour* l'environnement) ; structure qui conduit inéluctablement au comportement environnemental. C'est à cette fin qu'obéissent les différentes variables qui ont fait l'objet de notre enquête.

La variable extrant de notre modèle est le *comportement environnemental de l'élève*. Ce comportement environnemental peut prendre cinq dimensions : la promotion de l'environnement, le règlement de problème environnemental, l'embellissement, la sensibilisation et enfin le projet communautaire (tel que l'envisage Sauvé). En face, nous avons les intrants au comportement environnemental de l'élève qui sont le sexe, les valeurs et les intérêts de l'élève.

Construction du modèle basée sur le comportement environnemental de l'élève basé sur l'ErE

La construction du modèle basée sur le comportement environnemental de l'élève s'appuie sur les résultats de l'enquête que nous avons réalisée au cours de cette étude. Lors de cette enquête, il a été distribué un feuillet aux 156 élèves des 4 établissements visités (École Arras 3, École Lagune 1, École Selmer, École Vridi). Les résultats de ce questionnaire ont été traités à l'aide du logiciel Sphinx.

Le comportement environnemental, constitué de cinq dimensions dans le modèle, s'articule sur la distinction entre les rapports positifs et les rapports négatifs à l'environnement. Les rapports positifs à l'environnement sont basés sur trois dimensions de comportements environnementaux au lieu de cinq. Ce sont les aspects « *sensibilisation* », « *embellissement* » et « *résolution-problème* » du comportement environnemental des élèves. Les deux autres dimensions : positive (projet communautaire) et négative (promotion), contribuent moins au comportement environnemental des élèves.

Tableau 1 : Contributions des dimensions du comportement environnemental de l'élève ivoirien

	Axe 1 (+37.8%)		Axe 2 (+24.2%)	
CONTRIBUTIONS POSITIVES	sensibilisation	+32,0%	projet communautaire	+49,0%
	embellisement	+28,0%		
	resolution_problème	+16,0%		
CONTRIBUTIONS NEGATIVES			promotion	-49,0%

Source : Données d'analyse de la grille distribuée (2011)

On comprend dès lors que le modèle comportemental sur lequel prend appui le modèle éducationnel d'ErE (le premier étant la finalité du second) est significatif si ses dimensions optent pour un comportement axé sur la sensibilisation à l'environnement, à l'embellissement et à la résolution de problèmes environnementaux. Selon le tableau 1, il existe une corrélation négative entre le projet communautaire et la promotion. L'enseignant n'a donc pas intérêt à entreprendre des actions allant dans le sens d'un projet communautaire et associant la promotion, car cette action serait mal perçue par l'élève et les résultats escomptés (c'est-à-dire son comportement environnemental) seraient décevants.

Cependant, des actions environnementales allant dans le sens d'un comportement environnemental qui comporte les dimensions d'une résolution de problème, d'un embellissement et de la sensibilisation sont assez appropriées et bien appréciées des élèves. En outre, le tableau 2 nous fournit l'information selon laquelle, le comportement environnemental alliant la « *sensibilisation* » et « *l'embellissement* » (0,42) est davantage approprié aux élèves que le couple de comportement environnemental « *sensibilisation/résolution de problème* » (0,29).

Tableau 2 : Corrélations des dimensions du comportement environnemental de l'élève

	promotion	resolution_ problème	embellis ement	sensibili sation	projet com munautaire
promotion	1,00				
resolution_problème	0,23	1,00			
embellisement	0,31	0,10	1,00		
sensibilisation	0,21	0,29	0,42	1,00	
projet communautaire	-0,21	0,20	0,25	0,27	1,00

Source : Données d'analyse de la grille distribuée (2011)

On peut déduire que les modèles éducationnels comportant les dimensions couplées du comportement environnemental sont davantage efficaces que ceux ayant une visée de comportement environnemental unique.

Le modèle éducationnel recommandé par cette étude est celui ayant pour couple de comportement environnemental (sensibilisation/embellissement) et le couple (*sensibilisation/résolution de problème*) avec une nette considération pour le couple (*sensibilisation/embellissement*) par l'élève ivoirien.

Après le diagnostic des variantes de l'extrant (comportement environnemental) de notre modèle d'ERE, nous venons maintenant aux intrants ; c'est-à-dire aux différentes variables qui devraient pouvoir expliquer le comportement environnemental quel que soit le couple de comportement visé par l'enseignant ou adopté par l'enfant.

En analysant le comportement environnemental « *résolution de problème* », on observe que chez l'élève ivoirien, les facteurs « les maîtres nous font sortir », « *le sexe* » et la « *religion* » expliquent ce type de comportement. En outre, « *les maîtres nous font sortir* », explique davantage ce comportement environnemental chez l'élève ivoirien avec 22,5 pour cent du niveau d'apparition du facteur en question.

les maîtres nous font sortir	+ (53,47	+22,5%	
Je suis un garçon	+ (23,00	+20,5%	
J'aime tout ce qui est beau	- (8,42	-17,5%	
Je prie Dieu	+ (4,04	+15,0%	
Ma coopérative lutte contre ca	- (3,13	-6,5%	
A l'école tout le monde en parle	- (2,41	-5,0%	
Le directeur et les maîtres	- (1,92	-4,0%	
Les règles qu'on nou a montrés	- (1,20	-2,5%	
Mon ethnie dit que l'homme et la Nature sont égaux	- (0,72	-1,5%	
Je suis une fille	- (0,48	-1,0%	
Mon village m'y oblige	- (0,48	-1,0%	
Mon école m'y oblige	- (0,24	-0,5%	
On va me féliciter	- (0,24	-0,5%	
Sinon on va me punir	- (0,24	-0,5%	
Je ne prie pas Dieu	(*)	+0,0%	
Mon âge m'y oblige	(*)	+0,0%	
Les livres à l'école	(*)	+0,0%	

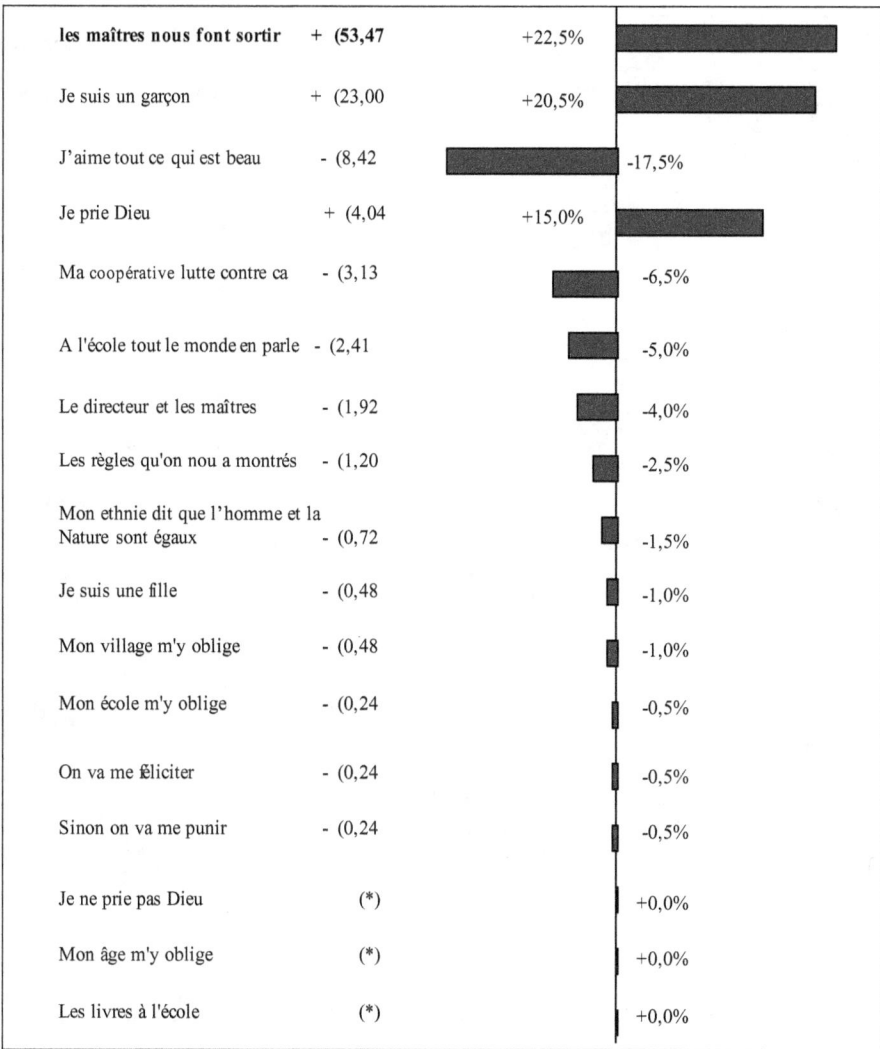

Figure 1 : Facteurs expliquant le comportement environnemental « Résolution-problème »
Source : Données d'analyse de la grille distribuée (2011)

En outre, l'analyse s'est penchée sur le comportement environnemental « *sensibilisation* ». Ainsi, il ressort de la figure 2 que le comportement environnemental « sensibilisation » est déterminé par les facteurs « *J'aime tout ce qui est beau* », « *Mon ethnie dit que l'Homme et la Nature sont égaux* ». L'action conduite par l'enseignant dans le cadre d'une « *sensibilisation* » n'aura un effet positif que si elle met un accent particulier sur le facteur « *J'aime tout ce qui est beau* » qui affecte 60,5 pour cent des proportions d'impacts positifs de l'ensemble des facteurs de ce comportement environnemental.

J'aime tout ce qui est beau	+ (3,16)	+60,5%
Mon ethnie dit que l'Homme et la Nature sont égaux	+ (3,16)	+7,9%
Mon âge m'y oblige	(*)	-0,7%
Mon école m'y oblige	(*)	-1,5%
Mon village m'y oblige	(*)	-2,2%
Ma coopérative lutte contre ca	(*)	-7,4%
Je suis une fille	(*)	-2,9%
Je suis un garçon	(*)	-4,4%
Je prie Dieu	(*)	-20,6%
Le directeur et les maîtres	(*)	-5,1%
Les règles qu'on nous a montrées	(*)	-5,9%
On va me féliciter	(*)	-3,7%
Les maîtres nous font sortir	(*)	-2,2%
A l'école tout le monde en parle	(*)	-8,1%
Les livres à l'école	(*)	-1,5%
Sinon on va me punir	(*)	-2,2%
Je ne prie pas Dieu	(*)	+0,0%

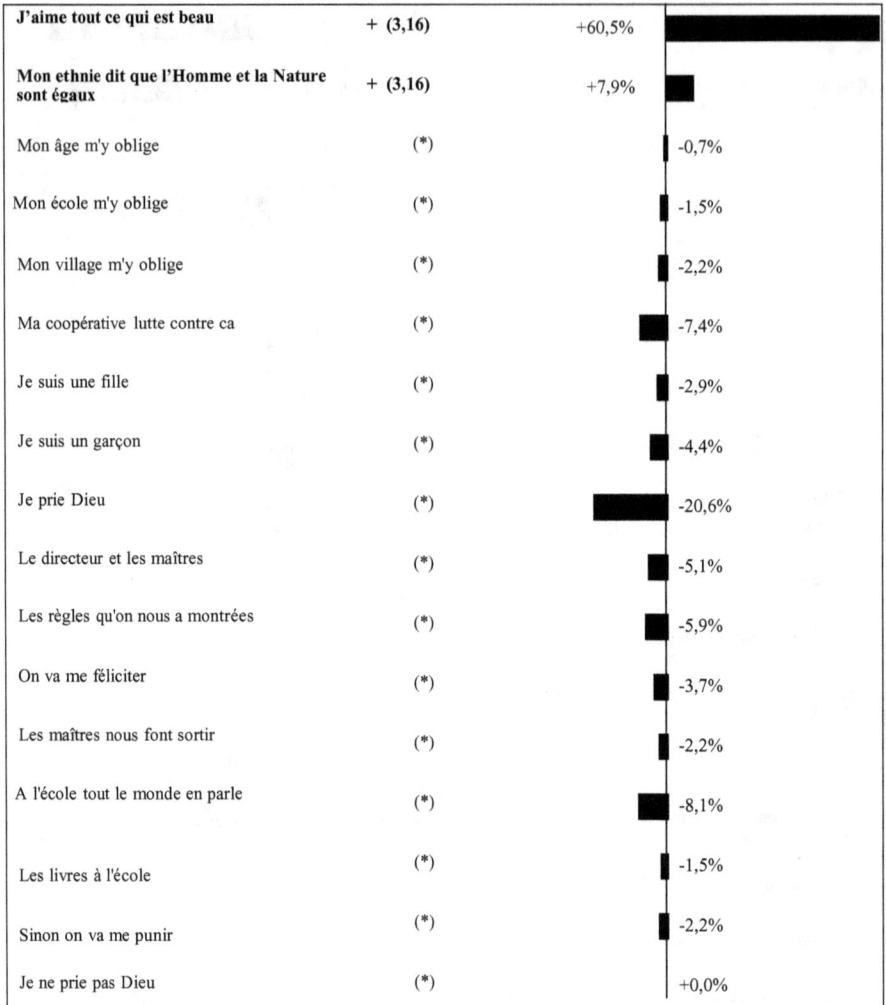

Figure 2 : Déterminants du comportement environnemental « sensibilisation » chez l'élève ivoirien

Source : Données d'analyse de la grille distribuée (2011)

Le modèle éducationnel d'ErE qui met l'accent sur un comportement environnemental « *sensibilisation* » doit mettre l'accent davantage sur « *J'aime tout ce qui est beau* » de l'élève que sur « *Mon ethnie dit que l'Homme et la Nature sont égaux* ». Cependant ces deux facteurs comptent dans l'atteinte de ce comportement environnemental.

Enfin, notre construction du modèle éducationnel nous conduit à visiter le comportement environnemental « *embellissement* ».

La figure 3 permet d'observer que « *J'aime tout ce qui est beau* » est le facteur unique et déterminant du comportement environnemental axé sur l'embellissement. Cette approche oblige l'enseignant à ne pas ignorer le facteur cognitif de l'élève, qui lui permet de s'approprier l'action d'embellir son environnement.

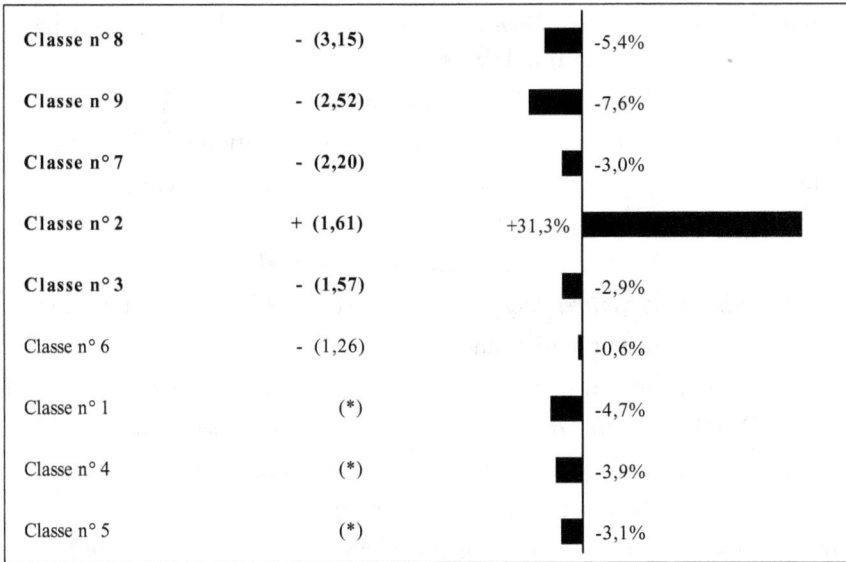

Classe n° 8	- (3,15)		-5,4%
Classe n° 9	- (2,52)		-7,6%
Classe n° 7	- (2,20)		-3,0%
Classe n° 2	+ (1,61)	+31,3%	
Classe n° 3	- (1,57)		-2,9%
Classe n° 6	- (1,26)		-0,6%
Classe n° 1	(*)		-4,7%
Classe n° 4	(*)		-3,9%
Classe n° 5	(*)		-3,1%

Figure 3 : Facteurs déterminants le comportement environnemental « Embellissement » chez l'élève ivoirien

Source : Données d'analyse de la grille distribuée (2011)

Ce facteur explique ainsi pour 31,3 pour cent la réussite de l'application d'un tel modèle d'adoption du comportement environnemental chez l'élève.

Au terme de cet exposé sur notre modèle, il nous apparaît opportun de faire une synthèse. Le modèle qui finalise cette production est avant tout une approche mathématique linéaire d'obédience positiviste et structuré dans le socio-constructif au niveau de ses variables, qui comprennent des intrants et un extrant (le comportement environnemental de l'élève).

De l'extrant (Ouput)

L'extrant de ce modèle est le comportement environnemental de l'élève du primaire. Ce comportement environnemental peut prendre trois types de variantes : sensibilisation (Y_1), embellissement (Y_2) et résolution de problème (Y_3).

Des intrants (Inputs)

Les inputs que nous présentons par variantes de l'extrant s'expriment suivant les facteurs qui les influencent favorablement.

Variante (Y1) [sensibilisation]

Intrant (X11) : *'J'aime tout ce qui est beau'* (Contribution positive forte)

Intrant (X12) : 'Mon ethnie dit que L'homme et la Nature sont égaux'.
(Contribution positive faible)

Intrant (X13) : *'Je prie Dieu'* (Contribution négative par absence : contribution latente)

Variante (Y2) [embellissement]

Intrant (X21) : *'J'aime tout ce qui est beau'* (Contribution positive forte)

ntrant (X22) : *'Je prie Die*u' (Contribution négative par absence : contribution latente)

Variante (Y3): [résolution problème]

Intrant (X31) : *'les maîtres nous font sortir de l'école'* (Contribution positive forte premier rang)

Intrant (X32) : *'le sexe'* (contribution positive forte deuxième rang)

Intrant (X33) : *'Je prie Dieu'* (Contribution positive troisième rang)

Intrant (X34) : *'J'aime tout ce qui est beau'* (Contribution négative par absence : contribution latente).

Au total, le modèle sur le comportement environnemental se présente sous la forme du tableau suivant :

Tableau 3 : Présentation du modèle de comportement environnemental basé sur l'éducation relative à l'environnement

Extrant (Y) (Visées de l'enseignant et/ou de l'élève)		Intrants (X) (attributs de l'élève)			
	Variantes	X1	X2	X3	X4
Comportement environnemental de l'élève	(Y1) sensibilisation	J'aime tout ce qui est beau	Mon ethnie dit que L'homme et la Nature sont égaux	Je prie Dieu	
	(Y2) embellissement	J'aime tout ce qui est beau	Je prie Dieu		
	(Y3) résolution problème	les maîtres nous font sortir de l'école	le sexe	Je prie Dieu	J'aime tout ce qui est beau

Source : Données d'analyse (2011)

Interprétation et conclusion sur le modèle

Le comportement environnemental de l'élève ivoirien est, selon notre approche, prédictif. Ainsi, si un enseignant veut obtenir une variante de comportement environnemental de l'élève, il faut qu'il agisse ou qu'il considère des facteurs essentiels à la détermination de ce comportement environnemental de l'élève, dont les dispositions doivent obligatoirement tenir compte des aptitudes et attentes de l'élève lui-même. En fait, il doit surtout tenir compte de la volonté d'agir de l'élève, qui fait appel aux intrants sumentionnés.

Ce modèle prédictif dans le contexte ivoirien montre que le comportement environnemental pouvant être défini dans le cadre du primaire ne comporte que trois variantes. Ces variantes partent de la sensibilisation en passant par l'embellissement, jusqu'à la résolution de problèmes environnementaux. On saisit ainsi que les comportements environnementaux des élèves ivoiriens ne tiennent pas suffisamment compte des variantes « *promotion* » et « *projet communautaire* » qui sont hors de leurs capacités et aptitudes selon les informations reçues dans la série d'enquête. Ces informations indiquent donc une baisse de la capacité d'agir de l'élève du primaire au niveau de ces deux dimensions.

Exposé sur les Intrants

Des intrants, le modèle prédictif conçu, met en exergue deux facteurs intrinsèques à l'élève (*J'aime tout ce qui est beau ; le sexe*), deux autres externes (*Mon ethnie dit que L'homme et la Nature sont égaux ; les maîtres nous font sortir de l'école*) et un dernier lié à la métaphysique (*Je prie Dieu*).

Les facteurs intrinsèques à l'élève

Les facteurs qui proviennent de l'élève, dans une prescription du comportement environnemental, sont marqués par deux variables clés.

J'aime tout ce qui est beau

La recherche de la précision dans une bonne disposition du paysage est une dimension essentielle à la définition de la beauté chez l'élève. Cette pratique le conduit à mettre en avant le cognitif dans cette quête de la beauté. Cependant, il importe de rappeler que si cette variable est dite intrinsèque, elle est une dimension culturelle de l'élève. Tout comme la dimension « *Je prie Dieu* », elle relève de ce dont la socialisation de départ en famille a pu imprégner l'enfant ; ainsi, l'enfant n'a pas une vision nette de la beauté. Ce sont les enseignements des maîtres, à travers les manuels qui l'aident à construire cette dimension de la beauté. La beauté se construit donc socialement à travers des formations ou une éducation par immersion dans un milieu social donné. Ceci conduit à la transformation des noyaux conceptuels de la vision sur la beauté. Il importe également de noter que l'enfant confond la beauté et la propreté. Cette attitude révèle que chez l'écolier ivoirien, l'absence de saleté constitue, avant tout, l'expression de la beauté dans le cadre de l'environnement. Cette attitude doit être perçue par l'enseignant afin de mieux saisir les schèmes à transformer chez l'élève.

Cette variable « *J'aime tout ce qui est beau* » est déterminante dans les trois variantes du comportement environnemental de l'élève du modèle. Ainsi contrairement aux deux premiers cas, où cette variante constitue une variable majeure à contribution positive, la dernière variante (résolution problème) expose cette variable comme latente dont l'absence complète produit un effet néfaste sur les résultats du comportement environnemental.

En outre, le facteur « *sexe* » est déterminant dans la définition du comportement environnemental de l'écolier ivoirien. Cette approche fait appel à la question du genre.

Le genre

Le facteur sexe est déterminant dans les rapports à l'environnement de l'écolier ivoirien. Ainsi selon qu'on soit garçon ou fille, on a une approche différente de l'environnement. Et cela tire sa source des rapports sociaux, culturels que les Africains et Ivoiriens ont avec l'environnement. En effet, dès leur naissance, les jeunes filles sont davantage amenées à être en rapport avec l'environnement que les garçons. Les questions de propreté de la maison, de la cour familiale, et parfois même de l'école sont largement imputées aux activités des filles. Les garçons, eux aussi, ont des rapports avec l'environnement, mais moins récurrents que les filles. Leurs activités sont davantage le balayage du salon de la maison familial, les coupes de gazons et le planting d'arbre. Aussi l'enseignant doit-il dès le départ reconnaître les activités qui sont supportables par l'élève (fille ou garçon) avant de se lancer dans une démarche d'ErE. Sur les variantes types de comportement environnemental que comporte notre modèle, seule une variante (résolution problème) tient compte du sexe ; les deux autres variantes n'en font pas cas.

Les facteurs externes à l'élève

Les facteurs externes à l'élève s'expriment clairement dans deux variables, une d'obédience culturelle « *Mon ethnie dit que l'Homme et la Nature sont égaux* », et l'autre suivant les dispositions pédagogiques pratiques à l'école.

-     *Mon ethnie dit que l'Homme et la Nature sont égaux*

Cette variable est avant tout culturelle. Elle prend sa source dans les savoirs locaux et endogènes dont les parents ont imprégné les élèves interrogés. En effet, elle fait son apparition dans la variante « *sensibilisation* » du modèle comme variable positive à contribution faible. Ainsi, selon cette modalité les enfants sont suffisamment informés sur les us et coutumes de leur région d'origine et sur ce que sont l'environnement et son importance quant à la construction de l'identité humaine. Cette dimension les aide à « sensibiliser » leur entourage sur l'adoption d'un comportement environnemental. D'où une expression de leur capacité d'agir envers l'environnement par la modification du comportement des autres. Les conditions familiales constituent une dimension pertinente dans la construction d'une telle intégration.

La variable « *les maîtres nous font sortir de l'école* » constitue l'autre dimension des dimensions externes à l'élève.

- *Les maîtres nous font sortir de l'école*

« *Les maîtres nous font sortir de l'école* » constitue pour les enfants une variable majeure de la résolution d'un problème environnemental par l'élève. Cette approche représente donc une dimension que l'enseignant doit prendre en compte dans l'atteinte de cette variante du comportement environnemental et de la dimension globale du modèle basé sur la perspective « *résolution problème* ». En effet, la connaissance de l'environnement externe de l'élève, son approche et son immersion, est l'une des démarches essentielles dans la construction de la variante du comportement environnemental basée sur la résolution de problèmes environnementaux. Cela suppose également que les chapitres du manuel consacrés à l'élève soient très explicites sur les problèmes environnementaux qui peuvent se poser au quotidien à l'élève.

Facteur lié à la métaphysique

Je prie Dieu

La variable « *je prie Dieu* » est identifiée dans toutes les variantes du comportement environnemental du modèle. Cette variable s'exprime soit avec des contributions positives, soit avec des contributions latentes dans le modèle. Elle devient à ce moment une variable critique dans la mesure où sa non-prise en compte engendre des conséquences graves sur la réussite du modèle. Elle s'avère ainsi cruciale dans la mesure où les attentes, les intérêts des enfants tournent autour de leur vision de Dieu et de leur rapport avec cet Être Suprême, créateur selon eux de la nature. Aussi, les mesures de sanctions suite à un mauvais entretien de l'environnement proviennent avant tout de la peur que les enfants ont de Dieu et des sanctions qui pourraient provenir de Lui. Les sanctions divines et inattendues sont les premières causes qui selon les élèves ivoiriens militent en faveur de leur adoption de comportements environnementaux.

Conclusion

Il s'agissait dans cette étude de montrer en quoi modéliser le comportement environnemental de l'élève du primaire à travers l'ErE posait un problème d'ordre épistémique et pratique. L'étude sur 348 élèves nous donne les enseignements suivants : d'abord, le comportement environnemental n'est pas statique, il est dynamique. Ensuite, suivant l'objectif de comportement environnemental visé, l'élève peut faire appel à plusieurs niveaux de variantes. Cependant, une variante dont la manipulation reste relativement difficile pour l'éducateur, est la variable « religion », qui apparaît dans toutes les composantes du comportement environnemental de l'élève. Cette variable, sensible du fait de la laïcité de l'État ivoirien, conduit à générer un *modèle prédictif* permettant de concilier la difficulté pratique de l'éducateur en ErE et la problématique épistémique du chercheur (choix entre le positivisme ou le socioconstructivisme) quant à la modélisation du comportement environnemental de l'élève.

Notes

1. Direction de l'extrascolaire et des activités coopératives.
2. Direction de la pédagogie et de la formation continue.

Références

Bressoux, P., 2011, *Modélisation statistique appliquée aux sciences sociales,* De Boeck, Bruxelles.

Côté, P., & M. Picard, 2003, « Représentations de l'environnement et de l'agir dans l'environnement chez des élèves du primaire des Îles-de-la-madeleine », *Vertigo – La revue en Sciences de l'environnement, 4* (2).

Essane, S., 1997, « Leadership and Managment », 9e Conférence générale de l'AUA, The African university in a rapidly changing global environment : facing the challenges of the 21st century, Lusaka, p. 1-25.

Kollmus, A., & J. Agyeman, 2002, « Mind the gap : why do people act environmentally and what are the barriers to pro-environmental behaviour ? », *Environmental Éducation Research, VIII* (3), p. 239-260.

Meunier, O., 2004, « Modèles d'approches didactiques en EEDD », in *Éducation à l'environnement et au développement durable*, Dossier de la veille, INRP.

Passeron, J.-C., 2006, *Le raisonnement sociologique. Un espace non popperien du raisonnement*, Albin Michel, Paris.

Robottom, I. & P. Hart, 1993, *Research in environmental education: Engaging the debate*, Deakin University Press, Geelong, Victoria.

Villemagne, C., 2008, « L'éducation relative à l'environnement en contexte d'alphabétisation des adultes : quelles dimensions critiques ? », *Éducation relative à l'environnement, Regards-Recherches-Réflexion*, p. 49-64.

13

Expériences de vie migratoire et capacités d'agir des enfants : cas des aides ménagères mineures dans la ville de Sikasso au Mali

Bra-Amba Dolo

Introduction

La littérature sur la migration des enfants est abondante et diversifiée. Les différentes acceptions du phénomène reposent sur des déterminants : géographiques, politiques, sociaux, économiques ou culturels, etc. Par exemple, sous un angle géographique, la migration est comprise comme le mouvement d'une ou de plusieurs personnes d'un endroit vers un autre, et le franchissement de frontières administratives ou politiques dans l'intention de s'installer, définitivement ou temporairement, dans un endroit différent de leur lieu d'origine (OIM 2011). Mais afin d'être plus opérant, ce travail adopte la définition ci-dessous, qui est largement partagée :

> La migration humaine est le déplacement du lieu de vie des individus. Les gens, conduits par leurs motivations, ont été en perpétuel mouvement d'une place à l'autre, en nombre élargi ou restreint, sur une courte ou une longue distance, dans un pays ou entre deux ou plusieurs pays, régions ou continents. (Camara, Traoré, Dicko & Sidibé 2011:4)

L'abondance de littérature et la multiplicité des définitions impliquent une diversité de visions de la migration. Mais une critique des écrits permet de constater la prédominance des visions protectionnistes, surtout concernant les enfants. À travers les différents travaux, on remarque aussi un regain d'intérêt pour la migration des femmes et des petites filles, dont les services domestiques sont de plus en plus sollicités dans les nouvelles familles africaines.

S'inscrivant dans ce dernier registre, cette étude sur la capacité d'agir des enfants s'intéresse aux filles qui migrent seules, sans être accompagnées de leurs parents ou d'autres adultes, pour offrir des services domestiques. Les propos de Mélanie Jacquemin (2003:24) traduisent bien ce regain d'intérêt pour la thématique :

> Si les pratiques anciennes de circulation des enfants dans les sociétés ouest-africaines constituent un cadre de référence essentiel, le recours aux services domestiques et marchands des enfants est devenu, avec la « crise », tout à fait central dans les stratégies familiales de survie.

Au Burkina Faso, Philippe et Ky (2003) constatent que tout semble se passer comme si migrer pour le travail en ville, et dès le bas âge, était devenu la nouvelle norme sociale.

Au Mali, des travaux se rapportant à la migration des femmes en général et à celles des filles en particulier existent (Konaté, De Koninck & Yaro 2010). Ils montrent que la situation des filles migrantes obéit à un contexte ouest-africain assez semblable : population majoritairement jeune et ressentant plus durement les conséquences de la pauvreté et des mutations sociales. Toutes choses de nature à faire prospérer le phénomène de la migration des filles. Konaté et ses collègues ont pu rencontrer dans le cadre de leur étude 1 039 filles en migration à Bamako, dans la capitale du Mali, ainsi que 1 065 filles en âge de migrer et 185 déjà de retour de la migration dans les zones de départ.

Or selon plusieurs perspectives, les protectionnistes surtout, les enfants séparés prématurément de leurs parents risquent de vivre des situations physiquement et psychologiquement dangereuses. Leurs besoins les plus essentiels d'affection, de protection et d'éducation risquent bien moins d'être satisfaits là où elles partent qu'en famille (Philippe & Ky 2003 ; Nöstlinger & Mathieu 1990). La migration présenterait ainsi des risques de vulnérabilité et d'exploitation. Elle serait une passerelle vers des fléaux comme la traite et le trafic contre lesquels il faut protéger les enfants (Save the Children Canada 2006). D'où la prédominance de l'approche protectionniste, au sens de la Convention relative aux droits de l'enfant (CDE) de 1989 ou de la Charte africaine des droits et du bien-être de l'enfant (CADBE). Le plus souvent, ces positions sont celles d'organismes internationaux qui s'appuient sur des travaux scientifiques sur le développement de l'enfant. À ce propos, on peut citer les travaux de psychopédagogie précurseurs de Wundt (1879, 1881), les théories psychopédagogiques de l'apprentissage de Skinner (1953) et de Piaget (1970).

Toutefois, les travaux qui animent le courant protectionniste adoptent dans le même temps une position théorique qui distingue les facteurs individuels et les facteurs environnementaux de vulnérabilité, introduisant ainsi un autre concept : la résilience. Celle-ci semble proche de la capacité d'agir des enfants (Garmezy 1985). Quelques modèles théoriques (Hawley & DeHaan 1996 ; Wolff 1995) mettent l'accent sur la dimension adaptative et évolutive du processus de résilience : l'individu ne naît pas résilient dans l'absolu, il devient résilient à quelque chose. Il est indispensable que l'enfant soit exposé à un certain nombre de facteurs de risque, de conditions considérées comme « adverses » afin qu'il développe une capacité ou une aptitude à une adaptation adéquate.

Les travaux de Théogène-Octave Gakubal (2000) portant sur les facteurs de la capacité d'agir à l'école des enfants rwandais réfugiés en France et en Suisse s'inscrivent dans la même perspective. L'auteur arrive à la conclusion que, malgré le drame du génocide qui engagea ces enfants dans l'exil, chaque enfant a gardé des ressources personnelles et sociales l'aidant à résister aux contraintes du nouvel environnement.

En somme, il existe des réflexions sur le développement de l'enfant dans les sociétés africaines qui envisagent la capacité d'agir des enfants. Néanmoins, elles semblent bien moins nombreuses que celles qui abordent la question sous l'angle exclusivement protectionniste. Mais la différence la plus fondamentale entre les deux est la place donnée à l'enfant lui-même dans la compréhension du processus de son développement. Face à un problème de société le concernant, quelle capacité de réaction l'enfant possède-t-il ? Est-il valable de le considérer, ainsi que le conçoivent les courants protectionnistes, comme un être en proie à la vulnérabilité et dépourvu de capacité d'autodéfense ? D'où le problème spécifique de cette étude.

Dans toutes les sociétés, il existe des valeurs qui justifient un engagement pour la protection des enfants. Car les enfants procurent du bonheur à leurs parents ; l'avenir de leur communauté et de leur pays repose sur eux. Toute situation qui tend à compromettre cette donne est un problème social. Ainsi, lorsque des filles de plus en plus jeunes s'adonnent à la migration dans différents pays africains et que l'on dispose de peu d'explications soutenues (Jacquemin 2009), il y a lieu d'en faire un problème de recherche. Au Mali particulièrement, on rencontre peu d'études abordant la migration des filles sous l'angle de leur capacité de réaction à l'adversité dans leurs nouveaux lieux d'accueil.

La perspective de recherche ici adoptée répond à la nécessité de comprendre comment les filles migrantes agissent sur les conditions de leur vie en situation de migration au Mali. Deux questions sont posées :

- Quelles sont leurs conditions de vie et de travail en contexte migratoire ?
- Comment réagissent-elles à ces conditions ?

Méthodologie

L'étude a visé la compréhension de la capacité d'agir des filles en situation de migration, à partir des récits de leurs expériences. Plus précisément, les circonstances ayant occasionné la migration, les conditions de vie et de travail en famille comme en milieu d'accueil, les stratégies de réaction aux réalités de la vie en migration, les perceptions des filles elles-mêmes ont constitué les objectifs de l'étude.

La ville de Sikasso est le site de l'étude. Chef-lieu de commune, de cercle et de région, Sikasso est la deuxième plus grande ville du Mali, après Bamako. En 2009, sa population était estimée à 225 753 habitants (RGPH 2009). À 100 km de la frontière ivoirienne et à 45 km de celle du Burkina Faso, Sikasso est une ville-carrefour entre des pays côtiers (Togo, Bénin, Ghana, Côte d'Ivoire) et continentaux (Burkina Faso et Mali). Avec son climat subtropical (près de 300 mm de hauteur de pluie en moyenne) favorisant une abondante production agricole, une urbanisation rapide et un développement de ressources socio-économiques, Sikasso reçoit un flux assez important de filles pour des emplois ménagers rémunérés. Elles proviennent de toutes les régions du Mali et souvent du Burkina Faso. Ces filles qui sont appelées aides ménagères constituent la population d'étude.

L'approche de l'étude est qualitative et se base sur des entretiens individuels à caractère de récit de vie, centrés sur les expériences de vie migratoire des filles. Une recension sélective de littérature a aidé à sa réalisation.

Quinze filles de moins de dix-huit ans ont été prises au hasard, sans préoccupation quantitative de population mère pour la réalisation des entretiens.

L'obtention d'informations utiles auprès des filles n'a pas toujours été facile, aussi bien à l'intérieur du domicile qu'à l'extérieur, dans les espaces publics. Très souvent, la liberté d'expression était entravée par la présence d'autres personnes, car il fallait trouver les filles en des lieux où elles sont en activité. Pour contourner de telles difficultés, nous étions deux : un enquêteur (déjà formé) prenait, chaque fois que cela était nécessaire, le temps de s'entretenir avec la patronne ou la personne devant qui la fille serait gênée de parler ; ainsi, nous conduisions l'entretien au même moment avec la fille. Certaines filles n'ont pas accepté l'enregistrement audio voire écrit, de leur discours, ce qui nous obligeait à déposer tout objet pour faire l'entretien qui était transcrit aussitôt après.

Les thèmes abordés concernaient les informations sur le milieu de départ (description du milieu familial, en lien avec le projet de migration), le processus migratoire, de la zone de départ aux zones de transit, l'expérience de vie de migrante en zone de destination, les sentiments personnels de mal-être ou de bien-être, les mécanismes de protection, les réseaux d'appartenance, les aspirations, entre autres.

Les données colligées ont fait l'objet d'analyse de contenu qui a permis de dégager les particularités des discours et leurs récurrences.

Résultats

Profil des filles : âge, niveau d'instruction, situation matrimoniale

Les quinze aides ménagères enquêtées sont de profils assez variés :

– Sur le plan de l'âge, les filles étaient réparties comme suit :

Répartition par âge des filles

Âge	17	16	15	14	13	10	Total
Nombre	4	2	3	3	2	1	15

– En matière d'instruction, les filles étaient réparties selon le tableau ci-dessous :

Répartition selon le niveau d'instruction

Niveau d'instruction	scolarisées	déscolarisées	non scolarisées	total
Nombre	6	9	0	15

Le tableau ci-dessous donne la répartition des filles selon leurs situations matrimoniales :

Situation matrimoniale	Mariées	fiancées	autres	Total
Nombre	2	10	3	15

Bien que les filles aient été interviewées au hasard, pourvu qu'elles aient moins de dix-huit ans, on observe une présence abondante de filles ayant l'âge de travailler – qui est de quinze ans dans la loi malienne. Aussi, avec 80 pour cent des filles déjà engagées dans un processus marital, on observe que la plupart d'entre elles ont déjà des responsabilités sociales. Cette situation est certainement un facteur d'encouragement du travail domestique des filles, mais n'est-elle pas également une indication de l'utilité sociale et de la pertinence de la migration laborieuse des filles ? Faut-il rester à la maison et pour y faire quoi, bien que non inscrite à l'école et vivant dans des conditions socio-économiques difficiles comme le tend à montrer l'enquête ?

À ce genre de questions posées aux filles, l'une d'elles, âgée de quinze ans, répond :

> Moi, mon âge ne m'inquiète pas. Je sais que je peux comprendre beaucoup de choses et je peux me défendre. La preuve, c'est que je suis parvenue seule jusque-là. Et puis, chez nous, l'âge n'empêche pas de travailler une fois qu'on a environ dix ans. Chez nous tout le monde est d'accord que ce qui est meilleur en ce moment est d'aller travailler en ville si on n'est pas à l'école, car bientôt il y aura le mariage qui attend les filles dans ce cas. Il faut aussi aider les parents : sinon à quoi bon d'être fille ou fils ? S'il s'agit des petites tâches que nous menons en famille, nous aurons le temps de le faire notre vie durant, une fois de retour ; et puis cela n'apporte rien. Donc il ne faut pas rester là à se croiser les bras et le mieux c'est de

commencer tôt. Ainsi, on peut avoir la chance de venir plusieurs fois en ville et on gagne davantage de ressources : de l'argent, la belle vie et on peut même avoir un bon mari en ville. Là au moins on se fatiguera moins qu'au village. Ce qu'une fille sérieuse apporte à sa famille, un gaillard ne peut pas s'il reste sur place. Raison pour laquelle nous souhaitons toutes aller travailler en ville. (Balakisa, 15 ans)

Non seulement ce discours constitue un élément de réponse aux questions de la vulnérabilité liée à l'âge et au danger supposé de la migration, mais il parle également de la capacité des filles. Les tenantes de ce discours tentent d'assurer que les filles ont bien des ressources de réaction aux aventures de la migration et que ces ressources ne dépendent pas nécessairement de l'âge.

Contextes et circonstances de migration

La décision, les modes de migration et le financement des voyages constituent une importante source d'analyse de leurs processus migratoires et de leurs capacités d'agir. Nous exploitons ici à titre non exhaustif, le cas d'Aminata Diarra, se donnant quatorze ans au moment de notre enquête et originaire du village de Son-Basin dans la commune rurale de Mahou, cercle de Yorosso, région de Sikasso. Le cas d'Aminata nous donne l'occasion de signaler que bon nombre des filles à Sikasso viennent des zones rurales (90 pour cent de notre échantillon) et qu'elles ont pour la plupart, des motifs de migration semblables à celui d'Aminata : 70 pour cent de celles que nous avons rencontrées ont eu une part décisive dans le processus migratoire parce qu'un problème socioculturel ou économique les y contraignait.

L'histoire d'Aminata, les faits :

Mon père est parti en Côte d'Ivoire pendant que j'étais petite, je ne le connais pas bien d'ailleurs. Ma maman et mes frères, nous sommes restés en famille, sans notre père, avec nos oncles. Il y a plus de deux ans, nous avons appris la mauvaise nouvelle qu'il serait tué là-bas. Des funérailles ont été aussitôt célébrées et ma maman fut proposée en remariage à un des plus jeunes frères de mon père. Maman a refusé...et suite à cette histoire, elle a été renvoyée de la famille. La vie était devenue dure alors pour nous et j'ai vraiment du mal à supporter cela, surtout la situation de ma maman. Finalement, je suis venue à Sikasso avec l'appui d'un jeune du village (rire).

L'histoire d'Aminata, son analyse :

Lorsque nous nous intéressons au lien entre Aminata, son milieu familial et la ville de Sikasso qui est son nouvel environnement social à la faveur de la migration, dans une « approche-milieu » (Marlo 2000), la décision de migration est bien loin des agissements innocents et anodins d'enfant. De cette décision d'Aminata, nous pouvons déduire que les causes de la migration des filles sont complexes : déconstruction de liens sociaux, éclatement de famille et instabilité des parents dans les ménages, causés ou aggravés par des conditions socio-économiques difficiles, des pratiques traditionnelles défavorables, ce qui est couramment évoqué, mais aussi une détermination personnelle, de la part des filles, d'opérer un changement dans le cours de leur vie. Et l'adversité des conditions de vie qui étaient celles d'Aminata n'a pas inhibé ses capacités, au contraire, elle lui a permis de s'ingénier à les changer. Aussi, le secret de la complicité entre elle et le sponsor de son voyage est bien un aspect profond de développement de capacité.

Conditions de vie et de travail des filles dans le processus migratoire

Les conditions de vie et de travail des filles sont largement décriées dans de nombreuses recherches. Les termes de l'emploi, les horaires, la multiplicité des tâches à exécuter, l'estime de leur personne, la modicité des salaires sont évoqués par des chercheurs et dénoncés par des activistes en matière de droits de l'enfant (Unicef 1999).

Certes, les filles vivent ces réalités à Sikasso. La plupart des filles exécutent toutes tâches demandées par leurs « patronnes », au point qu'il nous semble opportun de remettre en question cette appellation de filles domestiques ; elles travaillent à la maison mais sont aussi en dehors de la maison, dans la rue, dans les marchés en train de vendre divers articles, souvent dans le cadre même du commerce, au profit de leurs « patronnes ».

Dans l'enceinte des ménages ou même en milieu ouvert, il n'est pas difficile de les reconnaître non seulement à travers leurs activités, mais aussi leurs habillements, leurs causeries, leurs fréquentations, bref à travers leur intégration sociale.

Un des déterminants de prime importance des conditions de travail est le niveau de rémunération. À Sikasso, le salaire mensuel des filles tourne autour de 7 500 F CFA (14,40 $; 11,43 €) contre un Salaire minimum interprofessionnel garanti (SMIG) de 28 460 F CFA (43,37 € ; 56,29 $). Mais ces salaires sont contestés aujourd'hui en premier lieu par les filles. Le service domestique des filles est actuellement en mutation, situation ressentie par les employeuses/employeurs comme une crise. Puisque le salaire est bas, Sikasso, jadis zone de destination, est en train de devenir un transit pour beaucoup de filles. La plupart d'entre elles ont le projet de continuer vers Bamako ou Kayes, où une aide ménagère pourrait prétendre à un salaire qui avoisine même le SMIG, ou passent directement dans ces villes. Les femmes à Sikasso (« patronnes ») se plaignent de la difficulté actuelle à trouver une aide ménagère. L'offre de main-d'œuvre des filles n'est plus abondante comme par le passé et les négociations des termes de l'emploi leur deviennent par conséquent de plus en plus défavorables. Pourtant, ces changements de donne du marché sont beaucoup moins l'œuvre de nouvelles lois en faveur des filles ou de défenseurs des droits de celles-ci que celle des filles elles-mêmes. Toutes ces situations, synonymes de condition de vie et de travail pourraient être considérées comme difficiles ; nous étions personnellement de cet avis dans une de nos études consacrées aux filles domestiques à Bamako en 1999.

Cependant, cette étude nous conduit à un recul – les conditions peuvent-elles être considérées mauvaises à tout point de vue ? – un recul qui se fait à partir des points de vue des filles elles-mêmes et des conditions de vie dans leurs environnements « micro et méso-systémiques » d'origine, sans que l'on puisse ignorer que l'évaluation des conditions de vie et de travail doit tenir compte des normes fixées par la société, « le macro-système » de la perspective écologique (Bronfenbrenner 1979). Mieux, penser une condition de vie et de travail sans aucune difficulté semble utopique. La question intéressante est de voir comment les filles s'adaptent aux difficultés qu'elles finissent par transformer ou contourner : si Sikasso n'est plus favorable, pourquoi ne pas aller à Kayes, Bamako ou ailleurs ? Telle semble aussi la manifestation de la capacité d'agir des filles que nous examinons ci-après.

Stratégies de réaction aux circonstances de la vie en migration

Vis-à-vis de la question de savoir comment réagissent les filles en face des situations nouvelles qui pourraient se présenter à elles, l'on remarque que les filles ne sont pas totalement passives comme le fait croire une certaine littérature. Notre entretien avec Yamouyon Somboro, âgée de seize ans a été particulièrement éclairant :

> Je m'appelle Yamouyon Somboro, je viens du village de Goumouni. Notre commune est Soubala, nous, nous sommes de Bankass. Cela fait la troisième fois, je viens travailler ici à Sikasso. La première fois, je suis venue auprès de ma tante qui est mariée à un militaire dans le camp mais maintenant ils sont partis vers le nord du Mali. Puisque j'ai connu des personnes, je continue à venir, je ne rencontre pas beaucoup de problèmes dans la ville maintenant. Et même si je rencontre des problèmes, je connais comment les résoudre. Par exemple, j'ai l'habitude d'aller voir un monsieur qui est un policier dans un quartier où j'ai déjà travaillé. Il m'a aidé à récupérer mon salaire qui n'était pas payé par une dame. Après, je l'ai quittée pour me faire embaucher par une autre. Si ça ne va pas, on quitte, c'est comme cela. Même mes petites sœurs qui arrivent, je leur montre cela. En venant pour la première fois, dans notre village, les filles se renseignent : comment passer de porte en porte pour trouver du travail, comment négocier les salaires et d'autres conditions, par exemple si on doit passer la nuit dans la famille de la patronne ou pas. Moi personnellement, je n'accepte pas les patronnes qui exigent qu'on passe la nuit chez elles. Là, le travail ne finit pas et il y a toujours des bruits. Pour nous, il est préférable d'aller dormir en groupe, cela nous sécurise et nous donne l'occasion de jouer entre nous. Ici à Sanoubougou, nous sommes plus de dix dans cette situation.

Il ressort des entretiens avec Yamouyon que les filles ont révolutionné les modes de négociation des emplois ; elles sont, elles-mêmes, principales actrices de la négociation : soit la fille intéressée elle-même, soit une de ses paires tout au moins. Elles font preuve de solidarité : les plus âgées envers les plus jeunes, les plus expérimentées envers les néophytes ; la force du groupe au service de l'individu nécessiteux est un rempart contre les éventuelles adversités de la ville. Désormais, beaucoup de filles comme Yamouyon tiennent à leur liberté – Rokia, Massaran, Niélé et Koumba, qui faisaient partie de notre échantillon, l'ont particulièrement noté avec insistance. Décliner une offre de travail allant à l'encontre de cette liberté est possible, même courant. Au cours des négociations, beaucoup de « patronnes » proposent aux filles de dormir en famille une fois embauchée et présentent cela comme un des avantages gracieusement accordés. Mais, de plus en plus, les filles rejettent cette attitude de « bon samaritain » des patronnes. Ce rejet, semble-t-il, constitue une des meilleures stratégies pour se dérober à une définition sans limites du travail et des horaires de travail. Dans le pire des cas, la déclinaison pure et simple de l'offre de travail intervient. Si le volume de travail semble encore excessif, beaucoup de filles, en revanche, ne laissent plus passer sans correction exemplaire, les manquements aux clauses des contrats, qui sont pourtant informels ou tacites en général :

> Je sais ce que je suis venue faire et je sais ce que c'est de faire un travail domestique. Ce n'est pas de l'esclavage et moi quand même, je n'accepte pas tout, n'importe comment. (Koumba, 17 ans).

Perceptions des filles sur leur vie de migrantes

Les perceptions des filles sur leur vie migratoire ont plusieurs points communs malgré quelques divergences. Pour beaucoup comme Aminata, le moyen le plus sûr d'échapper aux hostilités sociales et économiques de leur milieu d'origine est « la migration laborieuse » et elle est un salut pour cela.

> Quand nous sommes en désaccord avec certains de nos parents, quand la nourriture, les vêtements nous manquent, nous courons vers la ville. En ville, on vit mieux, il faut le reconnaître, il faut simplement voir les gens ici et là-bas. (Ramata Koné, 15 ans)

Ce discours n'est pas un discours alarmiste portant sur la migration. Au contraire, c'est une idée de bonheur qui transparaît. Est-ce nécessairement une perception « enfantine » ? Non, parce qu'Aminata continue en disant que même si certains parents font semblant de les dissuader ils manquent de conviction et ils cèdent très rapidement. Ce propos est à notre avis digne de crédit car les tentatives d'opposition à la migration des filles constatées dans certaines communautés villageoises donnent paradoxalement comme résultat l'amplification du phénomène. Les filles malgré leur jeune âge semblent clairvoyantes dans leurs perceptions ; dans bien des cas, ce sont les mêmes perceptions qu'ont les parents ou les adultes. Ceci est d'autant vrai que si auparavant c'étaient les petites filles qui fuyaient en se cachant de leurs parents, aujourd'hui notre enquête nous a révélé que les filles ne se cachent plus ; les mamans sont au courant, ce sont souvent elles qui procurent le transport et beaucoup de pères sont même mis dans le secret. Comme si cela ne suffisait pas, les mères commencent à migrer en laissant leurs familles derrière elles, emboîtant le pas aux pères qui pensent souvent être seuls détenteurs du droit de migration. D'où une perception positive commune de la migration des filles, qu'elle soit avouée ou non, qui emporte notre conviction.

Quelles approches de migration des filles seraient-elles pertinentes aujourd'hui ?

Dès l'introduction de ce travail, nous avons évoqué la prédominance des logiques protectionnistes basées sur l'idée que les enfants en migration sont seulement vulnérables. Ce sont des logiques portées par des activistes dont le chercheur ne devra pas avoir forcément partager la vision, quand bien même elle a souvent bénéficié de légitimations scientifiques. Il faut noter en tout cas concernant les filles que les positions abolitionnistes – prolongement opérationnel des approches protectionnistes – longtemps adoptées, n'ont reçu paradoxalement comme réponse qu'un accroissement de la migration. Cela n'est-il pas un indicateur d'inefficacité de cette approche ? Comment penser que cette mobilité des filles est innocente, et que même si elle a une explication quelconque, celle-ci pourrait être ignorée ? L'histoire montre que les déplacements des hommes/femmes ont généralement comme mobile la recherche de meilleures conditions de vie. Pourquoi empêcher les filles – alors qu'on le permettrait aux autres – de migrer si c'est en cela qu'elles voient la solution aux adversités socio-économiques de leur environnement ? Oui, la protection des enfants ; ceci est un droit pour eux et un devoir pour ceux qui ont été à leur origine. Oui, ils sont vulnérables dans un monde où même les adultes n'ont pas la garantie de leur quiétude. Mais il nous semble également opportun d'accorder confiance aux ressources des filles (puis que c'est de cela qu'il s'agit) lorsque s'impose la migration. Il est à noter que dans plusieurs situations d'hostilité, les enfants ont fait la preuve de leur capacité, démontrant que le vieux principe pédagogique selon lequel l'homme/la femme s'ingénie en situation de problème ne saurait être l'exclusivité des adultes. Aussi bien dans les recherches scientifiques que pour l'action, la prise en compte de la capacité d'agir des enfants est vraisemblablement la nouvelle approche de la migration des filles vers laquelle il faut aller maintenant.

Conclusion

Cet article tente de mettre en relation l'expérience de vie migratoire et la capacité d'agir chez les filles domestiques appelées également aides ménagères. Il attire l'attention sur le fait que les filles, contrairement à ce qui se pense et se dit souvent, ont des forces, des stratégies de résistance afin de se sortir de leurs problèmes. L'article veut rapporter une vérité post-enquête qui commande d'atténuer les tableaux si souvent iniques de la migration et des travaux domestiques des filles qui sont présentés. La question de la migration, ajoutée à celle des services domestiques des filles est très complexe, parce qu'en pleine mutation sans être pour autant nouvelle. Des facteurs aussi nombreux que les crises économiques, la montée démographique avec l'urbanisation anarchique comme corollaire, les transformations dans les rôles et travaux des femmes, sont à prendre en compte.

Les filles domestiques rencontrent certainement des difficultés dans leur vie migratoire à Sikasso. Cependant, des changements notoires dans les conditions de vie et de travail des filles sont observables. Autant, certaines de leurs stratégies et capacités de révolution sont efficaces, autant un esprit de légitimation et d'approbation de leur migration laborieuse, ainsi que de bien-être – comparativement à leurs conditions de vie dans les milieux d'origine – domine les perceptions que rapportent leurs discours.

De tels changements et points de vue doivent être pris en compte dans les nouvelles recherches sur l'enfance africaine, et servir de moyens de rupture constructive avec des conceptions déjà au bout de leur limite. Car les discours des filles établissent clairement ces limites : les défenseurs de leurs droits, bras opérationnels des perspectives protectionnistes, sont plus visibles par leur nombre que par leurs résultats ; les mesures de dissuasion et même de répression aussi bien communautaires que juridiques de la migration des filles, ne sont célèbres que par leurs effets pervers, qui se constatent à l'accroissement du phénomène. Par conséquent, les efforts de compréhension, de maîtrise de la migration des filles et du développement même de l'enfant dans les sociétés africaines doivent être réorientés. Un recul critique doit être pris par rapport aux prescriptions normatives préétablies, distantes, voire idéalistes, au profit des leçons à tirer des contrecoups entre les enfants et leurs environnements.

Références

Binet, A. & T. Simon (1904-1905), 2004, *L'Élaboration du premier test d'intelligence,* L'Harmattan, Paris.

Camara, B., B. Traoré, B. E. Dicko & M. Sidibé, 2011, « Migration et tensions sociales dans le sud du Mali », *Rapport de recherche du Consortium for Development Partnership* (CDP), n° 9, CODESRIA, Dakar.

Coulibaly, B. & B. Dolo, 2007, *étude CAP sur le titre de voyage pour enfant de 0 à 18 ans tenant lieu d'autorisation de sortie,* Aide à l'enfance Canada/PACTE, Bamako

Dhondy, F., 1990, « Les enfants de l'immigration à Londres et leur pouvoir d'imaginaire », *Enfance,* tome 43, n° 1-2, p. 215-217.

Ebbinghaus, H., 1902, *Grundzüge der Psychologie,* 1. Band, 2. Theil, Veit & Co, Leipzig.

Gakuba, Théogène-Octave, 2000, « L'école : facteur de résilience des jeunes Rwandais réfugiés en France et en Suisse », in *L'éducation en débats : analyse comparée,* vol. 2, université de Genève.

Garmezy, N., 1985, « Stress Resistant Children : The Search for Protective Factors », dans *Recent Research in Developmental Psychopathology* (A Book Supplement to the *Journal of Child Psychology and Psychiatry 4),* sous la direction de J. Stevenson, Pergamon Press, Oxford, p. 213- 233.

Gesell, A., 1943, *Le jeune enfant dans la civilisation moderne*, PUF, Paris.

Grawitz, M., 2001, *Méthode des Sciences sociales*, 11ᵉ édition, Dalloz, Paris.

Hawley, D.R. & L. De Haan, 1996, « Toward a Definition of Family Resilience : Integrating Lifespan and Family Perspective », *Family Process, 35, 3*, p. 283-298.

Jacquemin, M., 2003, « Les petites bonnes de Côte d'Ivoire entre le village et la ville : l'exemple des jeunes migrantes du Nord-Est au travail à Abidjan », *Revue du GREJEM*, n° 2, p. 24-37. Disponible en ligne sur : http://horizon.documentation.ird.fr/exldoc/pleins_textes/pleins_textes_6/Attente/010033528.pdf. 20 septembre 2011.

Jacquemin, M., 2009, « Invisible Young Female Migrant Workers : « Little Domestics » in West Africa – Comparative Perspectives on Girls and Young Women's Work », Working Paper. Workshop Child and Youth Migration in West Africa. Research Progress and Implications for Policy, DRC on Migration, Globalisation and Poverty, University of Sussex/Centre for Migration Studies – University of Ghana, Accrawww. migrationdrc.org/news/.../Jaquemin%20Accra%20French.pdf.

Mali, RGPH, 1998, in Coulibaly B. & B. Dolo, 2006, *Étude d'approfondissement des connaissances sur les filles talibés dans les cercles de Sikasso et de Koutiala au Mali*, Save the Children.

Marlo, C., 2000, *Le modèle écologique du développement humain : conditions nécessaires de son utilité réelle*, Institut de recherche pour le développement social des jeunes, université de Montréal.

Microsoft ® Encarta ® 2009. © 1993-2008 Microsoft Corporation.

Morse, J. M., 2000, « Determining sample size », *Qualitative Health Reaserch* 10, p. 3-5.

Nöstlinger C. & F. Mathieu, 1990, « L'imaginaire dans la vie quotidienne des enfants », in *Enfance*, T. 43, n° 1-2, p. 219-222.

Organisation de l'unité africaine, 1990, *Charte africaine des droits et du bien-être de l'enfant.*

Piaget, J., 1970, *Psychologie et Pédagogie*, Gonthiers & Denoël, Paris.

Philippe, P. & C. Ky, 2003, Les filles domestiques au Burkina Faso : traite ou migration ? *Analyse de la migration laborieuse des enfants de la province du Sourou au Burkina Faso*, Terre des Hommes.

Rey, G., 2011, *Enfants migrants*, Institut international des droits de l'enfant (IDE), Sion. En ligne sur : http://www.childsrights.org/html/site_fr/

Save the Children Canada, Projet de lutte contre le trafic des enfants en Afrique de l'Ouest, 2006, *Que faisons-nous pour les filles et les garçons en migration ?*

Skinner, B., 1953, *Science and human behaviour*, Macmilland, New York.

Terrisse, B., F. Larose & M. L. Lefebvre, 2001, « La résilience : facteurs de risque et facteurs de protection dans l'environnement social et scolaire du jeune enfant », *Cahiers du Centre de recherche sur les formes d'éducation et d'enseignement*, numéro thématique, *École/Famille : Quelles médiations ? XIV*, p. 129-172.

Thorndike, E. L., 1903, *Educational Psychology*, Lemcke & Buechner, New York.

Unicef, 2005, *Principes directeurs pour la protection des droits des enfants victimes de la traite.*

14

Les causes du décrochage scolaire des enfants et leur réorientation au Bénin

Sandra Elvyre Loumedjinon

Introduction

Durant l'année 2007, le gouvernement béninois a entamé une réflexion pour appréhender les implications de l'abandon scolaire sur le niveau d'adaptation de l'élève après sa sortie du cycle scolaire. Les données sur le taux d'abandon à travers l'annuaire statistique du ministère de l'Enseignement de base montrent que le taux d'abandon augmente à partir du CE1. Il tournait autour de 9 pour cent en 2000-2001. Le phénomène semble plus accentué chez les garçons avant le cours moyen. Les recherches ayant abordé les facteurs influençant l'abandon ont fait émerger un peu plus d'une dizaine de variables pertinentes, à savoir le manque d'intérêt pour l'école, le manque de moyens financiers, le manque d'aide à domicile, la peur du maître, les fournitures et frais de scolarité impayés, l'école buissonnière, le nombre de redoublements, les activités extrascolaires, les problèmes de santé de l'enfant, la cantine scolaire et la langue d'enseignement (Sawadogo & Soura 2002). Certains auteurs (Koffi, Kouakou & Koné 2002) rapportent que 60 pour cent des enseignants évoquent le problème de moyens matériels ou financiers, mais ils ajoutent le faible suivi familial, les longues distances (17,4 pour cent), les problèmes de restauration (11,2 pour cent).

La question centrale qui guide notre étude s'articule autour de la préoccupation : « Quelles sont la disposition et la stratégie adoptées par l'enfant béninois issu du système scolaire face à son exclusion ? » L'objectif principal est d'analyser les causes de l'abandon scolaire chez les enfants. Un diagnostic des implications comportementales de l'enfant béninois suite à son décrochage (abandon) scolaire sera avancé : il s'agit de comprendre le niveau de vulnérabilité de ces enfants ayant abandonné l'école, en vue d'analyser les sources de leurs décisions se rapportant à leur réinsertion, et de décrire leurs stratégies de réinsertion. L'enjeu de cette recherche qualitative est de faire ressortir les déterminants de l'adaptabilité de l'élève à ses nouvelles conditions de vie après sa sortie du cycle normal de scolarité.

Le cadre de cette investigation est la ville d'Abomey-Calavi, située à vingt kilomètres de la capitale économique Cotonou. Cette ville a été retenue à cause de la pluralité de sa composition démographique. Elle est représentative en ce sens qu'on y retrouve beaucoup d'enfants ayant abandonné l'école, pour des causes variées. Des entretiens avec dix enfants « décrochés » de l'école béninoise ont été conduits selon les principes de la saturation à l'aide d'un guide d'entretien. Une analyse de contenu des discours obtenus lors des entretiens fut effectuée par le logiciel WeftQDA.

Niveau de vulnérabilité du décrocheur scolaire béninois : facteurs familiaux et institutionnels

Parmi les causes conduisant au décrochage scolaire de l'enfant béninois, il ressort nettement que la non-satisfaction des besoins physiologiques est une dimension critique de la rupture entre l'enfant et l'école. Les interrogations auprès des répondants ont permis de faire ressortir un manque de satisfaction de ces besoins humains primaires. « *Je ne trouvais pas à manger* », raconte Salim, un garçon de quinze ans ; cette position est confortée par les propos de Rodolphe (garçon du même âge) « *Je mangeais à peine à ma faim* ».

Un autre point saillant de l'analyse de contenu des répondants se situe au niveau des problèmes structurels liés à l'habitat et à la famille. De nombreux travaux soulignent le rôle des facteurs familiaux comme agent déstructurant de la présence de l'élève à l'école (Bachman, Green & Wirtanen 1971). Toute instabilité ou démission des parents rend vulnérable l'enfant dans sa qualité pérenne d'écolier. Ainsi, parmi les autres causes de son décrochage, Salim désigne l'absence d'« *électricité* ». La distance de la maison à l'école est aussi un facteur réducteur dans le maintien de l'enfant à l'école comme le mentionne Rodolphe, qui évoque un « *quartier très loin de mon école…* » La distance de l'école du lieu d'habitation constitue donc une dimension notable dans le décrochage de l'enfant béninois, tout comme l'emplacement de la maison où vit l'enfant : « *On vivait dans les Bas-fonds de Cotonou […] l'inondation de l'année passée a englouti tous mes cahiers* » (Arnold, garçon âgé de douze ans).

Dans ce contexte, la vulnérabilité de l'enfant béninois va plus loin que les conditions de logement. Le changement climatique ou les opérations d'assainissement constituent des variables auxquelles doit faire face l'enfant béninois.

Les propos de Rodolphe, qui déclare : « *tellement battu, j'ai décidé d'abandonner l'école* » ou ceux de Chantal, fille de seize ans qui rapporte : « *je sortais avec mes professeurs qui me donnaient des notes en échange de mon sexe...* », amènent vite à s'interroger sur la question de l'éthique dans l'enseignement scolaire béninois et de la conduite à l'école.

Ces facteurs, que nous caractérisons d'institutionnels avec Janosz (Janosz 2000:111), n'ont pas été développés par lui sous cet angle – en effet, selon lui, le décrochage est fortement lié à la communauté.

Or l'école qui est une institution d'éducation programmée, répond dans son développement à des règles d'éthiques que ces acteurs ne peuvent négocier. La démarche de harcèlement et de développement du droit de cuissage équivaut au piétinement de cette éthique. Ainsi, l'existence de rapports sexuels entre l'enseignant et l'enseigné déconstruit les rapports d'autorité et de gouvernance liés à l'enseignement en milieu scolaire et favorise en outre le développement de pratiques qui accélèrent le décrochage scolaire chez les élèves filles, les plus vulnérables.

L'enfant qui se retrouve piégé dans un cercle vicieux exclut davantage de son schéma représentationnel l'idée selon laquelle l'école est un transformateur social, reproducteur manifeste de la société, car il y retrouve des écarts de conduites majeures et décevantes. À ce stade, rien ne l'oblige à se maintenir dans le circuit scolaire, à cause du manque de confiance en l'institution scolaire elle-même.

L'âge et le redoublement

L'enfant béninois nourrit un sentiment de culpabilité et de résilience sur sa capacité de réaction face aux difficultés rencontrées lors de son parcours scolaire. L'âge et le redoublement intègrent une très forte corrélation et reviennent constamment dans les discours des répondants. Dans cette logique, un garçon de quinze ans construit une forte interdépendance entre la reprise d'une classe et l'âge, dimension discrétionnaire, non manipulable : « *le rendement était mauvais, j'ai dû abandonner* ». « *Arrivée en 3e, j'ai échoué trois fois au BEPC et mon âge était avancé, donc j'ai abandonné l'école* », a répondu une fille de seize ans.

Dans ces conditions, il devient impérieux psychologiquement pour l'enfant avancé en âge, de prendre une décision et de savoir si oui ou non, il désire continuer l'école. En effet, le fait de se retrouver dans une classe où les camarades sont plus jeunes que soi entraîne une fracture psychologique et un sentiment de frustration très difficile à digérer dans le cas béninois. Le droit d'aînesse étant de rigueur dans la société béninoise, il s'ensuit clairement que le plus âgé considère que le plus jeune mérite d'être dans une classe (sociale) inférieure à lui. D'où une tendance manifeste à considérer le plus jeune comme étant celui qui doit apprendre auprès du plus âgé. Se retrouver dans la même classe que ce dernier renforce, selon l'aîné, la perte de son autorité sur le plus jeune. L'honneur est retrouvé lorsqu'il abandonne la classe où se trouve le plus jeune, et décide d'entreprendre dans une aventure méconnue par le plus jeune : ce qui revêt une dimension mystique de supériorité pour le premier. Il conserve ainsi toute son autorité en adoptant un comportement de sacrifice suprême, celui de résilience, qui traduit tout simplement sa capacité de prendre une décision – toujours en face du plus jeune.

Au terme de notre analyse sur la vulnérabilité observée, il apparaît judicieux d'approfondir notre réflexion sur la prise de décision vis-à-vis de l'action de reconversion.

Prise de décision pour la reconversion

Selon Daniel K. Schneider, « la décision est un processus de résolution de problème qui met en œuvre des connaissances de nature très variée ». Partant de la « *décision simple* », Schneider indique qu'elle correspond à une classe de « *problème relativement bien défini* » :

« Un problème existe, si :
– Le décideur perçoit un état interne ou externe non désiré A.
– L'état de départ A non désiré doit être transformé dans un état de but B.
– Le décideur ne sait pas au départ, comment parcourir le « chemin » qui va du point de départ A vers le point de solution B. » (Schneider 1994)

Partant du modèle de Schneider nous observons que la prise de décision effectuée par le décrocheur béninois part d'une perception de son état primaire, la situation d'insatisfaction, qui le conduit à une volonté de changement.

Par insatisfaction, la présente recherche, qui met l'accent sur l'analyse de contenu, n'entend pas un niveau que les techniques de mesure d'attitude permettent de comprendre, mais une dimension des perceptions des répondants : « *Cette activité ne me plaisait pas trop parce que salissante. J'ai dû commencer à voler pour subvenir à mes besoins* », dit un garçon de quinze ans. L'assoupissement d'un désir d'apprendre y trouve également son fondement : « *Pour subvenir à ma faim j'ai commencé à voler les livres, l'argent ou toutes choses qui pouvaient me faire un revenu* ». Tout s'oriente alors vers une volonté de transformation d'un état en un état plus raffiné, plus accompli.

Volonté de changement

Les recherches de Janosz et le Blanc (1996) ont corroboré les travaux sur la pyramide de Maslow concernant les différents paliers de satisfaction des besoins humains dans la réalisation de l'épanouissement. Néanmoins cette théorie des besoins, affiche plusieurs faiblesses. Elle oublie les stratégies individuelles et collectives, les changements sociaux et les mutations structurelles permettant l'expression d'une revendication. Or ce type de mutation s'observe clairement dans le discours recueilli auprès d'un garçon de dix-huit ans : « *Je ne voulais plus continuer l'enseignement long, mais apprendre un métier pour vite gagner ma vie était ma préoccupation. Je dis à mon père que je veux faire l'informatique* ». La volonté de changement, de transformation du statut, est l'expression d'un ras-le-bol du passé, qui crée une fracture avec la volonté de réalisation des satisfactions mesurée par l'existence d'un projet de vie non réaliste au vu des conditions du présent.

L'existence d'un modèle sur la qualité de vie

La thématique de l'abandon de l'école fait généralement référence à la notion de qualité de vie. En effet, de nombreux travaux ont permis de comprendre que le rêve, la projection dans un modèle de vie ou dans une représentation sociale de la réussite, constitue l'un des fils majeurs de la décision de décrocher et même de la réinsertion dans la vie active. À l'évidence, elle constitue la dimension principale de gouvernance de la stratégie de reprise de confiance en soi après le décrochage scolaire, dans la réinsertion. Cette attitude donne de l'espoir lorsqu'on l'a permise : « *J'avais toujours rêvé d'être esthéticienne, donc j'ai demandé à l'un de mes professeurs, qui était un copain, de me payer la formation* » (fille de seize ans). Une autre fille de dix-huit ans explique : « *J'ai décidé de faire le « bonnage » c'est-à-dire aide ménagère. Avec l'économie je me suis payé l'école de la restauration* ».

Ainsi, la reprise de la confiance naît d'une volonté manifeste de réalisation d'un projet personnel de vie affirmant que l'école n'est pas la seule voie de réussite sociale ; mais elle reste déterminée par une qualité de vie qui émane, pour le décrocheur, d'un noyau représentationnel de la réussite. Cette dimension est étudiée dans les travaux relatifs au bien-être, au bonheur qui apporte la satisfaction et garantit la qualité de vie (Bradburn 1969). Il s'agit toutefois d'un sentiment peu stable, soumis à des fluctuations d'humeur. Le bonheur se distingue de la satisfaction par son caractère spontané et variable d'un jour sur l'autre. Nous en concluons que la quête permanente d'un modèle de vie allié, soit à un personnage social, soit à une représentation, conforte le décrocheur scolaire béninois dans sa décision de suivre un modèle de vie adapté à une trajectoire de vie dont aurait bénéficié leur personnage.

Sources de décision en vue de l'action

Nous allons maintenant nous attarder sur les sources de la décision des décrocheurs scolaires en vue d'une réinsertion sociale. À partir de ce que nous ont dit les répondants, nous avons regroupé les discours en différentes catégories à savoir :

- L'influence de la communauté ;
- la recherche de l'autonomie immédiate ;
- le traumatisme social ;
- et la volonté de réaliser un projet de vie.

L'influence de la communauté

Suivant le paradigme socioconstructiviste, toute activité individuelle émane d'un construit social. Nous pouvons ainsi postuler que la décision d'agir en vue d'une transformation du statut social émane avant tout de la société à laquelle appartient le décrocheur. En effet, la volonté de transformation du statut est renforcée par la présence de discours tendant à modifier le noyau stable de la représentation que le décrocheur se fait de sa propre condition sociale. L'un des répondants affirme ainsi l'influence exercée par sa famille élargie dans sa décision de reconversion et de rattrapage social après sa faillite du cursus scolaire. « *Mon oncle m'a proposé de le suivre pour travailler dans son atelier de mécanique* », raconte ce garçon de quinze ans.

La recherche de l'autonomie immédiate

La recherche d'une autonomie constitue également une condition latente de l'apparition de la prise de décision par le décrocheur béninois. Très présentes dans l'analyse de contenu du corpus de Rumberger (1987), la recherche de l'autonomie, de l'indépendance financière et sociale, et la volonté de se réaliser socialement se retrouvent ici également : « *Je ne voulais plus continuer l'enseignement long mais apprendre un métier pour vite gagner ma vie. C'était ma préoccupation. J'ai dit à mon père que je veux faire l'informatique* », explique un garçon de dix-huit ans.

L'autonomie est souvent difficile à atteindre dans un processus construit africain, dans la mesure où les usages de la société africaine font de l'individualisme une pratique asociale et difficilement accessible aux agents sociaux. En conséquence, toute décision qui n'a pas obtenu l'aval de la communauté revêt un caractère rebelle et non conforme à la logique sociale. C'est cette réflexion anthropologique qui distingue l'autonomie africaniste de l'autonomisation occidentale. En ce sens, dans la dimension africaine, l'autonomisation reste parcellaire et souvent dominée par le contrôle social.

Le traumatisme social

Le traumatisme perçu par le décrocheur social est apprécié par la communauté comme un laxisme aggravant de la part du décrocheur (Nordgren, Banas & MacDonald 2011). Considéré comme paresseux, le décrocheur scolaire extériorise auprès de sa communauté l'image d'un gaspilleur de ressources dont l'investissement financier et social n'aboutira jamais. Conscient de cette question sociale, le décrocheur se voit alors dans l'obligation de se racheter auprès de la société par l'affrontement de son propre traumatisme social. « *Tellement battu à l'école, j'ai abandonné et cherché une nouvelle activité…* »

Le traumatisme social, constitue donc un défi majeur du décrocheur scolaire dans la mesure où même s'il introduit le décrochage il peut devenir l'élément facilitateur de rattrapage social.

La volonté de réaliser un projet de vie

Nous avons pu, enfin, observer la dimension majeure prise par le projet de vie – qui articule les faits et gestes – comme source de décision. Nous l'avons notamment observé à travers le propos déjà mentionné d'une fille de seize ans : « *J'avais toujours rêvé d'être esthéticienne* », ou celui d'un garçon de douze ans : « *Je lui avais dit que je voulais aller à l'école jusqu'à être un ministre* ».

Enjeux de la réinsertion de l'élève décrocheur béninois

L'enjeu de la réinsertion de l'élève décrocheur présente trois aspects : économique, social et moral.

La nécessité d'acquérir une indépendance économique relève d'un défi personnel. Longtemps considéré comme un gouffre financier dont on n'entretient plus l'espoir d'un retour sur l'investissement, le décrocheur scolaire doit rapidement entrer dans la vie active afin de retrouver sa place économique – comme en témoigne le discours de Rodolphe (âgé de quinze ans) : « *Avec cette somme, j'ai pu ouvrir un bar et je suis le gérant.* »

L'enjeu social de la réinsertion se trouve dans la volonté de se faire reconnaître par ses pairs et membres de la communauté ; l'enfant est capable de surmonter le traumatisme social dont il a longtemps été l'objet, et qui l'a obligé à sortir de l'école. C'est alors une démarche de réintégration dans le schéma de la confiance placée en lui, et qui suscite une modification du noyau représentationnel qu'il avait de lui : « *Après ma sortie de l'école, j'ai fait « le bonnage » qui m'a payé la formation pour devenir la cuisinière d'un grand hôtel de Cotonou.* »

L'enjeu moral enfin, est la satisfaction que le décrocheur scolaire retire de la réalisation de sa réorientation, qui exprime sa capacité de dépassement face à une situation qui l'a avili socialement auparavant : « *L'esthétique… Ce métier est devenu une passion* » déclare Chantal, âgée de seize ans.

Conclusion

L'abandon ou le décrochage scolaire est un phénomène grandissant au Bénin. Il nous revenait d'élaborer un diagnostic de ses causes mais aussi de cerner l'adaptabilité de l'enfant béninois après sa sortie précoce du système scolaire. Les résultats indiquent que cette adaptabilité repose sur les décisions et les stratégies de reconversion. Les stratégies émanent avant tout du décrocheur scolaire et de la société dans laquelle il évolue, mais également de sa volonté de surmonter le traumatisme social l'ayant conduit au décrochage scolaire.

Bibliographie

Bachman, J. G., S. Green & I. D. Wirtanen, 1971, *Youth in transition : vol. 3. Dropping out : Problem or symptom ?*, Ann Arbor, University of Michigan.

Bradburn, N. M., 1969, *The structure of psychological well-being*, Chicago, Aldine.

Janosz, M., 2000, « L'abandon scolaire chez les adolescents : perspective nord-américaine », *Enjeux*, 122, p. 105-127.

Janosz, M. & M. Le Blanc, 1996, « Pour une vision intégrative des facteurs reliés à l'abandon scolaire », *Revue canadienne de psychoéducation*, 25(1), p. 61-88.

Koffi D., A. Kouakou & R. Koné, 2002, « Accès et maintien des élèves en Côte d'Ivoire et en Gambie : Côte d'Ivoire », in *Perspectives transnationales sur l'éducation de base en Afrique Centrale et de l'Ouest, accès, qualité et participation communautaire*, Rocare-Usaid, p. 11-33.

Nordgren, L., K. Banas & G. MacDonald, 2011, « Empathy gaps for social pain : why people underestimate the pain of social suffering », *Journal of personality and social psychology*, vol. 100(1), p. 120-128.

Rumberger, R. W., 1987, « High school dropouts : A review of issues and evidence », *Review of Educational Research* 57, p. 101-121.

Sawadogo, J. B. & A. B. Soura, 2002, *L'abandon précoce en milieu scolaire : analyse et recherche de modèle explicatif*, Rocare, Ouagadougou.

Schneider, D., 1994, *Modélisation de la démarche du décideur politique dans la perspective de l'intelligence artificielle*, thèse présentée pour l'obtention du doctorat SES, université de Genève.

15

Impact de l'incarcération d'un parent sur la vie de l'enfant au Cameroun

Hippolyte Héli Abanda

Introduction

L'incarcération est un moment vécu avec beaucoup de tristesse dans les familles dont un membre en éprouve la dure réalité. Celle-ci n'est pas sans conséquences pour l'enfant du détenu, victime de préjudices portant sur son développement à la fois mental, émotionnel et physique, et même sur son devenir dans la société. Cette étude est une entrée dans l'univers de l'enfant du détenu au Cameroun afin de comprendre et relever l'influence de l'absence du parent incarcéré, influence avec laquelle vit cet enfant. La réflexion sur la vie de l'enfant du détenu ne suscite pas toujours un grand intérêt de la part de la société, qui ne fait pas de distinction entre la faute commise par le parent et l'enfant innocent. Lorsqu'on parle des enfants vulnérables, celui du détenu est dans l'oubli total ; pourtant il appartient à un groupe qui souffre en silence. Parfois, lorsque la question de l'enfant du détenu est évoquée, c'est sans lui accorder grande importance, voire sans considération aucune, car il est victime d'une stigmatisation sociale liée au rejet.

Notre réflexion pose ainsi la problématique de l'enfant du détenu dans nos sociétés en général, et au Cameroun en particulier. Notamment celle de sa vie après l'incarcération de son parent. L'image que la société camerounaise a de lui est étroitement liée à celle de son géniteur. Des enquêtes menées sur le terrain révèlent que l'entourage de ce type d'enfant pense qu'il n'est capable de rien sinon de ressembler à son parent incarcéré. En considérant ce regard social, ce jugement subjectif animé par la volonté de rejet, la présente étude s'interroge sur l'influence de l'absence du parent sur la vie de son enfant et les différentes stratégies que celui-ci met en place pour pouvoir surmonter les difficultés liées à l'incarcération de son parent. Deux hypothèses deviennent nécessaires à la compréhension de la vie de l'enfant victime de l'incarcération de son parent : la vie de l'enfant est influencée par l'incarcération de son parent. Face à cette incarcération, l'enfant développe des stratégies pour surmonter le rejet dont il est victime. Ces hypothèses permettent de clarifier la situation des enfants des détenus. Pour les tester, le cadre théorique de notre recherche s'appuiera sur la psychologie sociale, qui s'intéresse « à l'étude scientifique du comportement social de l'homme, analysant aussi bien les composantes psychologiques des phénomènes que leur dimension sociale […] et qui permet de prendre en compte aussi bien les facteurs individuels que contextuels, sociétaux et culturels » (Baggio 2008:13).

À partir d'une approche opportuniste – qui combine plusieurs théories – notre travail se veut une analyse systémique multiniveau qui intègre différents aspects de la réalité de l'impact de l'incarcération d'un parent sur la vie de son enfant. Nos données empiriques, telles que le questionnaire et les entretiens, nous permettront de donner la parole aux enfants dont l'âge varie entre dix et dix-huit ans et à ceux qui sont âgés de vingt et vingt et un ans – dont la majorité n'est pas souvent efficiente dans tous les cas – qui malgré leur jeunesse, ont connu des influences dans leur vie en tant qu'enfant.

Notre enquête a été menée à Yaoundé au Cameroun pour des raisons de proximité géographique et de facilité, car nous y résidons. Nous avons délibérément opté pour une approche combinée, qui intègre à la fois les approches quantitative et qualitative. La rencontre avec les enfants s'est déroulée dans le cadre familial, pour la collecte des données.

Après la perception sociale de l'incarcération, qui nous mènera à la vie influencée de l'enfant du détenu, seront présentés ses droits et ses besoins spécifiques et une analyse des différentes stratégies qu'il développe pour surmonter ses difficultés. Une conclusion, loin de prétendre faire une étude entière de la problématique de l'enfant du détenu, apporte quelques recommandations adressées à ceux qui vivent autour de lui.

La perception sociale de l'incarcération : punition et marginalisation

Dans l'organisation de la société, les prisons sont construites dans l'optique de punir ceux qui sont en conflit avec la loi. C'est donc une forme de punition que la société met en place pour différencier les personnes en phase avec la loi et celles qui sont en déphasage avec celle-ci. La prison est ainsi perçue comme un lieu de correction, un lieu où l'état exerce son pouvoir. On tolère d'ailleurs tous les discours sur les prisonniers à condition qu'ils soient tenus par d'autres. Ce qui est intolérable, c'est un prisonnier qui parle à la première personne de ce qu'il vit (Foucault 1971).

Dans une perspective sociohistorique, relevons que cette idée remonte à nombre d'années avant la nôtre car dans certaines sociétés, il était question de se débarrasser de celui qui était fautif, soit en l'isolant dans le village, soit en le chassant et des personnes étaient chargées de le conduire à la frontière. Il apparaît que la prison est non seulement une forme de punition, mais aussi une raison de marginalisation de la société. Le prisonnier est un être à part qui perd l'estime de toute la société. C'est un être souillé qui n'a pas droit de cité, qui perd même ses droits naturels comme celui de vivre avec ses enfants, les voir. Il subit les préjugés et la discrimination de la société qui entretient envers lui des impressions négatives, un comportement négatif, le rejette (Baggio 2008).

Actuellement, au Cameroun, les enfants n'ont pas le droit d'entrer à la prison régionale de Yaoundé pour une visite à leur parent ; les autorités avancent plusieurs raisons pour le justifier. L'incarcération est donc une forme d'exclusion sociale plus ou moins légale ; celle-ci, en plus de la solitude du prisonnier, détruit ses liens familiaux surtout ceux qu'il entretient avec ses enfants. Dès qu'il est incarcéré, le parent n'espère plus voir ses enfants, parler avec eux, leur marquer son affection (Badinter 2008). Tout ceci influence profondément l'enfant qui est attaché au prisonnier par la fibre parentale, très importante pour son développement.

Enfant de détenu : une vie influencée

Faite de souffrances psychologiques, matérielles, de stigmatisation, de honte, la vie de l'enfant du détenu est un chemin de croix capable de le déséquilibrer. Pierrette et Viviane, des enfants de détenu nous ont accordé des entretiens qui le confirment.

> Pierrette – Notre famille paternelle a trouvé que notre mère avait tué son mari et notre oncle par le biais de sa fortune a tout manigancé jusqu'au tribunal au point où notre mère a été condamnée à 20 ans de prison. Nous n'avions rien à dire ; d'ailleurs nous étions encore tout petits et nos oncles et tantes nous interdisaient de rendre visite à notre mère sous peine de bastonnade. Après nous nous sommes rebellés et avons décidé de rendre visite à notre mère en prison même si on devait subir la bastonnade. Actuellement, nos petits frères sont dans un autre village où notre grande sœur est en mariage. Quant à moi, je vis avec mon petit ami ici à Yaoundé et je ne vais plus à l'école pourtant j'ai un baccalauréat en série Industrie d'habillement. Je veux poursuivre mes études mais il n'y a pas de moyens. Notre famille maternelle a dit qu'elle ne se mêlait pas de cette histoire sans raisons évidentes, car elle n'a pas une personne influente qui puisse prendre les devants.

> L'incarcération de notre mère nous a beaucoup influencés. Tout le monde nous a abandonnés ; pas d'aide financière, pas de conseils ; seules les personnes de dehors essayaient de nous supporter, pas d'amour. Notre mère nous demande seulement de beaucoup prier.

En écoutant Pierrette, on note qu'effectivement l'incarcération de leur mère laisse des séquelles sur les enfants, et le comportement de la famille confirme l'idée selon laquelle la prison signifie rejet, exclusion – et cela influence remarquablement les enfants qui vivent le stress dans sa dimension psychosociale (Moser 1995).

Le deuxième entretien que nous avons mené s'est passé avec Viviane[1], 20 ans mais qui lors de l'arrestation de son père était un peu plus jeune.

> Viviane – Notre père est allé en prison pour des raisons que je ne veux pas évoquer avec vous s'il vous plaît. Après son incarcération, notre mère a été victime d'une grave maladie que l'on dit mystique car on a déjà fait le tour des médecins et des guérisseurs. Ayant vu cela, il n'y avait personne pour s'occuper de mes petits frères et de mon père en prison à qui on devait apporter au moins de quoi manger. J'ai abandonné mes études et j'ai commencé à vendre les beignets avec du haricot pour supporter la famille. Avec cette activité, je paye la scolarité de mes trois petits frères et sœurs et j'envoie à manger à mon père qui heureusement va sortir bientôt car il a été condamné pour cinq ans et il lui reste deux semaines. L'incarcération de notre père a eu beaucoup d'influence sur notre vie ; mes petits frères sont difficilement encadrés car je ne peux pas faire tout ça à la fois. Nos familles maternelles et paternelles ne nous regardent pas sous prétexte que notre père ne rendait visite à personne lorsqu'il était dehors et avait les moyens. L'absence de notre père, je peux le dire est une perte pour nous car moi par exemple j'ai arrêté les cours et l'éducation de mes petits frères n'est pas assurée car notre mère est malade.

L'entretien avec Viviane nous montre l'impact de l'incarcération d'un parent. Elle a abandonné les cours pour s'occuper de ses frères et de ses parents. Elle est devenue ainsi un « leader démocratique » de sa famille et a utilisé ses caractéristiques personnelles, comme l'intelligence et le dynamisme (Lewin, Lippit & White cités par Baggio 2008:35). Personne ne s'intéresse à eux pour des raisons peu évidentes, preuve que l'enfant du détenu a peu de place dans les cœurs et qu'il peut même payer pour les agissements jugés négatifs de son parent.

Moyennant un questionnaire, nous avons également vérifié les domaines dans lesquels la vie de l'enfant du détenu est influencée. Nous avons soumis un questionnaire à 50 enfants qui ont un parent en prison. Ceux-ci ont un âge compris entre dix et dix-huit ans. Cette tranche a été retenue parce que nous avions l'assurance qu'elle comprend le principe de réponses sans aide aux questions.

Au sein de la famille

Tableau 1 : distribution des enfants selon l'affection de leur parent avant son incarcération

Le parent donnait de l'affection	Effectif	Pourcentage
Oui	30	60
Parfois	19	38
Non	01	02
Total	50	100

Sources : questionnaire

Tableau 2 : distribution des enfants selon le comportement des membres de la famille envers eux

Comportement des membres de la famille	Effectif	Pourcentage
Bon	3	6
Passable	18	36
Mauvais	29	58
Total	50	100

Source : questionnaire

Des enfants interrogés, 58 pour cent pensent que le comportement des membres de la famille est mauvais et 36 pour cent le trouvent passable. Cette absence d'affection a des répercussions sur leur vie surtout que 60 pour cent d'entre eux déclarent que leurs parents leur accordaient de l'affection et 38 pour cent bénéficiaient parfois de cette affection. Le seul enfant qui estime ne pas avoir bénéficié de l'affection de son parent en liberté assure que, malgré cette situation, il préfère voir son père à la maison plutôt qu'en prison ; déclinant ainsi un aspect de sa personnalité extravertie car il est sensible (Jung cité par Dortier 2009) à la situation que vit son parent.

À l'école

L'influence de l'incarcération d'un parent sur la vie de son enfant se ressent à deux niveaux. D'abord celui des résultats scolaires comme le démontre le tableau ci-dessous.

Tableau 3 : Distribution des enfants selon leurs résultats à l'école

Résultats à l'école	Effectif	Pourcentage
Bons	10	20
Passables	22	44
Mauvais	18	36
Total	50	100

Source : questionnaire

Les mauvais résultats à l'école proviennent de raisons multiples :

- suivi mal assuré par les tuteurs ;
- absence de répétiteur ;
- exécution des tâches domestiques de manière permanente ;
- absence du matériel didactique ;
- déconcentration liée aux histoires concernant l'incarcération du parent ;
- rappel de leur statut par leur tuteur ;
- manque d'accompagnement psychosocial.

Toutes ces causes sont le fait de l'incarcération du parent dans la mesure où les tuteurs les plus généreux accordent le minimum qui parfois se résume à des cahiers, la scolarité, les stylos, les crayons. Les éléments importants qui constituent la vie scolaire d'un élève ne sont pas toujours réunis, surtout sur le plan psychologique et mental. Les besoins primordiaux, sociaux et de sécurité (Maslow, cité par Dortier 2009) de ces enfants de détenus ne sont pas assurés par les tuteurs et cela justifie l'absence de performance à l'école.

Ensuite, l'autre aspect de la vie de cet enfant qui à l'école subit l'influence de l'incarcération de son parent est sa relation avec ses camarades, comme nous le confirme le tableau.

Tableau 4 : distribution des enfants selon que leurs camarades savent que leur parent est en prison

Les camarades savent que le parent est en prison	Effectif	Pourcentage
Oui	11	22
Non	39	78
Total	**50**	**100**

Source : Questionnaire

Pour leur stabilité morale, une large majorité de ces enfants préfèrent que leurs camarades ne soient pas au courant de la situation de leur parent pour des multiples raisons :
- la honte ;
- la différence du regard porté sur eux ;
- l'isolement ;
- la moquerie.

Ils ont peur du rejet car leurs camarades, qui se comportent comme des racistes, les repoussent et les considèrent comme des intrus (Baggio 2008:39-40).

Tableau 5 : distribution des enfants selon qu'ils ont honte d'avoir leur parent en prison

Ils ont honte d'avoir un parent en prison	Effectif	Pourcentage
Oui	39	78
Non	2	4
Parfois	9	18
Total	**50**	**100**

Source : questionnaire

Ce fort taux de pourcentage du « oui » se justifie par le fait que ces enfants ont de la peine à accepter cette réalité et vivre avec elle. Celle-ci leur impose une ligne de conduite qui les prédispose à agir ou avoir des comportements qui leur sont spécifiques. Cet aspect confirme la théorie de Jean-Paul Sartre sur le Regard lorsqu'il dit qu'Autrui est ce qui nous définit le mieux.

Au sein de la société

L'enfant du détenu subit le regard social, qui se fige à l'idée de « tel père, tel fils » ou encore « telle mère, telle fille ». La société ne fait pas de différence entre le parent détenu et son enfant qui, pourtant, est un être à part, différent de son parent. Elle se comporte comme si l'enfant était le principal responsable de la faute commise par le parent pour se retrouver en prison. Le regard social met les enfants des détenus dans une poubelle, la referme pour qu'on n'en parle pas car ils n'ont pas voix au chapitre. Ils sont considérés par la société comme des « brebis galeuses » (Baggio 2008:61-62), des membres socialement indésirables.

Les dirigeants également ne considèrent pas ce groupe d'enfants comme des enfants vulnérables. L'attention est tournée vers les autres couches, telles que les enfants de la rue, les orphelins, les handicapés… Pierrette, au cours de l'entretien mené avec elle, dit « *tout le monde nous a abandonnés ; pas d'aides financières, pas de conseils* » ; elle souligne aussi que les personnes qui s'intéressent à leur sort « essayent » de les « supporter ». Cette position, ce regard social, influence de manière négative l'enfant du détenu qui se sent exclu et rejeté par une société qui ne le reconnaît pas dans sa souffrance psychologique ; pourtant c'est un enfant, qui a aussi ses droits et des besoins spécifiques qui doivent être pris en compte.

Les enfants sont deux fois victimes : d'une part ils sont séparés de leurs parents incarcérés, et d'autre part, ils souffrent eux-mêmes de la stigmatisation du délit, de la honte et du rejet (Wolleswinkel 2002).

Iko'o (2008) fait une analyse froide de la situation en général et dans la société camerounaise en particulier. Elle soutient que les enfants des détenus sont victimes de stigmatisation, de raillerie et de maltraitance. Une fois leur parent incarcéré, ils reçoivent plusieurs étiquettes marginales et subissent des moqueries ; ce sont des enfants à la vulnérabilité établie. Dans notre échantillon, 11 d'entre eux dont la tranche d'âge oscille entre seize et dix-huit ans sont traités de domestiques dans les familles qui leur font la « faveur » de les recueillir après l'incarcération de l'un de leurs parents. Ils sont même envoyés au village – car la situation de leur parent est une souillure qui ne leur donne pas le privilège de rester en ville mais plutôt chez les grands-parents au village. Parfois, ce sont des enfants qui se contentent des restes de nourriture, qui sont envoyés à l'école dans une écurie, contrairement aux autres enfants de la maison d'accueil. Iko'o (2008) constate que ce sont des enfants qui n'ont que des devoirs et pas des droits ; ce sont des parias de la société qui sont repoussés par leurs camarades à l'école sous le fallacieux prétexte qu'ils vont leur transmettre la condamnation de leur parent.

Droits et besoins spécifiques des enfants des détenus

Les droits de l'enfant du détenu

L'enfant du détenu est un enfant à part entière au même titre que tous les autres ; les droits de l'enfant sont aussi les siens. Trois articles de la Convention internationale des droits de l'enfant (CIDE) des Nations unies retiennent l'attention à leur sujet.

Article 3

Dans toutes les décisions qui concernent les enfants, qu'elles soient le fait des institutions publiques ou privées de protection sociale, des tribunaux, des autorités administratives ou des organes législatifs, l'intérêt supérieur de l'enfant doit être une considération primordiale.

Cet article est l'un des plus importants de la Convention car il interpelle toutes les sphères de prise de décision à s'incliner sur la problématique de la place de l'enfant en général, y compris celui du détenu ; d'ailleurs, il place « l'intérêt supérieur de l'enfant » au-dessus de tout et comme priorité.

Article 9

Le droit de l'enfant séparé de ses deux parents ou de l'un d'eux d'entretenir régulièrement des rapports personnels et des contacts avec ses deux parents, sauf si cela est contraire à l'intérêt supérieur de l'enfant.

Ici l'on appelle les États à éviter toute séparation de l'enfant de ses parents ; à part si le délit commis concerne l'enfant. Or en ce qui concerne les enfants des détenus, cette séparation est évidente soit du fait de la justice soit du « partage » que les membres des familles font des enfants, car souvent le parent resté en liberté n'a pas les moyens nécessaires pour assurer la survie des enfants. Il « bénéficie » ainsi de la solidarité africaine qui renvoie à un type de valeur lié à la tradition (Schwartz 1992). Malheureusement, l'avis de l'enfant du détenu est ignoré (Brown 2001) comme nous le prouve l'entretien avec Pierrette. Généralement cette séparation ne tient pas compte de « l'intérêt supérieur de l'enfant » du détenu qui, selon certains tuteurs, bénéficie ainsi d'une faveur.

Article 12

… leurs opinions étant dûment prises en considération eu égard à leur âge et à leur degré de maturité.

Cette partie de l'article rappelle aux États parties que les enfants doivent être libres de donner leurs avis sur les problèmes les concernant.

On comprend donc à partir de ces articles que les enfants des détenus ont droit à la parole lorsqu'il s'agit d'une décision qui les concerne et que leurs avis doivent être pris en compte et au sérieux. Ils ne les excluent pas ; ils ont les mêmes droits que tous les autres enfants cités dans la CIDE. L'incarcération de leurs parents n'est en aucun cas une raison pour quelque forme de discrimination que ce soit. Il faut d'ailleurs signaler que ces droits sont d'ordre social, familial et psychologique car l'incarcération est une perte d'affection pour l'enfant, d'où son déséquilibre et ses besoins spécifiques.

Les besoins spécifiques de l'enfant du détenu

L'enfant du détenu, comme tout individu, a des besoins humains (Maslow 1970) ; mais il y en a qui sont spécifiques et propres à sa vulnérabilité :

- La vérité : certaines familles cachent la vérité aux enfants par rapport à la véritable destination de leur parent ; d'autres leur disent qu'il ou elle les a abandonnés, ou leur font croire qu'il ou elle est en Europe. L'enfant devient ainsi « un voyageur sans bagages » Bouregba (2008) car une partie de son histoire est voilée, pourtant il doit la connaître parce que notre passé est avec nous (Dortier 2009).
- La reconnaissance en tant que personne capable de participer à la construction de son avenir.
- La reconnaissance sociale en tant qu'enfant à part entière.
- La non-assimilation au statut de son parent.
- Le suivi permanent des services sociaux dans la famille, à l'école et dans la société tant que son parent reste en détention.

Bouregba (2008) met en exergue cet aspect des besoins spécifiques de l'enfant du détenu. Il pense que l'éloignement entre un enfant et son parent incarcéré n'est pas sans conséquences surtout sur son état psychologique et que cet enfant a besoin que l'on s'intéresse à ses spécificités, liées à l'absence de son parent. C'est pour cela que les actions comme les accompagnements, les suivis psychosociaux sont d'une importance capitale. On peut faire en sorte qu'il se rende compte de sa véritable histoire par un récit, lui trouver des tuteurs tels que ses grands-parents, oncles, tantes et frères, qui puissent lui servir de modèle et l'aider à réussir.

Stratégies de survie des enfants des détenus

Malgré l'attitude de rejet développée par son entourage, l'enfant du détenu pose des actes qui démontrent sa capacité à surmonter l'absence du parent incarcéré.

À l'analyse des informations recueillies lors des entretiens et des réponses obtenues dans le questionnaire, il apparaît que l'enfant du détenu a une capacité morale remarquable, qui sous-tend ses actions, lesquelles lui permettent de contourner l'absence de son parent. Il garde la tête froide et développe une force psychologique nécessaire à sa survie. Ces actions sont à la fois morales et physiques.

Les actions morales

D'un entretien avec une femme de détenu à propos de ses enfants, il ressort la capacité d'agir de deux enfants âgés de 8 ans et de 12 ans.

Propos de Myriam :

> Je sais que c'est mon mari qui vous a envoyé. J'ai décidé qu'il ne verra plus ses enfants parce que s'il avait pensé à eux, il n'aurait fait ce qu'il a fait. Il s'est comporté comme un irresponsable et pourquoi veut-il que mes enfants aillent le voir en prison ; ce qui va d'ailleurs les traumatiser. Le garçon de douze ans me harcèle chaque fois qu'il veut voir son père mais c'est moi qui le refuse car je trouve que la prison n'est pas un endroit pour enfants. Je suis contre le fait que les enfants entrent dans la prison même si c'est pour rendre visite à leurs parents qui s'y trouvent et cela est ma philosophie. Parfois la fille de huit ans exige qu'elle ne mangera [sic] que si je l'emmène voir son père. Je leur ai dit que leur père est en prison et que c'est un mauvais endroit pour les enfants. Je sais que ça les influence psychologiquement et peut-être ils ne sont pas équilibrés mais moi j'ai décidé que c'est comme cela et je crois que c'est pour leur bien.

Les attitudes des deux enfants relevées dans cet entretien montrent que pour voir leur père incarcéré, ces deux enfants développent chacun sa stratégie ; s'engageant dans des comportements relevant de leur capacité d'agir. Pendant que le garçon utilise le harcèlement comme action visant à le mener vers son père, la fille, quant à elle, a comme moyen le chantage. Ces stratégies ont porté leurs fruits car la mère a accepté de confier les enfants aux volontaires de l'association Relais Enfants-Parents du Cameroun qui devaient les accompagner à la prison centrale de Yaoundé afin qu'ils y rencontrent leur père.

Une autre action morale prouvant que l'enfant du détenu a des capacités est l'acceptation de la situation de son parent. Dans le tableau 5, nous avons vu que 2 enfants sur les 50 enquêtés déclarent qu'ils n'ont pas honte d'avoir un parent en prison et ils vont plus loin en déclarant que cette incarcération n'a pas d'influence sur leur vie. Il ressort donc que même si le pourcentage (4 pour cent) de ce groupe d'enfants est bas, il n'est pas non plus à négliger car cela démontre qu'ils ont une capacité psychologique à surmonter la situation et cela se confirme avec le tableau 3 dans lequel on peut lire que 20 pour cent (soit 10/50) de ces enfants ont de bons résultats et 44 pour cent (22/50) ont des résultats passables. Ces chiffres prouvent que certains enfants, malgré l'incarcération de leur parent, ont une capacité d'agir, sont capables de réussir dans leurs études. Nous en avons la confirmation avec Pierrette qui, lors de l'entretien, a révélé qu'elle a un baccalauréat série IH (Industrie de l'habillement) obtenu alors que sa mère était déjà en détention.

La troisième stratégie morale de l'enfant du détenu est la prière, qui est une assise psychologique capable de lui permettre de surmonter l'incarcération de son parent. Si la mère de Pierrette demande à ses enfants de prier, c'est parce qu'elle sait qu'ils en sont capables.

Les actions physiques

On a noté chez les enfants de détenu que nous avons rencontrés qu'ils ont aussi développé des stratégies physiques pour surmonter l'absence de leurs parents :
- L'abandon des études pour supporter le poids de la famille à travers la création d'une AGR.
- Le mariage pour des raisons non évoquées ; mais après analyse de la situation, il apparaît que c'est pour se mettre à l'abri de certains besoins ; c'est donc un mariage d'intérêt.

L'action économique

La mise sur pied d'une AGR afin de subvenir aux besoins de la famille et d'assurer la scolarisation des plus petits. C'est le cas de Viviane.

Malgré l'incarcération de leurs parents, l'on voit clairement que les enfants des détenus, consciemment ou inconsciemment, sont capables de surmonter la situation dans laquelle les plonge le statut de leurs parents à travers des stratégies variées. Par cette capacité d'agir, ces enfants déconstruisent le discours social qui prétend qu'ils ne peuvent que suivre la voie de l'infraction de leurs parents.

Conclusion

Cette étude nous a permis de voir que l'incarcération d'un parent influence la vie de l'enfant en général et les domaines sensibles pour son développement.

En Afrique, le développement de l'enfant se fait dans la société et avec la société, dans la famille et avec la famille. Pourtant, nous avons constaté que ces deux espaces ne sont pas favorables au développement de l'enfant du détenu qui devient ainsi un être à part qui paye le délit commis par son parent. L'incarcération devient donc un alibi qui permet de marginaliser l'enfant du détenu. Pourtant, pour sa survie, il développe des stratégies qui sont à la fois morales, physiques et économiques. Par ailleurs, il faut signaler que toutes les incarcérations des parents ne sont pas négatives pour l'enfant.

Nous suggérons donc :
- Que l'enfant du détenu ne soit pas condamné au même titre que son parent.
- Que l'enfant du détenu bénéficie aussi de l'accompagnement psychosocial comme toutes les autres couches vulnérables (les enfants de la rue, les orphelins, les enfants handicapés…)
- Que l'enfant du détenu ait la parole dans la société.
- Que l'entourage de l'enfant du détenu soit sensibilisé sur les droits et les capacités de ce dernier.

Note

1.   Prénom fictif selon sa volonté.

Bibliographie

Badinter, R., 2008, « Préface », in Ayre, E. & A. Bouregba, *Enfants de parents incarcérés. Guide de bonnes pratiques : perspectives européennes*, Eurochips, Paris.

Baggio, S., 2008, *Psychologie sociale*, de Boeck, Bruxelles.

Bouregba, A., 2008, in Ayre, E. & A. Bouregba, *Enfants de parents incarcérés.*

Brown, K., 2001, *Personne ne m'a jamais rien demandé : les jeunes face à l'incarcération d'un membre de la famille*, Londres, Federation of Prisoners' Families Support Group.

Dortier, J.-F., 2009, *Les Sciences Humaines. Panorama des connaissances*, Auxerre, Sciences Humaines Éditions.

Foucault, M., 2001 (1971), Préface à « Enquête dans vingt prisons », Paris, Champ libre, coll. « Intolérable », n° 1, 28 mai 1971, p. 3-5, publié dans *Dits et Écrits, T. II* texte 91, p. 196, Gallimard, Paris.

Iko'o, S., 2008, Rapport de la deuxième conférence annuelle organisée par l'Association Relais Enfants-Parents du Cameroun, « L'enfant face à l'incarcération de son parent », Yaoundé.

Moser, G., 1992, *Les stress urbains*, Paris, Armand Colin.

ONU, 2009, *Convention internationale des droits de l'enfant.*

Schwartz, S. H., 1992, « Universals in the content and structure of values : theoretical advances and empirical tests in 20 countries », in M. P. Zanna (Ed), *Advances in experimental social psychology, 25*, Academic Press, San Diego, p. 1-65.

Wolleswinkel, R., 2002, « Children of Imprisoned Parents », in J. C. M. Willems (éd), *Developmental and Autonomy Rights of Children ; Empowering children, Caregivers and communities*, Anvers, Oxford, New York, Intersentia.

16

Conclusion: Agency, Realities and the Future of African Childhoods

Yaw Ofosu-Kusi

Introduction

Africa's most important resource is human beings, with children being the gem in the crown. This gives a lot of hope for the future of the continent. But the potential of African children would be immeasurable only if they are properly groomed. However, the current notion of the African child is one of misery and endless suffering, as portrayed by Non-Governmental Organisations (NGOs) and even UNICEF. While some of these notions are caricatures of the reality, the imagery of wars, natural disasters like droughts, floods and the resultant famines and destitution is compelling. What is distressing is the impact of such activities in tandem with outmoded social and cultural practices on children. These negative images represent despair and victimhood because of the over-representation of negativities.

The 2011 Child and Youth Institute sought a different perspective to the conventional view of childhood in Africa by re-orientating and placing African children in a developmental process that recognises their socio-cognitive and physical potential. The thrust of the theme was children's ability to initiate actions as a way of mitigating some of the persistent challenges in their own lives and those of their families. This positions them as capable beings able to act in their interest, at least some of the times if not all the time. The claim of agency implies an empowerment that underlies many of the positive and sometimes negative behaviours some children exhibit around the continent. There is sufficient evidence of children's engagement in activities that are usually reserved for adults because of the failure of adults to perform their responsibilities towards children. While not disputing the reality, that is, legal incapacity of children in some situations, we must also acknowledge their ingenuity and potential to confront challenges, be creative, adaptive, resourceful and capable beings in the labour fields, under-resourced classrooms or destitute homes.

But the projection of this view would be a herculean task, since the majority of adults believe that children should be passive recipients of adult knowledge, and must have no opinion, even in matters that concern them and when they clearly have their own opinions. This calls for a reconstruction of African childhood, possibly through a concerted exercise of deconstruction and interrogation of the orthodoxy. For example, viewed from the perspective of age, children's agency becomes problematic because the legal age sets limits on what they can and cannot do. The UNCRC, ACWRC and national constitutions legally define a child as anyone below the age of 18 years; within that social space, they are expected to be in school, stay with their parents or family members, not engage in hazardous work, and so on. It is therefore contradictory to argue that children should be accorded the status of competency in aspects of their lives when they are concurrently being protected by law because of their physical and psycho-social underdevelopment. However, authorities that set the limits on childhood tend to be lethargic or fail dismally in providing the necessities of childhood for the majority of African children. Many of them, having developed social skills and experiential abilities are then propelled into action. As social actors, what they do may or may not be in their interest, but that is not peculiar to children, it applies to adults as well.

Realities

African childhoods can be dichotomised into rural and urban categories. The majority of children still live in rural communities, (e.g. only 37% of sub-Sahara African population was urbanised in 2010), where there are fewer developmental projects, schools are severely deficient of resources and qualified teachers while the local economy is characterised by widespread unemployment and under-employment (UNICEF 2012). There is therefore a higher tendency for poverty to transcend generations. These conditions weigh heavily on children's decisions to migrate to the cities or neighbouring countries for work, pursue education and the elusive attractions of the urban centres (Hashim and Thorsen 2011; Ofosu-Kusi and Mizen 2012). While rural childhood is traditional, embedded in arcane culture and, to some degree, hidden from the limelight, urban childhood is generally in the limelight and less saddled with the strictures of culture. Accessibility to school, health facilities and other imperatives of child development is much better. It is in such spaces and its corresponding schools, play grounds and homes that some children experience privileged childhoods to become the future 'African aristocrats'. At the other end, however, are children of the urban poor. Together with their families (or alone), they live in slums or under slum-like conditions, with many of them in Lagos, Accra, Cairo, Nairobi and other African cities, simply squatting on public lands (Davis 2006). Their saviour is principally not African governments but the ubiquitous informal sector. However, the persistent 'informalisation' of urban African economies poses a threat to millions of children in the urban areas. Deriving much of its steam from the neo-liberal policies of the 1980s and 1990s, the informal sector is a direct consequence of the decline and, in some cases, collapse or total failure of the formal sector to generate employment and regulate the economy (Verlet 2000; Ofosu-Kusi 2002; Lindell 2010). Those policies not only impoverished families but decimated, and continued to erode developmental opportunities for many children. Moreover, its arbitrariness provides opportunity for children to be part of the economic arrangements in the vastly unregulated social and economic space, thereby affecting their schooling.

In both contexts, poverty and destitution are major hurdles for many families and, by association, children. Between 2000 and 2009, 42 per cent of Africa's population lived below the international poverty line of $1.25 per day. In sub-Sahara Africa, the rate was 49 per cent and even higher for Western and Central Africa, at 52 per cent (UNICEF 2012). The corrupt tendency of African elites to systematically deplete public resources for their private gain engenders pervasive poverty and creates a vicious cycle of social and political instability in the form of wars and conflicts, economic mismanagement, diseases and failure of public health systems.

Faced with such structural difficulties and adversities, we see evidence of children's reflexive actions in various chapters of this volume. Whether it is children and young people seeking a presence in the streets and markets of Accra (Ghana) or young girls seeking work in Sikasso (Mali) as house-maids; or foster children working at the expense of their education in various markets in Lagos (Nigeria), or on cocoa plantations in the cocoa-growing areas of Ondo State (Nigeria); or dropping out of school in Abomey-calavi (Benin), we see both positive and negative actions on the part of children. Another pressing concern is AIDS, HIV transmission, death of parents and the pressures of premature adulthood. According to UNICEF (2012), the estimated adult HIV prevalence rate for Africa as a whole in 2009 was 3.9 per cent, while for sub-Sahara Africa it was 4.8 per cent. The prevalence of diseases and other causes of death resulted in 57.6 million children aged between 0 and 17 years being orphans, out of which 15 million were orphaned through AIDS (UNICEF 2012). In Malawi and Lesotho, countries that have had elaborate encounters with the pandemic, we again see evidence of how children are managing meagre resources as family-heads upon the deaths of their parents through AIDS. We also see the pervasiveness of children's vulnerability to HIV infection and how they develop propellant forces to overcome temptations and protect themselves against infection. In South

Africa, young African girls refuse to be objectified as helpless beings at the mercy of sexual predators, even if the orthodoxy portrays them as passive recipients of pain and infection within a social construction that sees girls as soft and boys as hardy, robust, boisterous and entitled to the patriarchal dividend.

Social indiscipline has led to environmental degradation in many communities and is as problematic for adults as it is for children, as exhibited by Ivorian children who are willing to take on the responsibility of redeeming their school environments from destruction. The motivation for their actions lies in the significance of physical, social and political environments in the way children represent themselves and construct their identities. For example, in the Democratic Republic of Congo, children in two contrasting environments shape their lives and aspirations according to the dominant images of their environment. Thus, while education and other modernising influences may be exerted by school authorities and parents, it is the children's own perception of reality that is most crucial. Similarly, Kenyan children frame images and perceptions of their political leaders in relation to iconic representations such as trees, animals, landmarks and buildings in their environment. Though construed by adults as incapable of forming political opinions, they are able to pigeon-hole leaders according to what they glean from society. Finally, a demonstration of children's capacity to manage their affairs, whether in schools or homes, is evident in children's involvement in school governance in Cameroon, or the children's assembly in Kenya where they make resolutions and decisions about national issues affecting their welfare and future.

In all these cases, the centrality of ability, capacity, or agency is evident in children's pursuit of status, dignity and material resources. However, the tangential relationship between agency and vulnerability is equally evident, since there are many factors that obfuscate their identity and place in society. The reality is that children do not control resources, do not make and enforce laws, hence they have to contain their potential within the demands of adults. The helplessness is embedded in the failure of the state to provide care, widespread destitution, disintegrating family and the changing roles of parents. For example, in terms of urban childhood, since the state is either unwilling or unable to fully regulate the informal sector – especially in relation to children – a process of informal regulation of childhood emerges in the street through gender, physicality, class and ethnicity. In this process, some children become antagonists while others are culprits.

And the Future

The potential of Africa is unquestionable. The way and manner in which we have exploited and utilised our opportunities is the major problem of the continent. Children are the most important social, economic and cultural capital of the future and so need full protection from African societies, governments and continental organisations to ensure their holistic development. The need to re-orientate ourselves to the global best practices for children is an imperative in Africa's quest for development and respect around the world.

The most obvious way to give protection and succour to children is to prioritise formal and informal education as a major mode of socialisation. Even though some people argue that the rewards of schooling are not that obvious for many children, it would be infantile to lower our guard on the singular task of achieving a hundred per cent enrolment and attendance rates for children around the continent. It is important, in educating our children, to recognise the fluidity of children's socio-cognitive and physical development. Hence, we must re-invent curriculum design by developing emergent or living curricular that are consistent with the present, rather than the rigid, thematic and often outdated ones, so that learning will be an exciting experience. The social and economic dividends of having literate populations have been dramatic for the developed world and the newly-industrialised Asian and South American economies. Moreover, in order to initiate and sustain the development of African children and their societies, we must develop stable socio-economic and political systems, ensure equitable distribution of resources – especially between rural and urban communities, and between the demands of adults and those of children – and seek an immediate end to the profligacy and unbridled squandering of public wealth and opportunities, and corruption by politicians and technocrats.

In that spirit, the future of African children can be further championed by constantly placing the global discourse in the African context while at the same time evolving African childhood that is grounded in its ontological realities. But this must be done in tandem with the paradigm shift in our understanding of children and childhood. Surely, children are evolving beings, both physically and mentally; they will mature some day and assume the mantle of leadership and adulthood. Until then, we must recognise them for who they are in the here and now, what they are capable of achieving contemporaneously in their development, rather than what they may or may not become in the future.

Innovative ideas in science, technology, arts, and so on, have been created and developed by children, sometimes in secondary schools, in other places. African children are equally ingenious and can shape the future of the continent through their thought processes but they need to be nurtured and recognised for their capacity to influence society through constructive engagement in the teaching-learning environment in schools, work, family life and community development. If the future of the continent is its children, then the future of those children hinges on the degree to which we empower them through care, love, attention and legislations to enable them blossom as children today and leaders in the next generation.

Nevertheless, there is the need for a nuanced appreciation of children's agency, to avoid dualisms, in order not to fall into the trap of pursuing binaries. In this respect, elevating children's potential as significant social actors without conceding the corresponding false sense of well-being and an illusion of independence would be reckless. That recognition will help us protect children better while giving them space to blossom.

References

Davis, M., 2006, *Planet of Slums*, London: Zed Books.

Hashim, I. and Thorsen, D., 2011, *Child Migration in Africa*, London: Zed Books.

Lindell, I., 2010, 'Between Exit and Voice: Informality and the Spaces of Popular Agency', African Studies Quarterly, Vol. 11, No. 2 & 3, pp. 1-11.

Ofosu-Kusi, Y. and Mizen, P., 2012, 'No Longer Willing to be Dependent: Young People Moving Beyond Learning', in G. Spittler and M. Bourdillon, eds., *African Children at Work: Working and Learning in Growing Up for Life*, Berlin: Lit Verlag.

Ofosu-Kusi, Y., 2002, 'Migrant Child Labourers in Ghana: A Case Study of the Making of an Adjustment Generation', unpublished Ph.D Thesis, University of Warwick, UK.

Verlet, M., 2000, 'Growing Up in Ghana: Deregulation and the Employment of Children', in B. Schlemmer, ed., *The Exploited Child*, London: Zed Books.

UNICEF, 2012, '*The State of the World's Children, 2012*', New York: UNICEF.

Index

Nigeria, viii, 6–7, 33–35, 37–39, 41, 43–47, 49–50, 52–53, 55, 57, 59–61, 63–64, 124, 211
Nigerian Demographic, 34
noise, 25, 60, 130
NPC (National Population Commission), 47, 63–64

O

Odigbo LGA, 56, 59–62
Ofosu-Kusi, 1–32, 127, 135, 209–14
Oke Igbo LGA, 56–61
Okunola, 34, 37, 39, 47
Old Fadama, 16, 20, 22–23, 25–26, 28
Olufemi- Educational Challenges Facing Children, 49, 51–64
Ombati, 107–22
Ondo State, 7, 49, 51–64, 211
orphans, 46, 66, 78, 81, 94–96, 98, 101, 211
Orphans and Vulnerable Children. See OVC
OVC (Orphans and Vulnerable Children), 81, 94, 96, 98, 103–4

P

parental death, 94, 97
Parenthood, 46–47
parents, 9–10, 19, 27–28, 33–34, 37–38, 40–45, 49, 52–53, 56–63, 94–95, 97–104, 108, 127–29, 143–47, 210–12
surviving, 37, 44
Parents National Educational Union (PNEU), 133
Paris, 135, 176, 188
participants, 11–12, 20–25, 27, 40–41, 44, 52–53, 57, 77, 79–84, 86, 88–91, 99, 101–3, 114–16, 140–43, 146–47
active, 11, 124, 128
female, 43, 60–61, 145
participation, viii, 10–11, 78, 80–81, 108, 124–25, 127–28, 132, 134, 137–41, 143, 147–48
participatory, 80–81, 91, 140

passivity, 8, 67, 71
Pattman, 65, 67–74
perceptions, 10, 13, 15, 39, 55, 72, 88, 109–17, 212
performative, 80–81, 91
performative research, 80–81
person, 24, 29, 85, 87, 91, 116–17
perspectives, 10, 12, 18, 67, 78, 117–18, 126, 137, 139–40, 196, 209–10
children's, 51–52, 109–10, 149
Peter, 142–44, 146
PNEU (Parents National Educational Union), 133
political leaders, 10–11, 108–9, 113, 212
Political Socialization, 118–19
politics, 46, 55, 64, 67, 72, 74, 108, 111, 116, 119
population, viii, 2, 18, 29, 31, 36, 46–47, 52, 63, 99
poverty, 18, 23, 38, 62, 66, 71, 93, 95, 105, 188, 210–11
power, 7–8, 21, 46, 71–72, 84, 109, 112, 115–16, 119, 129–30, 135, 138–39
male, 67, 70–71
President, 109, 111–17, 141
President Kibaki, 11, 111–13, 115
primary school level, 51
Prime Minister, 109, 111, 113–15, 117, 129–33
Prime Minister Raila, 113, 115
programmes, 19, 78, 97–98, 104, 127, 129–30, 135
project, 77, 79–82, 89, 98, 103, 127, 131, 134, 139–40
Promotion, 77–92
properties, 95–96, 112–13, 117
protagonist, 86, 88, 90
protection, 26, 35, 49, 78, 92, 94, 99, 102–3, 110, 127, 140, 213
Prout, 3, 123–24, 129, 132, 135, 137, 149
provision, 50, 60, 78, 85, 99, 102, 140
psychological problems, 102–3
punishment, corporal, 11, 147–48
pupils, 11, 62, 110, 127–33

www.ingramcontent.com/pod-product-compliance
Lightning Source LLC
Chambersburg PA
CBHW050644280326
41932CB00015B/2778